Palaeoethnobotany of Princess Point, Lower Great Lakes Region, Southern Ontario, Canada

Della Saunders

BAR International Series 1790
2008

Published in 2016 by
BAR Publishing, Oxford

BAR International Series 1790

Palaeoethnobotany of Princess Point, Lower Great Lakes Region, Southern Ontario, Canada

ISBN 978 1 4073 0278 2

BAR Publishing is the trading name of British Archaeological Reports (Oxford) Ltd.
British Archaeological Reports was first incorporated in 1974 to publish the BAR
Series, International and British. In 1992 Hadrian Books Ltd became part of the BAR
group. This volume was originally published by Archaeopress in conjunction with
British Archaeological Reports (Oxford) Ltd / Hadrian Books Ltd, the Series principal
publisher, in 2008. This present volume is published by BAR Publishing, 2016.

Printed in England

BAR
PUBLISHING

BAR titles are available from:

BAR Publishing
122 Banbury Rd, Oxford, OX2 7BP, UK
EMAIL info@barpublishing.com
PHONE +44 (0)1865 310431
FAX +44 (0)1865 316916
www.barpublishing.com

Acknowledgements

I thank Dr. Gary Crawford and Dr. David Smith, both of the University of Toronto, for the opportunity to participate in the Princess Point Project, and appreciate Dr. Crawford generously sharing his extensive knowledge of past plant use. The Princess Point Project was made possible by a Social Sciences and Humanities Research Council (Canada) grant awarded to Dr. Crawford and Dr. Smith. Ialso thank the University of Toronto for supporting my work. Thank you to Dr. Gyoung-Ah Lee, University of Oregon, and to Dr. Steve Monckton, University of Toronto, for theoretical and statistical insights, and to Ms. Sandra Poaps for assisting with statistical analyses. I thank Mr. Jeff Bursey for his hard work floating hundreds of litres of soil samples, together with University of Toronto archaeological field school students. I thank Dr. Chen Shen, Royal Ontario Museum, for generously providing computer and equipment to allow me to photograph the ancient seeds recovered in this research. Finally, thank you to my husband, Mr. Steve Shepherd, for everything.

Table of Contents

List of Tables

List of Figures

List of Plates

Chapter One

Introduction

Introduction

This work explores the interrelationship between humans and plants within the Princess Point culture. Princess Point is the archaeological cultural context in which a shift from an economy based on foraging to one that incorporated horticulture occurred in what is now southern Ontario. The earliest dates for evidence of corn horticulture in Ontario are from the Princess Point period (ca. 1570 to 970 B.P.) (Crawford *et al.* 1997).

Plants are essential to human existence. In the past, people depended on plants for many purposes, including food, medicine, shelter, and tools. Plants often had symbolic importance, which mediated people's interaction with them and added to their technical, nutritional, and medicinal importance (Ford 1979). The natural environment affects cultural development by providing cultural groups with a particular set of resources and, for this reason, the study of ancient plant remains is crucial to gain a balanced understanding of past lifeways. Local plant resources provide both limits and potential.

An understanding of prehistoric subsistence is impossible without the retrieval, identification, and interpretation of plants that were used. Palaeoethnobotany is the analysis and interpretation of ancient plant remains that can provide information on the interaction between people and plants (Yarnell 1964; Ford 1979). This interrelationship between people and plants is dynamic rather than static, and palaeoethnobotanical issues are complex as a result.

Plants play a fundamental role in human economic systems and people can have a profound impact on their environments (Butzer 1990; McGlade 1995:113-132). Anthropogenic communities are, therefore, an important component of human systems (see Yarnell 1964 Asch and Asch 1985; Ford 1985; Smith 1992, 1995a,b; Crawford 1997). Understanding past cultural adaptations to the plant world and the impact of plants upon prehistoric populations is important, as opposed to simply making identifications of useful plants (Yarnell 1964; Ford 1979; see also Crawford 1997; Hammett 1997). Cultures define which plant resources are appropriate to use. The behavioural consequences of the cultural definition of a useful plant can modify, to a lesser or greater degree, the structure and composition of the local environment.

Through a relationship, which starts with the gathering of wild plants, humans intervene in the growth cycle of the plant population. Human intervention can enhance a plant population's competitive advantage and chances for reproductive success. If the plant is transplanted or stored and seeds are dispersed to assure their availability for germination, these tended plants may develop morphological changes indicative of intensive human manipulation in their life cycle. The plant-human interrelationship can vary significantly from an occasional interaction to an intimate relationship where one is dependent on the other. Domesticated plants are dependent on humans and can be seen as cultural artifacts that result from human selection for genetically controlled features (Ford 1979). Human activities, constrained by cultural prescription, impact on plants and the environment; and, plants, within a dynamic and symbiotic relationship, affect human culture. Plants and people can have a profound impact upon each other, that is, from the activity of gathering wild plants to intensive agriculture (Yarnell 1964; Ford 1979). People do not select and use plants at random but plants are collected and gathered within the cultural context of each society. The use of each plant is culturally prescribed and archaeobotanical remains reflect these activities (for example, see Black 1980; Moerman 1998). Often these activities are preserved only by the microscopic evidence left from decayed or burned plants (Ford 1979:286).

The basis of this study of the Princess Point is to explore the origins of agriculture, together with plant use generally in southern Ontario, and to gain a better understanding of a time when people were changing their subsistence pattern from one based on wild plant resources during the Middle Woodland (Spence *et al.* 1990; Fox 1990) to one that incorporated crops (Crawford *et al.* 1997; Smith and Crawford 1997). Ounjian's (1998) study of Glen Meyer and prehistoric Neutral palaeoethnobotany encompasses a period when people were practicing horticulture. This Princess Point research deals with the period directly preceding the Glen Meyer. The Princess Point inhabited an area to the north of the eastern reaches of Lake Erie and west of the western shores of Lake Ontario (Smith and Crawford 1997). The study concentrates on two geographic areas: the lower Grand River valley and Cootes Paradise (see Figure 1). The Glen Meyer sites studied by Ounjian (1998) are located in the western corner of southern Ontario.

With these temporal and spatial differences in mind, I evaluate the role that plants played for Princess Point inhabitants within the context of what is known about plant resource exploitation before and after this time within southern Ontario. I explore the affiliations and impacts of populations to the south in eastern North America, as they relate to the Princess Point. My goal is to contribute to an understanding of what Hodder (1992:241) terms the "practical factors", that is, economic patterns and subsistence behaviours. This research explores the dynamics of change in human behaviour by examining patterns of plant resource exploitation over time and space.

As gardening or agricultural activities are introduced into a population's subsistence pattern, people tend to maintain their established pattern of gathering and hunting while gradually incorporating crop plants. As the population increases, agricultural crops can become increasingly important to sustain greater numbers of people and intensification occurs (see Rindos 1984). A feedback situation may occur so that, with the availability of more food resources, a larger population can be supported and, with a larger population, increasingly complex agricultural practices occur, resulting in the availability of more food resources (Ford 1985; Keegan 1987; Smith 1990, 1992; Price and Gebauer 1992; Scarry 1993; Gebauer and Price 1995; Rogers and Smith 1995; McNutt 1996; O'Brien and Dunnell 1998). This then leads to a wide range of cultural changes, including a shift towards permanent settled villages, and an increasing and ongoing reliance on agriculture and domesticated crops. Cultural changes and a florescence of technological activities can occur. However, even though subsistence activities, social patterns, settlement patterns, and technology can experience great change, wild plant foods are not necessarily eliminated from a population's diet (Butzer 1990:171-190; Monckton 1990, 1992; Ounjian 1998). To the contrary, the opposite is often true and an increased reliance on specific wild plants may develop (for example, see Crawford 1983; Monckton 1990, 1992; Crawford 1997; Ounjian 1998). Some weedy species, such as chenopod, purslane, and American nightshade, would thrive in an environment disturbed by agricultural activities and longer term, more permanent settlements (Smith 1992; Harlan 1995). These plant species would occupy the margins of fields and disturbed soils close to permanent structures and would provide an attractive, easily attainable food resource for a growing population. (The scientific and common names of plants pertinent to this research are set out in Table 2.)

Princess Point assemblages contain large numbers of these weedy plants and these species also occur in Glen Meyer samples. The difference perhaps being that, by Glen Meyer times, an economic pattern that included horticulture was better established. The trend toward growing and consuming greater quantities of indigenous and introduced crops was well underway but still supplemented by an array of wild plant foods, especially fleshy fruits (Ounjian 1998). Conversely, evidence suggests that the Princess Point supplemented their staple foodstuffs and dependence on wild plant foods with maize. Princess Point sites contain a higher density of weedy plants than maize and the later Glen Meyer assemblages produced a higher density of maize than weedy plants (Ounjian 1998). Both assemblages produced a wide diversity of individual plant species, although more species are identified from the Glen Meyer

samples. Several taxa that occur in Princess Point sites do not appear in Glen Meyer, while others that are found in Glen Meyer are not present with the Princess Point.

Differences emerge in the analyses of these two populations; each population exhibiting its own distinctive subsistence pattern with an underlying pattern of continuity. These differences provide evidence of localized and temporal variability existing between the Princess Point and the Glen Meyer cultures. The differences I identify in this study are typical of the regional cultural adaptations that are seen throughout other parts of the eastern woodlands of North America during the Middle and Late Woodland (Scarry 1993). This regional variability, both cultural and ecological, tends to be overlain with a sense of temporal continuity and uniformity in settlement and subsistence patterns.

Palaeoethnobotanical Evidence

Palaeoethnobotany is a comparatively recent addition to the study of past cultures and over the past 20 years it has expanded to include a diverse range of techniques, analyses, and results (Hastorf 1999). The key to reconstructing subsistence is to use multiple lines of evidence (Pearsall 1996:234). The relationship between evidence and explanation is key (Pearsall 1996:234). Although no single set of steps achieves a solid explanation, the more evidence accumulated, the better the final argument. An approach using multiple lines of evidence is based on a strategy that is not single-context dependent (see Wylie 1994) but rather is based on a convergence of independent research techniques that would provide stronger evidence for the ultimate interpretation of data than with the use of a solitary technique.

This research considers macrobotanical analysis of plant remains. Substantial understanding of past plant use, as well as cultural change, can be gleaned from macrobotanical analysis. Macrobotanical remains are investigated morphologically and histologically with the aid of a light microscope. Ethnographic studies on plants provide a guide to the use of individual uses of plants in the past. Although no ethnographic material is available regarding Princess Point, written accounts are available regarding the Iroquoian and their subsistence activities. The Iroquoian are believed to be descendant from the Princess Point (Crawford and Smith 1996; Smith and Crawford 1997). A solid body of empirical data allows for the findings from this research to be compared to other populations, including the Glen Meyer and groups further south in the Eastern Woodlands.

Ancient plant remains can help address many archaeological questions and, to this end, improvements on collection, methodologies, data presentation, and technologies should be ongoing. Some topics, such as the cultural value and ritual meaning of specific plants, are difficult to explore in prehistory, but together with regional studies on the origins of agriculture, are worth pursuing.

Previous Research

Over the past several years, a number of University of Toronto graduate dissertations and theses have focused on Princess Point or studies closely related to this research. Bowyer (1995) examines plant remains from the Lone Pine and Grand Banks sites and her findings are incorporated into this study. Ormerod (1994) and Shen (1997) provide a better understanding of Princess Point lithic technology. Shen (1997) characterizes Princess Point lithic production and explores changes during this time period. Bekerman (1995), through ceramic analysis, details the relative chronology of Princess Point sites. Dieterman (2001) explores settlement patterns and the Princess Point landscape by contrasting local Middle Woodland and Late Woodland systems. Ounjian (1998) provides a comprehensive analysis of the palaeoethnobotany of the Glen Meyer and prehistoric Neutral. The palaeoethnobotany of the temporally later Huron is the focus of Monckton's work (1990, 1992).

The origins of Princess Point as a cultural construct are traced to Thomas Lee (1951, 1952) and Richard MacNeish (1952). At that time, Lee defined MacNeish's Ontario Owasco designation as transitional from Point Peninsula (Middle Woodland) to Glen Meyer (Late Woodland). Lee based this designation on several New York state Owasco style sites in southern Ontario that were excavated in the early 1900s by William J. Wintemberg. These sites produced ceramics that Wintemberg documented as being non-Iroquoian.

Many years later, David Stothers (1977) defined the Princess Point Complex; so named after the type site, Princess Point (AhGx-1), in Cootes Paradise. Stothers' definition was based on exploratory excavations conducted between 1969 and 1974 in southern Ontario. This included excavation of the Princess Point site by Noble and Stothers in the late 1960s. Survey and test excavations were conducted around Cootes Paradise in 1972 and in the lower Grand Valley between 1969 and 1974. On the banks of the Grand River, at the Cayuga Bridge (AfGx-1) and Grand Banks (AfGx-3) sites, Stothers excavated sections of the river bank and concluded the stratigraphy showed three distinct periods of Princess Point occupation. Thus, on the basis of a limited number of radiocarbon assays, pottery seriation, and stratigraphy, Stothers initially dated Princess Point from 1400 to 1100 B.P. He divided this time period into three phases: Early (1400 to 1250 B.P.), Middle (1250 to 1150 B.P.), and Late (1150 to 1100 B.P.) (Stothers 1977). He determined that Princess Point was transitional between Middle Woodland and the Late Woodland Ontario Iroquoian Tradition in southern Ontario (Stothers 1977). Furthermore, from the distribution of 35 assumed Princess Point sites, Stothers isolated three contemporary regional concentrations in southwestern and south central Ontario: Point Pelee, Ausable, and Grand River. Stothers identified what he termed Princess Point sites covering the area from Burlington Bay on Lake Ontario to the Grand River watershed and the Lake Erie shoreline (Stothers 1977:41-42).

Stothers used three characteristics to distinguish Princess Point from other cultures. First, he proposed the material cultural assemblage, including pottery and projectile points, differed from the antecedent Middle Woodland in both manufacture and style (Stothers 1977:42-43). Second, as indicating incipient horticulture, Stothers noted the presence of one maize kernel from the Grand Banks site, four or five maize kernels from the Princess Point site at Cootes Paradise, together with 44 maize kernels from the more westerly Porteous site (Stothers 1977:117). Last, settlements were located in riverine/lacustrine environments that Stothers interpreted to be spring to summer seasonal aggregation camps (Stothers 1977:43-44). Stothers described the subsistence pattern as consisting of seasonal foragers who also practiced horticulture, lived in small communities near bodies of water in the warm weather, and dispersed to uplands in cold weather (Stothers 1977:43-44; Stothers and Yarnell 1977).

From the time of Stothers' work in the 1970s to the initiatives of Crawford and Smith in the 1990s, archaeologists did not conduct any large-scale research on Princess Point. However, several researchers and institutions added new data and interpretations and cultural resource management operations also contributed (for example, Lennox and Morrison 1990; Timmins 1992). Fox (1984, 1990) narrowed the scope of Princess Point both spatially and temporally. He restricted the geographical zone to what Stothers had termed the Grand River focus, that is, from the region south of the western half of Lake Ontario and to the north of the eastern half of Lake Erie. On the basis of a distinct material assemblage, Murphy and Ferris (1990) reassigned the Point Pelée focus in the most southwesterly corner of Ontario to the Rivière au Vase Phase of the Western Basin Late Woodland sequence. The Ausable focus near Lake Huron remains too poorly known to classify.

Stothers' initial work identified 18 sites as having a Princess Point affiliation within the Grand River focus (Surma, Orchid, Martin, Jordan Harbour, Reimer, Selkirk 5, Selkirk 2, Port Maitland, Newman, Cayuga Bridge, Grand Banks, Indiana, Middleport, Glass, Porteous, Mohawk Chapel, Princess Point, and Rat Island). Princess Point now is identified as forming a collection of some 90 archaeological sites situated from the Niagara River on Lake Ontario to the southeast, to the Credit River drainage to the northeast, and to Long Point on Lake Erie to the west (Fox 1982, 1984, 1990; Smith and Crawford 1997). Fox (1990:174) also restricted the chronology to 1300 to 1100 B.P. Timmins (1985) re-examined the radiocarbon dates from Princess Point sites and concluded there was insufficient evidence to support

Stothers' three-phase chronology. Recent detailed ceramic attribute analysis also supports a single continuous culture period (Bekerman 1995).

Beginning in 1993, a multidisciplinary research project at the University of Toronto has been investigating the transition from Middle to Late Woodland in southern Ontario and the origins of horticulture in the Northeast Woodlands. Princess Point is the primary focus of this research, which has lead to the amendment of Princess Point chronology to as early as 1570 B.P. and as late as 970 B.P. The amendment is based on accelerator mass spectrometer (AMS) dates on maize kernels recovered from the Grand Banks site (Crawford et al. 1997) and a number of recalibrated radiocarbon dates on late Princess Point sites (Smith 1997). The earliest corn so far in Ontario dates to cal. 1570±90 B.P. from the Grand Banks site (Crawford et al. 1997). Upriver from Grand Banks at the Meyer site, a corn fragment dates to about 1270 B.P., and another maize fragment from Forster dates to circa 1200 B.P. (Crawford and Smith 2001). These dates indicate a shift to a mixed economy that included horticulture, gathering, hunting, and fishing (Crawford and Smith 1996; Crawford et al. 1997). Research continues to accumulate more evidence regarding such significant developments as incipient maize horticulture, the appearance of larger settlements, concomitant with accelerated population growth.

The terminal date for Princess Point is an arbitrary date as late Princess Point overlaps with early Glen Meyer in time. Glen Meyer dates from 1100 to 700 B.P. (Williamson 1990) and, to compound the complexity, distinguishing late Princess Point from early Glen Meyer is difficult (Crawford and Smith 1996; Smith and Crawford 1997). Although their relationship to one another is still in question, Ounjian (1998:11) suggests that Princess Point and Glen Meyer are both part of one large cultural group responsible for the continuum of occupations present in the region.

Princess Point is viewed as an early phase of Late Woodland and Wright (1966) considered it closely related to the Ontario Iroquoian Tradition. Significant cultural and social changes marked the end of the earlier Middle Woodland period and these changes are hypothesized to lay the groundwork for subsequent Iroquoian cultures (Smith and Crawford 1997:28). The origin of Princess Point continues to be debated.

Stothers initially argued that the Princess Point were affiliated with a Hopewell population that migrated into the area from the western basin region at the west end of Lake Erie, bringing the practice of maize horticulture, and subsequently settling throughout southwestern and south central Ontario (Stothers 1977; see also Stothers and Yarnell 1977). A few years later, he reversed his migration theory and now argues that these people represent an in situ development from Middle Woodland populations (Stothers and Pratt 1981). However, although late Middle Woodland and early Princess Point cultures appear to be contemporaneous, they have different artifact assemblages (Smith and Crawford 1997), which negates Stothers' in situ hypothesis. Snow (1995) argues that the Princess Point people were Algonkian speakers who were displaced near the end of the Middle Woodland by migrations of maize-based Iroquoian groups from the south. Refuting this theory, Crawford and Smith (1996) note that Princess Point peoples practiced maize agriculture earlier than Snow's migration hypothesis would allow. A culture from the south may also have diffused into, or was assimilated by, local Ontario populations (Smith and Crawford 1997). Fox (1990) argues that the practice of maize agriculture diffused into the area and was adopted by local Middle Woodland groups.

Princess Point is mostly known from sites along the Grand River and, until recently, research did not focus on subsistence patterns. One exception is the Varden site on Long Point that provided subsistence data. The site was stratified with distinct occupation levels and the deepest two contained Princess Point components (MacDonald 1986; Fox 1990).

Environment

The Princess Point Complex is restricted geographically to south-central Ontario; extending from Long Point to the Niagara River along the north shore of Lake Erie, and around the western end of Lake Ontario to the Credit River. The Grand River Valley and Cootes Paradise are within the mildest climatic area in Ontario, which is categorized as humid continental (Brown et al. 1974). This area is located within the northernmost reaches of the Carolinian Biotic Province or what is also known as the Deciduous Forest Region. The ecological zone is marked by a climax hardwood forest dominated by nut-bearing trees and Carolinian species that normally are found only to the south in eastern United States. The geographical area of this study exhibits considerable environmental diversity as a consequence of its relatively recent deglaciation (for more information on the environment see Dice 1943; Rowe 1977; Chapman and Putnam 1984; Allen et al. 1990).

Pollen records help to interpret the vegetation and climate histories in southern Ontario. From the Middle Holocene to about 1000 years ago, the pollen record from Crawford Lake is dominated by beech, maple, elm, oak, and birch (McAndrews and Boyko-Diakonow 1989). This mixed hardwood forest shifted slightly to a pine-oak-birch dominated forest about 600 years ago.

The Grand River Valley drains nearly 6,700 square kilometres, making it one of the largest watersheds in southern Ontario. The river drains nearly 300 kilometres south from its source near Georgian Bay to Lake Erie, dropping some 352 metres as it flows. The hummocky glacial topography gives rise to many habitat types, including extensive uplands, swamp forests, bogs in kettle depressions, fens, and remnants of prairie and oak savannah (Chapman and Putnam 1984). The lower Grand River is an entrenched river valley that flows onto the low-lying plain along the north shore of Lake Erie. Movement of the river channel is restricted in some places by bedrock or resistant glacial materials. Elsewhere, floodplains are evident and are comprised mainly of accreted lateral bars and point bars built from river-transported silts and sands (Crawford *et al.* 1998). Prior to 1500 B.P., during time periods associated with Late Archaic through to Middle Woodland, significant alluvial accumulations occurred. However, Crawford *et al.* (1998) identify the period from about 1500 to 200 B.P. as a time when the Grand River was relatively stable with little alluviation. Princess Point falls within this time period. The floodplains of the lower Grand River likely provided suitable locations for occupation at this time as there would have been a relatively low risk of flooding, compared to the preceding Middle Woodland. A relatively stable floodplain environment facilitated and coincided with occupation along the floodplains of the Grand River at the onset of horticulture in Ontario (Crawford *et al.* 1998).

Cootes Paradise, just west of Hamilton Harbour on Lake Ontario, is a 250 hectare marshy water body. In the past, Cootes has been described as a small lake, a river, or a marsh, and usually in conjunction with the mention of the presence of wild rice, water lilies, ducks, other water fowl, and animals. In 1669 Jesuit accounts describe the area as a small lake, and in the late 1700s Lord Simcoe's wife described Cootes as a small river or lake (Fraser 1997).

The characteristics of any landscape are essential components in archaeological interpretations. This research concerns two geographic areas situated within riverine, wetland, and floodplain environments (see Crawford *et al.* 1997; Walker *et al.* 1997). Rivers provided attractive settlement locales for prehistoric populations in northeastern North America (Walker *et al.* 1997), and floodplain occupations are relatively common during the period of some 1500 years ago in Ontario, as well as in neighbouring Pennsylvania and New York (see Stothers 1977; Stothers and Yarnell 1977; Ritchie and Funk 1973; Stewart 1994; Crawford *et al.* 1998). This pattern contrasts with that of the later Iroquoians who tended to settle in upland locations away from major rivers and closer to springs or small creeks (Walker *et al.* 1997:866).

The continual transformation of rivers by spring floods and meandering forces shaped the floodplain landscapes that were the setting for the initial development and subsequent entrenchment of prehistoric food producing economies (Smith 1992). Edgar Anderson (1956) was the first to argue that floodplains provided open habitats that would support diverse weedy plants. Otherwise, open habitats are quite rare in the natural environment. Weedy plants would have been very competitive and successful in natural open habitats, as well as in disturbed open areas created by human settlement. The Floodplain Weed Theory (Anderson 1956) helps to explain anthropogenesis, plant domestication, and human settlement patterns throughout much of eastern North America (cf. Harlan *et al.* 1973; de Wet and Harlan 1975; Smith 1992).

The open habitat caused by floodwaters is particularly pertinent to archaeological investigations as flooding can occur with some consistency every year in spring or early summer. This can create a more or less reliable habitat for weedy plant species that, in turn, can provide a degree of dependability for the forager extracting these resources. These weeds are susceptible to various levels of human manipulation and intervention along the continuum leading to domestication and food production (cf. Anderson 1952; Smith 1992). Floodplains provide productive vegetation, are rich in annual weedy plants, and can provide areas ideally suited to human habitation.

Organization of Study

This study is organized into six chapters. The text refers to plant species by common names. Scientific names are provided in Table 2. In this, the first chapter, the reader is introduced to the objectives of the research. Princess Point is reviewed from a spatial and temporal perspective. Scholarly research of Princess Point began about 50 years ago with Richard MacNeish and data have been garnered incrementally since then.

In Chapter Two, I provide information from previous research on cultural groups that came before and after Princess Point to provide a spatial and temporal perspective. Princess Point is one of a number of prehistoric populations that lived in the Lower Great Lakes region and I review details about the individual sites explored in this study. The chapter also outlines the emergence of agriculture as it applies to the Eastern Woodlands of North America, from the Archaic to the Late Woodland.

Chapter Three, Plant Evidence: Sampling and Methods, reviews the sampling strategy and method used to conduct archaeobotanical analysis on soil samples. I also explore the inherent challenges in the subdiscipline of palaeoethnobotany. Details of the methods of recovery followed in this research are provided.

Chapter Four, Identification and Quantification of Plant Remains, summarizes the results of the botanical analyses. The chapter delineates important factors involved in identifying plant remains and explains the method used to quantify and categorize the remains. The frequency that plant categories and taxa appear within individual samples and sites is provided by absolute numbers and percentages. Density ratios are calculated. Tabulated results are provided and bar graphs depict site-to-site and feature-to-feature comparisons. Photographs of selected plant remains are included.

Chapter Five, Princess Point Plant Use, explores how the Princess Point may have used plants that were available to them on a day-to-day basis. The dietary and medicinal aspects of plants are detailed, taking into account nutritional and chemical compositions, which could provide clues as to the past uses of some plants. In the section on plant taxa, I review individual plant taxa for which there is archaeological evidence.

Chapter Six, the final chapter, summarizes the findings and explores the significance of these conclusions as they apply to the Princess Point in southern Ontario in relation to the later Glen Meyer. I also compare subsistence patterns to Middle and early Late Woodland populations to the south in the Northeastern Woodlands. Macrobotanical analyses resulted in the identification of thousands of seeds and 36 species. The Princess Point population used corn, together with a suite of wild plants. There is substantial evidence for the use of fleshy fruits and the use of greens and grains, specifically, starchy and oily-seeded plants. Evidence also indicates that wetland plants were important during Princess Point times.

The underlying concept of this study is that changes in subsistence are dynamic and complex; and there is a broad range of possible interactions with local environments that vary on a continuum from minimal effect to extensive agricultural changes. In exploring the human-plant interrelationship of the Princess Point in southern Ontario, I conclude that there was a general shift from an economy based on foraging to one that incorporated horticulture at this time.

Regional variation with underlying continuity is a defining concept of the subsistence economies of the Eastern Woodlands of North America, and the results of this study add to what is known about populations from this area. The Princess Point relied on a variety of plants, had a good understanding of both wild and cultivated plants, and had a distinctive economic pattern that is regionally and temporally significant. This study explores the depth and breadth of plant use by the Princess Point and considers how their use of plants ultimately would lead to the intensive horticultural subsistence pattern of the Glen Meyer. Princess Point subsistence is similar to that of populations living during the Middle and Late Woodland periods of the Eastern Woodlands to the south. This general pattern led to intensive agriculture and cultural fluorescence throughout eastern North America.

Chapter Two

Princess Point

Introduction

Princess Point is one of a number of prehistoric populations that inhabited the Lower Great Lakes region and is likely ancestral to later Iroquoian horticultural societies (Crawford *et al.* 1997; Crawford and Smith 1996; Smith and Crawford 1995; Fox 1990; Trigger 1985; Wright 1984; Stothers 1977; Noble 1975). Princess Point dates from about 1570 to 970 B.P., in the early Late Woodland period of southern Ontario (Crawford *et al.* 1997; Smith 1997), and represents the first shift to a subsistence pattern that incorporated horticulture into a hunting, fishing, and plant collecting lifeway (Smith and Crawford 1997). This early horticultural population made significant use of floodplains in particular along the Grand River (Walker *et al.* 1997), at wetlands, such as Cootes Paradise, and at riverine, lacustrine, and upland locales (Smith and Crawford 1997). Crawford and Smith (1996:7) argue that a transition to centered communities was occurring at this time, concomitant with a shift in subsistence patterns. Over time and with the intensification of horticulture, a more sedentary, village-based lifeway would emerge in Early Iroquoian times. This chapter provides a synopsis of what is known about this past population.

Middle Woodland

Antecedent to Princess Point is the Middle Woodland period, which covers a time span from about 2000 to 1300 B.P. (Spence *et al.* 1990; Smith 2001). This period includes three cultural complexes: Couture and Saugeen in southwestern Ontario, and Point Peninsula in south-central Ontario and into eastern Ontario and New York State. Ceramics, settlement and subsistence systems, and mortuary practices characterize the period. Pottery style variation differentiates the individual cultural complexes (Spence *et al.* 1990:142; Smith 1997:55), but the geographical borders and the material culture of these three groups are not well-defined. Some feel it best to explain Couture, Saugeen, and Point Peninsula in terms of cultural continuity (Spence *et al.* 1990). Most researchers describe the Middle Woodland subsistence pattern as seasonally scheduled with late spring to early summer macroband encampments on large water bodies and later summer to early spring microband dispersal. Large, dense artifact scatters, typically by lakes or large rivers, distinguish the material culture from Early Woodland (Spence *et al.* 1990).

The Grand River serves as an arbitrary boundary between designating a site as either Saugeen or Point Peninsula. Although little is known about Point Peninsula, the Saugeen culture is fairly well documented, especially along the shores of Lake Huron (Spence *et al.* 1990). On the Grand River, sites are attributed to both Saugeen and an indeterminate Middle Woodland culture. Like Princess Point, Saugeen sites are in the Carolinian forest ecozone and the Grand River drainage system. This section reviews the Saugeen culture within the context of its possible connection to Princess Point. Researchers agree that early Middle Woodland is antecedent to Princess Point and that later Middle Woodland culture overlaps with Princess Point (Smith 1997).

Saugeen groups practiced a settlement-subsistence pattern involving late spring to early summer riverine macroband camps. People dispersed from late summer to early spring into microband camps inland, or on or near the Lake Huron shore (Finlayson 1977; Timmins 1985). Researchers more recently suggest that Middle Woodland practiced a relatively stable residency (Spence *et al.* 1990). Macrobands aggregated at riverine-oriented, semi-permanent settlements from early spring to fall. As evidenced by the recovery of fish remains, macroband occupations by riverine settings appear to focus on the intensive exploitation of spawning fish (Spence *et al.* 1990:167). Mammalian and avian remains are also present. From fall to spring, smaller group forays likely were made inland to key resource locations, using the riverine settlement as a base camp.

Plant use by these Middle Woodland peoples remains essentially unknown. The Inverhuron-Lucas site, close to the shores of Lake Huron, is the only site to have floral remains recovered by flotation. The floral remains identified consist primarily of bramble, butternut, elderberry, and dogwood (Finlayson 1977:554-557; Spence *et al.* 1990:151). Princess Point cord-wrapped stick ceramics are rare or absent on late Saugeen sites (Spence *et al.* 1990:151).

Princess Point

Background

Princess Point is one of a number of transitional Middle to Late Woodland cultures in the Northeast dating from about 1570 to 970 B.P., and is seen as ancestral to later Iroquoian societies in the area (Stothers 1977; Fox 1990; Crawford and Smith 1996; Smith and Crawford 1997; Smith 2001). This transitional period is defined on the basis of changes in ceramic vessel attributes (Fox 1990:172). Earlier coil construction is generally replaced by a paddled vessel production technique where vessels are formed from large clay masses. Vessel body form changes from elongated, with a cone-shaped base, to a more globular form. Cord-wrapped stick impressions replace simple and dentate tool impressions (Williamson 1990; Smith and Crawford 1997).

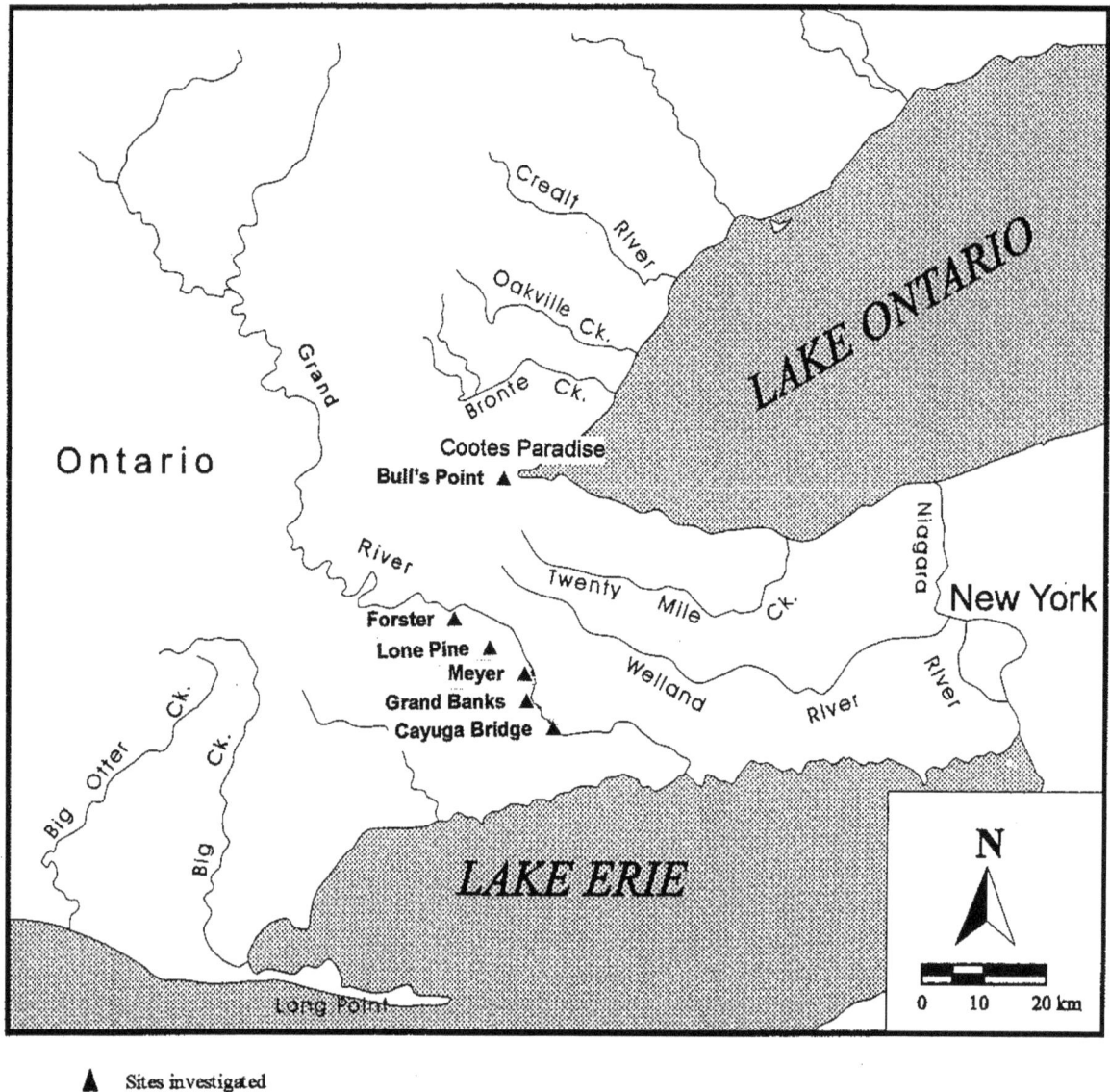

▲ Sites investigated

Figure 1 Map of Princess Point Study Region

Princess Point peoples may have seasonally exploited riverine bars and marshland sites at an early date and more intensively with time (Crawford *et al.* 1998). A diverse mix of hunting, fishing, gathering, and agriculture describes their subsistence pattern. The plant component included corn, starchy grains, greens, fleshy fruits, wetland plants, weedy annuals, and nut. The earliest evidence of horticulture in Ontario is from Princess Point (Crawford *et al.* 1997; Crawford and Smith 2001).

This research explores the palaeoethnobotany of six Princess Point sites: Grand Banks, Lone Pine, Cayuga Bridge, Meyer, Forster, and Bull's Point (see Figure 1). Monckton (1999) provides a recent analysis and summary of the botanical remains of another Princess Point site, Holmedale, which is located on the floodplains of the Grand River. Holmedale's environmental context, settlement pattern, artifact assemblage, and plant remains are similar to sites that are the focus of this study. Holmedale is defined as Princess Point on the basis of a

single rim-sherd bearing cord-wrapped stick impressions characteristic of the period. At Holmedale, 885 charred seeds and fragments were recovered from samples representing 21 features. Monckton (1999) identified a suite of plants common to the Northern Mixed Economy, including maize, fleshy fruits, greens and grains, and other taxa: similar to the archaeobotanical assemblages analyzed in this study.

Material Culture

Earthenware, the main diagnostic feature of Princess Point, is decorated with cord-wrapped stick in oblique, vertical, and horizontal rows arranged in bands (Stothers 1977; Fox 1990; Smith and Crawford 1997). Pottery is mainly constructed by the paddle and anvil technique formed from a large clay masses. This technique is in contrast to earlier Middle Woodland coil-produced pottery, although a few coil pieces still are recovered from Princess Point sites (Fox 1990; Crawford and Smith

1996). Vessel shapes are variable but generally have semi-conical bases and collarless, out-flaring rims. Many vessels have large exterior punctates around the neck that produce interior bosses.

Ceramic smoking pipes are present but not common (Fox 1990:175; Smith and Crawford 1997). At the Lone Pine site (about 1100 B.P.) archaeologists recovered nine pipe bowls, accounting for nearly one-third of all ceramics at this site (Smith and Crawford 1997). The Holmedale site produced 34 pipe fragments (Pihl 1999). Princess Point pipe bowls tend to be either barrel or cylindrical in shape. The pipe bowls are plain and smooth, or are decorated with rows of punctates, cord-wrapped stick impressed geometric patterns or incised motifs. Stems are round or D-shaped. Elbows are both right- and obtuse-angled (Fox 1990; Stothers 1977; Smith and Crawford 1997). Smith and Crawford (1997) characterize these pipes as fully functional, but not elaborate. What was smoked in these pipes is not known.

This study did not produce tobacco seeds; however, Monckton identified eight tobacco seeds from the Princess Point Holmedale site. Carbonized tobacco seeds associated with carbonized wood from a hearth feature, at the Stratford Flats site, date to about 975 B.P. (Fecteau 1983). Fox (1990:178) suggests that tobacco may have entered Ontario along with corn and also may have been grown by Princess Point; but there is no evidence to support this view yet. Other plant materials also may have provided the alkaloids that were sought through smoking (Yarnell 1964).

The Princess Point lithic assemblage consists of a limited range of bifacial chert tools and a variety of cutting and scraping tools (Stothers 1977; Fox 1990; Shen 1997). Levanna-like triangular projectile points and T-based drills are found. Ground stone tools are rare; but chisels, adzes, and steatite pipes are present. Roughstone artifacts include anvil/hammerstones, cobble hammerstones, and notched pebble netsinkers (Stothers 1977; Fox 1990). Princess Point lithics of the lower Grand River valley are almost exclusively composed of dark gray Onondaga chert (Fox 1990; Ormerod 1994; Shen 1997). Worked bone, antler, and shell are rare at Princess Point sites compared to Middle Woodland, but some bone awls, antler tine points, antler flaking tools, and marginella shell beads are reported (Fox 1990).

Shen (1997:297) notes that variability in lithic technology may be a direct response to a change in subsistence strategies and with subsistence diversification lithic production tended toward generalized patterns. Shen (1997) found that Princess Point people tended to adopt a non-standardized core reduction strategy, and predominantly produced and used flake tools for the requirements of mixed economic activities. Shen (1997) concludes that the occurrence of generalized stone tool production during Princess Point is one of a series of consequences arising from the origins of agriculture. This change in lithic technology could have been caused by a combination of external factors (such as sedentism, population increase, and availability of raw materials) and internal factors (such as time-stress, productive organization, and land use), rather than by a single factor. If these elements are enabled by the emergence of food production, patterns of lithic production are also likely affected (Shen 1997:299).

Burial patterns are not well known. No burials have been discovered on single component sites, and none of the potential Princess Point burials have been radiocarbon dated. The few purported Princess Point burials are individual graves with the body placed in a flexed, articulated position and accompanied by grave goods (Fox 1990). At the Surma site, eight of eleven burials contained Levanna-style triangular points and grave offerings suggestive of a Princess Point provenience (Fox 1990:182). The only other possible grave site having a Princess Point affiliation is the Monarch Knoll burial in the Kitchener vicinity (Fox 1990:182).

Settlement and Scheduling

Stothers (1973, 1977) proposed a subsistence pattern for Princess Point represented by a seasonal round of a large spring to fall riverine or lacustrine aggregation and small fall to spring upland, interior hunting camps. In the spring and summer, people subsisted through limited horticulture, plant gathering, hunting, and fishing. Stothers argued that the floodplain of the Grand River valley provided an environment conducive to agricultural pursuits, but at certain times habitation of the floodplains would have been unsuitable (Stothers 1977:117). Stothers based this seasonal pattern supposition on the preceding Middle Woodland seasonal round proposition, arguing that Princess Point practiced a similar warm season macroband agglomeration and cold season microband dispersal. However, the validity of this proposal is questionable; the Middle Woodland subsistence cycle itself was not based on palaeoethnobotanical data but on inferences, assumptions, and suppositions. This aggregation and dispersal pattern is reported in ethnographic accounts of modern hunting and gathering groups, such as the Montagnais-Naskapi Cree culture in northern Quebec (Rogers 1953).

Earlier subsistence models proposed for Princess Point were based on limited animal and plant evidence (cf. Stothers 1977; MacDonald 1986; Fox 1990). The recovery and identification of floral remains only recently has become a more or less routine component of archaeological excavations, and the palaeoethnobotany of Princess Point sites is recorded on some recently excavated sites, including Varden (MacDonald 1986, Fox 1990), Stratford Flats (Fox 1990), Bull's Point and Bull's Cove (Smith et al. 1996; Kuris 1998), Grand Banks and Lone Pine (Bowyer 1995), Holmedale (Monckton 1999), Forster, Sassafras Point, and Meyer (reports on file at the University of Toronto, Department of Anthropology).

Throughout eastern North America, floodplains and riverine ecology are significant factors in models of agricultural origins (Smith 1992; Crawford *et al.* 1998). Upland sites may be later ones indicative of a shift to the Iroquoian pattern of upland villages (Smith and Crawford 1997; Crawford *et al.* 1998). Like many others in northeastern North America, several Princess Point sites are located adjacent to water. Sites are commonly located on the floodplain of the lower Grand River and a number of sites have been identified on the shores of lakes or embayments, such as Cootes Paradise. Recent research suggests that these floodplain settlements may have been occupied year-round (Crawford *et al.* 1998).

Smith and Crawford (1997) caution against basing Princess Point settlement models on unsubstantiated Middle Woodland patterns. They emphasize that the particulars of riverine geomorphology must be fully studied before concluding that natural cycles, such as flooding, helped determine Princess Point scheduling decisions. A preliminary geomorphological investigation of the stratigraphy and site formation of the Grand River floodplain explores these concerns (Crawford *et al.* 1998). This investigation concludes that during Princess Point times the floodplains of the Grand River appear to have been relatively stable and would have provided a favourable habitat environment. Future research should consider crop production logistics (Smith and Crawford 1997:25) and models that take into account more stable communities as short term, special purpose sites should be explored (Smith and Crawford 1995; Crawford and Smith 1996).

Subsistence

Crawford and Smith (1997) call the diverse subsistence pattern of the Lower Great Lakes region a Northern Mixed Economy. This subsistence pattern is a mix of agriculture, hunting, fishing, and gathering from a variety of resources and biotic zones. The plant component of the pattern includes cultigens, fleshy fruits, grains, greens, nuts, and numerous weedy annuals and perennials. These plants would have been used for subsistence, as well as for medicinal, ritual, ceremonial, clothing, and household purposes.

The floodplains along the Grand River and around Cootes Paradise would have provided attractive settlement locales for precontact populations, particularly for early horticulturalists (Walker *et al.* 1997). The alluvial soils provided high quality land for cultivation and also riverine resources, such as water, fish, shellfish, and amphibians, were nearby. Bone preservation at Princess Point sites is often poor. Analysis of faunal remains most commonly yields white-tailed deer and fish (Fox 1990; Smith and Crawford 1997). Although evidence is limited, it reflects the usual range of important subsistence-related and fur-bearing species generally found on precontact sites in Ontario (Fox 1990:176). Other species reported include bear, fox, raccoon, beaver, muskrat, grey squirrel,

woodchuck, chipmunk, rabbit, lemming, mice, bald eagle, ducks, shorebirds, songbirds, turtles, snakes, and clams (MacDonald 1986; Fox 1990; Cabeceiras 1994; Quin 1994). Fish remains include sturgeon, bass, freshwater drum, pike, walleye, bowfin, sucker, catfish, burbot, yellow perch, and pumpkinseed.

Crawford *et al.* (1997) argue that the shift to a mixed economy was complete in the Lower Great Lakes by 900 B.P. This does not suggest, however, that maize and other cultigens became so important to exclude the exploitation of other plant resources. Many researchers have suggested that cultigens eventually became the dominant food for Ontario native populations and the gathering of wild plant foods declined sharply (Heidenreich 1971; Stothers 1977, 1979; Stothers and Yarnell 1977; Sykes 1981). Recent work disputes this opinion (see Monckton 1990, 1992; Ounjian 1998). Smith and Crawford (1997) calculate that some 20% of archaeologically recovered plant remains from Late Iroquoian times are cultigens. The remaining 80% are from wild plants. Smith and Crawford (1997) contend that rather than simply replacing wild plant foods, cultigens augmented the prehistoric diet. In support of this view, Monckton's (1990, 1992) research shows that, although the Huron were intensive maize agriculturalists, they also relied on a significant amount of wild plant food, especially fleshy fruits. Crawford's (1985) study of the Seed site indicates a considerable reliance on wild plant foods and Ounjian's (1998) extensive floral analysis confirms a broad array of plants, both wild and cultivated, was used in Early and Late Iroquoian times.

The first detailed and systematic examination of plant use in southern Ontario during the early Late Woodland was conducted by Bowyer (1995). Prior to Bowyer's research, the only flotation of archaeological samples done on early Late Woodland sites in southern Ontario was at the Varden site (MacDonald 1986; Fox 1990) and Stratford Flats site (Fox 1990). At the Varden site, the analysis did not produce any evidence for cultigens, but bramble, sumac, strawberry, elderberry, wild plum, wild cherry, and wild grape were identified (MacDonald 1986; Fox 1990). At Stratford Flats, one tobacco seed is reported associated with carbonized wood dating to 1075 B.P. (Fox 1990). The analysis also produced four maize kernels. From the original excavations at the Grand Banks site, one maize kernel was recovered (Stothers and Yarnell 1977). From the late Princess Point/early Glen Meyer Porteous site, Stothers (1977) reports 44 carbonized maize kernels and one cob fragment.

In 1997, Smith and Crawford (1997) noted that recent detailed research had produced a plant remains assemblage that included one cultigen (maize); three types of nuts (acorn, butternut, and hickory); four fleshy fruit taxa (American nightshade, bramble, ground cherry, and strawberry); grasses and greens (chenopod, purslane, switchgrass, and other grasses); and other taxa (arrowhead, cleavers, and sumac).

The analysis of the Holmedale site identified the cultigens maize and tobacco (Monckton 1999). The maize remains were very fragmented but some kernels were present. The study concluded that the most common fleshy fruit was bramble. One strawberry seed was identified, and chenopod, spikenard, sumac, cleavers, and cat-tail were present. Erect knotweed, purslane, and small grass seeds were not recovered. Walnut, oak, and hickory represented the nut remains. Although, wild plant foods were more common, the quantity of maize suggests some degree of reliance on the cultigen.

The archaeological record documents five cultigens that northern Iroquoian groups grew in Ontario: maize, bean, cucurbit, sunflower (*Helianthus annuus* var. *macrocarpa),* and tobacco (Fecteau 1985; Monckton 1990, 1992; Crawford and Smith 1995; Smith and Crawford 1997; Ounjian 1998). Maize was the first cultigen to reach southern Ontario (Crawford *et al.*1997) and, by Glen Meyer times, all five cultigens were present with maize being widespread (Ounjian 1998). Agricultural origins in south-central Ontario are the result of secondary processes and none of the plants involved in crop production are native to Ontario (Crawford *et al.* 1998).

Early theories proposed that cultigens were introduced slowly and gradually, and were not established until Middle Ontario Iroquoian (650 to 600 B.P.) (Caldwell 1958; White 1963; Wright 1966). Later theories suggested an early rapid introduction of cultigens in early Late Woodland (1500 to 1000 B.P.) (Noble 1975; Stothers 1977; Trigger 1981). Later theories now are supported by a series of accelerator mass spectrometry (AMS) dates on maize from the Princess Point Grand Banks site that gives a range from 1570 to 970 B.P. (Crawford *et al.* 1997). The AMS dates on kernel and cupule fragments from Grand Banks (see Table 1) are the earliest direct dates for corn in the Great Lakes area, and provide evidence that this crop was cultivated in the lower Grand River valley by the sixth century A.D. (Crawford *et al.* 1997). The Meyer site produced a corn fragment dating to 1270 B.P., and another maize fragment from Forster dates to almost 1200 B.P. (Crawford and Smith 2001). The Surma site is of interest because human bone from there indicates the presence of a relatively high C_4 plant (perhaps the tropical cultigen corn) (Katzenberg *et al.* 1995). However, the date of 1300 B.P. for the bone is not radiocarbon dated and is surmised from pottery seriation.

How and why maize came to Ontario is still a matter of debate. Horticulture in Ontario is best examined within the context of secondary origins, that is, diffusion and migration models (Crawford and Smith 2001). The earliest theory postulated that Hopewell people or their descendants migrated into southern Ontario from the Midwest bringing maize with them, and a timely climatic amelioration allowed the successful introduction of maize

to Ontario (Stothers 1977; Stothers and Yarnell 1977; Jackson 1983). However, Middle Woodland horticulture in the Midwest was not based on corn; therefore, this early argument does not hold (Crawford and Smith 1996, 2001). Fox (1990:185) points out that the reassignment of the Point Pelee Focus to the non-Princess Point Western Basin Tradition weakens the tie between Princess Point and the Ohio Hopewell manifestations. This reassignment led more recent research to reject the Ohio population migration hypothesis in favour of *in situ* development from the Middle Woodland. The cultigen may have been introduced either by migration of a southeastern group or through diffusion of ideas that were incorporated into the Middle Woodland subsistence pattern and ultimately adopted by Princess Point (Fox 1990; Snow 1995; Smith and Crawford 1997). In 1995, Snow argued that a northward migration of Iroquoian people brought maize horticulture with them, hypothesizing that this migration occurred after 1100 B.P. Snow (1996) subsequently accommodated more recent evidence (see Crawford and Smith 1996; Crawford *et al.* 1997) into his argument and, most recently, contends that Iroquoian people were migrating northward by about 1500 B.P. At this point, not enough is known about Middle Woodland subsistence in southern Ontario on which to base a firm argument regarding the introduction of maize into the area.

The extent to which maize played a role in Princess Point subsistence is not known, but its presence at a number of sites suggests that maize was becoming an important component of Princess Point diet some time before 1000 B.P. (Smith and Crawford 1997). It generally is accepted that corn remains found in Ontario are the Eastern eight-row variety, also known as eight-row Northern Flint (Noble 1975; Smith and Crawford 1997; Ounjian 1998). This variety was critical to northern Iroquoian horticulture and, in her study of Glen Meyer, Ounjian (1998:62) identifies Eastern eight-row.

In this study of Princess Point, corn density varies from site to site. For example, the Grand Banks site, particularly Feature 210, was rich but few remains were recovered at Bull's Point. Smith and Crawford (1997:26) contend that, with the range of radiocarbon dates from Grand Banks (1570 to 970 B.P.) (Crawford *et al.* 1997) and the highest densities of corn coming from the 1000 B.P. range, the site may represent occupations from the initiation of corn husbandry through the initial intensification of agriculture in the lower Grand River valley. Smith and Crawford (1997:27) speculate that the introduction of the cultigen to southern Ontario was introduced through Princess Point communities, either by migration or diffusion, as early as 1500 to 1400 B.P. Its arrival probably was not much earlier considering the dates of its introduction in areas to the south (Crawford *et al.* 1997). Crawford *et al.* (1997) suggest that initially limited cultivation was practiced, coinciding with the development of large river bar sites, such as Grand Banks.

Table 1 Princess Point Radiocarbon Dates

Site	Lab Number	Sample	Radiocarbon Date (BP)
Grand Banks, 729-671	TO-5307	cupule	1570±90
Grand Banks, 729-670	TO-5308	cupule	1500±150
Meyer, 573-514	TO-8150	cupule	1270±100
Grand Banks, 729-671	TO-4585	kernel	1250±80
Forster	TO-7039	cupule	1150±100
Cayuga Bridge, Fe. 5	TO-7293	butternut	1110±50
Grand Banks, Fe. 1	TO-4584	kernel	1060±60
Lone Pine, 460-500	TO-4586	kernel	1040±60
Grand Banks, Fe. 210	TO-5875	cupule	970±50
Bull's Point	TO-6341	kernel	960±60
Cayuga Bridge, Fe. 18	TO-7445	hickory nutshell	980±110
Meyer, Fe. 56	TO-8964	dog phalanx	890±60
Cayuga Bridge, A2	TO-7446	wood charcoal	120±50

Princess Point represents the first shift to a subsistence pattern that incorporated horticulture into a hunting, fishing, and plant collecting lifeway that was practiced by earlier peoples. At this time of economic change, a transition to centred communities was occurring, concomitant with a shift in subsistence patterns. By 1000 B.P., with the intensification of cultivation, Princess Point became dependent on a food production subsistence regime. This economic pattern was accompanied by the development of more centred communities, providing the basis for a more settled, village-based lifeway, which would clearly emerge during Iroquoian times (Fox 1993; Smith and Crawford 1997). For whatever reason maize agriculture was adopted, this change ultimately would affect populations through increased sedentism, changes in ceramic production, population aggregation (Crawford and Smith 1996), matrilocality, territoriality, and warfare (Stothers and Yarnell 1977). The adoption of agriculture would have far-ranging effects on the lifeway and social organization of a culture and its adoption generally is associated with cultural complexity.

Late Woodland

Crawford and Smith (1996; Smith and Crawford 1995, 1997) support the argument that the later Late Woodland Glen Meyer is part of a continuum from and is descendant to Princess Point. Earlier researchers had speculated on this cultural continuity (Noble 1975; Fox 1982, 1990; MacDonald 1986; Williamson 1990) and, although growing evidence supports this view, the relationship still is not entirely clear. The date of

inception for this Early Ontario Iroquoian tradition is debated, but most researchers agree on a termination date of about 700 B.P. The generally accepted time range for Early Ontario Iroquoian is from about 1100 to 700 B.P. (Smith 1990; Williamson 1990:310; Ounjian 1998). Smith and Crawford (1997:24; Smith 1997) point out that the transition from Princess Point to Glen Meyer was not abrupt. Some Princess Point communities may have persisted until at least 1000 B.P. or later, overlapping Glen Meyer.

An area encompassing southwestern Ontario, extending east from Long Point on the north shore of Lake Erie, as far north as the Ausable River, and to the southeastern shore of Lake Huron, defines the geographic area of Glen Meyer (Williamson 1990:304). This area overlaps Princess Point, but extends further west. Initially, researchers saw the Glen Meyer as an Ontario variant of New York Owasco and thought it to be an *in situ* development based on horticulture (Lee 1952; Ritchie 1944). James Wright (1966) then defined the Early Ontario Iroquois tradition as being comprised of two regional variants: Glen Meyer in the west and Pickering in the east. Researchers believed that both these two branches shared much in common with contemporaneous phases of Owasco in New York State, and that the origin of all three developments could be traced back to the Middle Woodland period, in their respective regions of the Lower Great Lakes (Wright 1966:94; Williamson 1990:293). Both Ritchie (1961) and Wright (1966) agreed that the centre of Iroquoian development was in Ontario and New York. Wright (1966) argued that in later

Ontario Iroquoian times, the Pickering tradition conquered and absorbed the Glen Meyer tradition. This theory is contested by Williamson (1990:295) who suggests that the argument to support a division of these two branches fails to adequately consider the variability between regional populations. Pickering and Glen Meyer may simply represent two spatially different but culturally similar traditions. Clearly, in southern Ontario, settlement, subsistence, and material culture have considerable regional variability (Williamson 1990:295). Williamson (1990:313) argues that Early Ontario Iroquoian was a time of regional cultural adaptations overlain with uniformity in settlement and subsistence patterns.

Archaeologists consider the Porteous site to be either early Glen Meyer or transitional between Princess Point and Early Ontario Iroquoian (Fox 1990:178; Williamson 1990:308; Smith and Crawford 1997). The site is described as a small village situated on an elevated sandy knoll, with rectangular houses, central hearths, and storage areas (Noble and Kenyon 1972). Porteous represents one of the earliest moves away from the previous Princess Point floodplain settlement pattern to one that tended to be focused on elevated sandy knolls. Spence *et al.* (1990) suggest that the Early Ontario Iroquoian settlement pattern generally involved permanent villages, together with seasonally occupied camps, that were occupied in the fall for hunting and in the spring for fishing.

Structured, settled village life is evident in early Glen Meyer (Ounjian 1998), and recent research suggests a trend toward year-round settlement during the earlier Princess Point (Crawford *et al.* 1996; Smith and Crawford 1997). Early Glen Meyer houses were relatively small and elliptical, increasing in dimensions through time (Williamson 1990:304). Glen Meyer villages were generally small in size (under one hectare), palisaded with one or two rows, and contained long houses of various shapes and sizes (Noble 1975; Williamson 1990:306). Williamson (1990) proposes that these settlements were base villages, occupied only during winter, and small groups left the villages during the summer months to travel to specialized resource sites for hunting, gathering, and fishing.

The material culture of early Glen Meyer contains several elements that resemble Princess Point. For example, early Glen Meyer pottery is similar to Princess Point's in its paddle construction, conoidal bases, and collarless rims, with cord-wrapped stick decoration (Smith and Crawford 1997). Early Iroquoian vessels, however, are more likely to be thin-walled, compared to Princess Point. The vessels tend to be globular in shape, with more rounded bottoms, than in earlier times (Fox 1990; Williamson 1990). Early Iroquoian vessels are made by modeling a large lump of clay into the vessel shape (Williamson 1990). Vessel rims are normally collarless or have a slight collar development. Vessels tend to be decorated,

often on both exterior and interior rims, as well as on the exterior necks and lips. The most common exterior rim motif is oblique lines that are produced by linear and dentate stamping. Cord-wrapped stick impressions are prevalent in early assemblages. Punctate decoration occurs on both interior and exterior vessel surfaces. The use of punctation, dentate stamping, and cord-wrapped stick impressions suggests continuity from preceding Princess Point ceramics (Fox 1990; Williamson 1990; Smith and Crawford 1997).

Smith and Crawford (1997) identify some smoking pipes dating to Princess Point and pipes become more prevalent in the Glen Meyer (Williamson 1990). Glen Meyer pipes are roughly made, with obtuse- or right-angled elbows. The stems are plain. The bowls tend to be barrel- or cylindrical-shaped. Most pipes are undecorated, but a few are punctated and occasionally are incised. Some sites have yielded effigy pipes, including effigies of a human face, a snake, a quadruped, and a turkey (Williamson 1990:299). Ounjian (1998) found substantial botanical evidence for tobacco use, identifying tobacco seeds at 80% of Glen Meyer sites. This is a significant finding indicative of the growing importance of plant material that was likely used for ritual, ceremonial, or recreational purposes.

Early Glen Meyer tool assemblages are similar to those of Princess Point. Projectile points are triangular, but smaller than earlier points, with concave bases and downward projecting corner spurs (Williamson 1990:299). Generally, the triangular points are smaller than the Levanna-style point associated with Princess Point sites. However, like Princess Point sites, flake tools dominate the assemblages. Worked bone assemblages are poorly known, compared to later Iroquoian sites.

Faunal remains from early Glen Meyer sites are similar to those of Princess Point; deer, small mammals, birds, fish, and amphibians are found (Berg 1988; Ounjian 1998). Williamson (1990:317) notes that faunal resources exploited from Glen Meyer sites include deer, raccoon, squirrel, wild turkey, river-dwelling mammals, fish, and turtles.

Although plant remains reflect greater diversity for Glen Meyer (see Ounjian 1998) than for Princess Point, this study and others (Bowyer 1996; Smith and Crawford 1997; Ounjian 1998) provide evidence for a continuum of use of many plant species. Williamson (1990:317) notes the recovery of a variety of nuts and other wild plant foods from Glen Meyer sites. However, Glen Meyer shows evidence for an increasing reliance on agriculture. The Glen Meyer were growing five cultigens: maize, common bean, cucurbit, sunflower, and tobacco (Ounjian 1998). Nutmeats, especially acorn, are present and fleshy fruits are well represented in Ounjian's (1998) study. The most common fruits are bramble, elderberry, strawberry, and American nightshade. These plants likely flourished in a human-impacted landscape, largely due to increased gardening activities (Crawford *et al.* 1998). Ounjian (1998) reports evidence for the use of all species of the Eastern Agricultural Complex (see Linton 1924), with the exception of maygrass. This suite of plants includes little barley, erect knotweed, chenopod, sunflower, and marsh elder. The most frequently recovered seed is purslane. Ounjian (1998) argues that, despite including wild plant foods in their diet, the Glen Meyer were not casual horticulturalists but extensively practiced agriculture, giving them economic stability and allowing them to remain year-round in their villages.

Anthropogenesis

People altered their landscapes, and anthropogenesis, as an influence on habitats in the Great Lakes region, is recognized as an important factor affecting plant resources (Yarnell 1964). Fire, land clearance, settlements, agriculture, and building are a few of the human factors that disturbed the natural landscape. These disturbed-soil open settings were not representative of a pristine wilderness but were a mix of weeds, opportunistic species, and, often, cultigens. Disrupted habitats provided the opportunity for human experimentation with colonizing species of plants, ranging from simple toleration and various forms of encouragement to cultivation (Asch and Asch 1985; Ford 1985; Smith 1992, 1995a,b).

Manipulation of plants, through weeding, gardening or cultivation, may have begun with the establishment of more permanent settlements. In river valley areas, such as the Grand River valley, the transition by hunter-gatherer groups from having relatively short-term camp sites to less mobile sites and sedentary settlements would occur over time. Settlements would represent disturbed-soil open habitats that were occupied throughout the growing season and reused year after year, sometimes over long periods of time (Smith 1995b:201). Plants that grew abundantly in floodplain environments, had substantial harvest yield potential, and were storable would be attractive resources. A new, anthropogenic habitat (one that was continually disturbed and open) would enrich local resources (Smith 1995b:201).

Along a continuum of increasing intervention in the life cycles of plants, a critically important point was the annual cycle of harvesting, that is, the storing of seed and planting the stored seed at the beginning of the subsequent growing season. The deliberate planting of harvested seeds over time could shift plant species into the domesticated category. Sowing seed stock added a human behavioural component to open habitats, imposing a new and different set of selective pressures on plants, and created a new environment that was different from any found in nature (Smith 1995b:198). Bye (1985) notes that in the Southwest United States, weeds are encouraged to grow among crops and are harvested as edible greens, suggesting a conscious melding of wild plants and cultigens in gardens, as well as in diets. These

activities would constitute a conceptual framework for the manipulation of wild plants and the intervention in the life cycles of plants (Smith 1995b:211). The conceptual framework of plant manipulation and encouragement, establishment of open-habitats, and increasing intervention in the life cycles of plants would make the efforts needed to tend and cultivate the cultigen maize readily accepted.

Agricultural Emergence

In 1924, Ralph Linton was the first to suggest that farming economies based on indigenous small-seed plants may have existed prior to the adoption of maize agriculture in eastern North America. Linton (1936:214) also suggested that river valleys provided an ecological area favourable for growing crops, as they are rich and are replenished with silt brought down by floods. This view has come to be supported by the archaeological record (Smith 1992). Fritz (1993:55) notes that the most thoroughly developed model for the domestication of these plants involves the creation and maintenance of open, disturbed, and enriched human habitation areas on river terraces. Eastern North America was an independent centre of plant domestication with substantial food production economies well under way prior to the introduction of maize and bean from Mesoamerica. Archaeological evidence is distributed in riverine areas, from eastern Kentucky and Tennessee, west to the Ozarks, and north to Illinois (Smith 1992; Fritz 1993).

Researchers consider that horticulture in the Lower Great Lakes, New York, Pennsylvania, and New England is the result of secondary domestication processes (Smith and Crawford 1997; Crawford 1999). Secondary domestication or intensification is a more common process than primary domestication and can be the result of diffusion, migration, or both (Cowan and Watson 1992a). One route to secondary agriculture is when a suite of domesticated plants is introduced into an area where economies are dominated by foraging. Agriculture then slowly replaces the foraging lifeway. Secondary developments or intensification may also occur with the introduction of a new crop into a cultural system that is already dependent upon some indigenous cultivated plants, with the new crop plant often becoming dominant. This type of secondary horticultural origins took place in eastern North America, where the native starchy and oily-seeded plants of the Eastern Agricultural Complex were supplanted by the cultigen maize (Cowan and Watson 1992; Smith 1992, 1995). This secondary process also occurred in Japan, where the Jomon pattern of multicropping was replaced by rice cultivation (Crawford 1992).

Geographically, the domestication of plants in eastern North America appears to have covered a broadly distributed area without a specific core. A trend towards more intensive exploitation of a diversity of plant foods is seen in the archaeological record, dating over 3500 years ago (Fritz 1993), with the importance of tending and maintaining early native crops gradually increasing from the Late Archaic period onwards. Populations relied heavily upon wild plant foods, augmented with a small suite of plants produced from small-scale cultivation. Sunflower, chenopod, and marsh elder provide the earliest signs of plant management in the Midwest by Archaic societies (Asch and Asch 1985; Yarnell 1987; Chapman and Watson 1993; Fritz 1986, 1993). Small, starchy seeds were an important component of the subsistence base and evidence for the early exploitation of chenopod is documented (Crawford 1982; Asch and Asch 1985; Fritz 1986; Smith and Cowan 1987; Yarnell 1987), together with maygrass (Chapman and Shea 1981; Heiser 1985; Smith 1992, 1995; Yarnell 1993).

The subsistence practices of the Archaic continued into the Early Woodland period, and dating from 2500 years ago, gardening played an even more vital part of the subsistence base (Fritz 1993:39). Evidence for the ongoing process of domestication is provided by the seed coat of chenopod seeds becoming progressively thinner (Smith 1992, 1995), and increasingly larger sunflower seeds being recovered (Fritz 1986; Yarnell 1993:22-25). Fritz (1993:43) reports that flotation samples yielded thousands of charred starchy and oily seeds of native crops, especially chenopod. Some 2200 years ago, cultures grew and stored native crops in considerable numbers. Corn was brought into some indigenous gardening systems in small quantities; however, no evidence exists for consumption of appreciable amounts of corn until after the end of the Middle Woodland (Fritz 1993:55-56). The earliest dated corn in eastern North America comes from the Holding site in the American Bottom area, about 2000 years ago, and other dates are attributed to the second century A.D. (Riley *et al.* 1994). The introduction of the cultigen corn came at a time when the Eastern Agricultural Complex was already well developed (Cowan and Watson 1992a), and for the next 600 years, corn was grown, but only in small amounts. Yarnell (1993:22) notes that most of the corn remains from this time period are very fragmentary.

With the emergence of Middle Woodland, production of native crops increased dramatically and there is a recurring group of small and large starchy and oily-seeded plants (Yarnell 1974; Chapman and Shea 1981; Johannessen 1984; Asch and Asch 1985). Yarnell (1993:25) suggests that the Middle Woodland emergence resulted from more effective subsistence practices based largely on native plant husbandry. Chenopod often is the most abundant of these species, but maygrass (Cowan 1978), little barley, and knotweed (Fritz 1987) are numerous and common in flotation samples (Fritz 1993:39). Some evidence of knotweed domestication appears about 800 years ago and continues for 500 years (Fritz 1987; 1993). Marsh elder and sunflower are well represented in rock shelter deposits (Fritz 1993:39). These six species are part of what is known as the Eastern Agricultural Complex and, in the Middle Woodland,

these seed species increasingly become an important, storable dietary staple (Fritz 1993:47). Although there is regional variability, Fritz (1993:49) notes that a recognizable archaeobotanical pattern arises with small grain seeds remaining below 30% of the total seed sample until near the end of the Archaic, and then dramatically increasing to 90% during the Middle Woodland.

Although significant during the Middle Woodland, corn dramatically increases in importance, and eventually displaces other plant foods, only well into the Late Woodland (Yarnell 1993:22). Evidence for the increasing socioeconomic importance of plant husbandry systems over a broad area, during a time of considerable cultural change, is clear. Population levels rose markedly from about 1700 to 1000 B.P. with widespread growth and dispersal of populations especially within river valley landscapes (Smith 1992:111). Hart (2001) argues that at some point after the adoption of maize agriculture (or the migration of agriculturalists), some families adopted matrilocal residence. More than patrilocal residence, matrilocal residence may have helped ensure the continuation of agricultural traditions and innovations, thus perpetuating favourable maize gene complexes (Hart 2001:169).

In most early Late Woodland sites at this time, there is a combination of plants and considerable evidence for a continuum of small-scale seed crop cultivation leading up to and throughout the Late Woodland. The small starchy, oily seeds, especially chenopod, but also knotweed, little barley, and maygrass, are most common and sometimes very abundant. A few sunflower seeds and tobacco seeds are also recovered. There are enough corn fragments appearing in the early Late Woodland assemblages to indicate that corn was grown, but perhaps not to the degree that it was a staple (Johannessen 1993:60). Major plant foods appear to be fleshy fruits and nuts (Johannessen 1993:64). Other Late Woodland seeds that are found in the Eastern Woodlands, as well as at Princess Point sites, include hackberry, bramble, sumac, grape, elderberry, cleaver, purslane, American nightshade, and members of the grass family and mint family. Evidence for plant cultivation is characterized by numerous nut remains and chenopod seeds, which are often the only seed present in quantity. For example, at the Holding site in Illinois, chenopod seeds average over seven seeds per litre, the only seed taxon present in quantity (Riley *et al.* 1994). Corn fragments are identified in the northern area of the Eastern Woodlands, as well as sunflower (Johannessen 1993:66-67). This pattern is comparable to that found in Princess Point, with the notable exception that Princess Point assemblages contain relatively small amounts of nut.

Corn production increases dramatically and rapidly replaces starchy and oily-seeded plants about 1100 to 1000 B.P. (Smith 1992:111). After this time period, cultivated crops truly become important staples.

Although the earliest dates for macrobotanical evidence of maize in northeastern North America date back about 2000 years ago, it appears that maize played a minor role in plant husbandry systems during the first 600 years after its initial introduction (Smith 1992:110). By 1200 B.P., the appearance of maize is widespread in the archaeological record. By 850 B.P., agricultural economies dominated by maize were well-established in river valleys throughout eastern North America (Smith 1992). Hart (1999) argues that it cannot be determined whether maize remains reflect a gradual increase in use or a relatively high use at the time the crop was adopted. The presence of maize remains in the archaeological record reflects the level of use at a particular location, together with charring, deposition, and favourable preservation (Hart 2001:170), making the intensity of maize use generally throughout the Northeast difficult to determine.

In southern Ontario, AMS radiocarbon dates on corn indicate that the introduction of maize occurred as early as 1570 B.P. (see Table 1), with maize becoming a significant crop throughout the Lower Great Lakes after 1100 B.P. (Crawford *et al.* 1997), and with the emergence of the Glen Meyer (Ounjian 1998). Crawford and Smith (1996) suggest that, in studying the emergence of food production in southwestern Ontario, a multifactorial approach should be taken that incorporates sedentism, population increase, and competition over localized resources. Localized variability of populations and increased pressures on local wild resources have the potential to lead to the development and intensification of horticulture. Regional variations of different populations would emerge, and Princess Point represents one phase of a localized variability of populations (Crawford *et al.* 1997).

No single accepted general theory explains the origins of agriculture but, rather, variability and regional developments are the general concepts that underlie explanations for primary and secondary agricultural origins. Smith (1992:250) explains that although maize gained significant importance in Northeastern subsistence strategies, maize itself did not precipitate a major change in social structure or economic systems. Societies adopted maize as an addition to an already well-established food producing economy, and the existing horticultural system was transformed by the introduction of the new crop. Crops of the Eastern Agricultural Complex were small-seeded annuals of both starchy and oily varieties. Maize was introduced when the Eastern Agricultural Complex was already entrenched. It took several hundred years for maize to gain importance and dominance in the horticultural systems of Northeastern populations. Cowan and Watson (1992:210) explain this long gap between the time when maize was first introduced and the time when it became the focal point of subsistence patterns in genetic terms. Initially, maize was a tropical cultigen, adapted for much different growing conditions than those in eastern North America. The early

maize from the area likely represents a diversity of gene pools, and these gene pools were manipulated through selection for desired characteristics. About 1000 years ago, in conjunction with the expansion of maize horticulture, the variety grown in the north adapted to the cooler mean annual temperature and shorter day-length of the Northeast. This variety of maize then grew easily and was at least as productive as the annuals of the Eastern Agricultural Complex.

Hart (1999) suggests that many incidences of the adoption of maize simply ended in its extinction over varying lengths of time in different areas. Hart argues for a coevolutionary relationship between humans and maize, where maize fitness increased as the human population sowed more kernels, thus increasing the number of plants in the ecological system. Then, because of increased food availability through higher maize yields and corresponding changes in human consumption, human fitness may also have increased. Fritz (1993) sees the adoption of maize horticulture as a continuing trend that began during the Late Archaic with the domestication of gourds, marsh elder, sunflower, and chenopod (Asch and Asch 1985; Smith 1990; Chapman and Watson 1993; Yarnell 1993). Fritz (1993) argues that we know little about early corn in the Eastern Woodlands. With considerable regional variability in the crop, whether dependency increased as a result of the availability of newer or better varieties is difficult to determine.

A number of researchers attribute the increase in crop production to subsistence stress (e.g., Ford 1974; Muller 1987; Welch 1990), such as climatic fluctuations or population growth. On the other hand, others argue that the adoption of maize caused population growth (Stothers 1977:164-167; Crawford and Smith 1996). Trigger believes there is no relationship between the adoption of maize agriculture and population growth (Trigger 1985:86-7). Crawford (1999:230) contends that we are not yet able to explain the process of agricultural intensification. The process may be linked to the evolution of northern tolerant maize (Eastern eight-row maize) but by 1850 to 1450 B.P., maize was already adapted to temperate zones (Crawford 1999:230; see Fritz 1990:490). Crawford (1999:230) notes that explanations linking intensification to climatic amelioration and population growth are minimalist proximate causes. These are weak explanations for primary agricultural origins and, likely, for secondary origins too. In Ontario, population pressure seems not to have stimulated the adoption of maize horticulture, as population growth occurred after 1100 B.P., well after the first evidence for maize (1570 B.P., see Crawford *et al.* 1997). The Medieval Warm Epoch in Ontario left no strong signature in the pollen record (Crawford *et al.* 1998), although its impact may be visible in pollen records elsewhere in the Northeast (Crawford 1999:230).

Scarry (1993:88) suggests that changing social relations and competition between groups may have led to intensified crop production to support prestige-building activities. Surplus foods may have been used for ceremonial feasts and, over time, expectations of reciprocity led to the crop being traded over some distance. Scarry (1993:88) suggests that corn may have been a special plant that was introduced and dispersed through an exchange network, carrying ritual or social status connotations. Hart (1999) agrees that ceremonial or religious reasons may have encouraged a population group to adopt and manage the cultigen. Hart (1999) contends that there are significant obstacles to the initial establishment of maize as a crop. It was likely not just one event responsible for the adoption of maize in the Eastern Woodlands. Rather, there were probably many examples of maize being adopted in several different locations. Hart (2001) also explores the affects of post-marital residence and settlement patterns on maize production evolution, concluding that matrilocality and agriculture coevolved among ancestral northern Iroquoian populations. Crawford (1999:230) notes that the sociopolitical context of horticulture is difficult to assess and is exploring other conditions in which intensification occurred, such as the floodplain setting and how people interacted with floodplain dynamics (see Crawford et al. 1998).

Scarry (1993) recognizes that there was considerable variability in subsistence economies and crop production strategies throughout the Northeast, and that there were differences in the relative importance of corn and native seed crops. However, after 1000 B.P., corn became the dominant crop. The reasons for the adoption of a cultigen such as maize into a subsistence pattern are difficult to determine. The ultimate answer likely does not lie with one reason but is best explained by several dynamic, interconnected reasons.

Sites

Five sites (Grand Banks, Lone Pine, Meyer, Cayuga Bridge, and Forster), situated within the Grand River valley, and one site (Bull's Point), located along the shores of Cootes Paradise, are the targets of this study (see Figure 1).

Grand River Valley

Grand Banks Site (AfGx-3)
Investigations over the past twenty years identify more than forty Princess Point sites along the lower Grand River (Crawford and Smith 1996). The Grand Banks site (see Figure 2 and 3) is located on a ten-hectare floodplain bar on the southwest bank of the Grand River near Cayuga, Ontario, some 35 kilometres upstream from Lake Erie. At the site, the width of the river varies between 75 and 200 metres. The alluvial soils provided high quality land for cultivation, while allowing access to riverine resources (Walker et al. 1997)

Recent excavations at Grand Banks were divided into Areas A, B, and C (see Smith and Crawford 1997). The bedrock is at about 2.5 metres, above which is alluvium, followed by 20 to 30 cm thick palaeosol (PI) or sheet midden (see Figure 3). Overlying PI is one metre of alluvium, followed by another palaeosol (PII). Palaeosol II is capped by about 55 cm of alluvium and is historic. Archaeologists excavated 18 square metres in Area A, and most units were excavated until there was no further evidence of Princess Point occupation. The most northeasterly units (730-670 and 730-671) were excavated below this level. Area A deposits revealed artifacts to a depth of nearly two metres, with two pit features and no evidence of posts.

Area B consisted of a 17-square-metre trench. Archaeologists excavated the centre of the trench until sterile deposits were reached at a depth of two metres. The trench produced a high density of artifacts, together with pits and post moulds. One cylindrical pit, Feature 210, contained exceptionally well-preserved pottery, plant, and animal remains.

Area C revealed some 93 post moulds in at least two levels in this 45-square-metre excavation area. Four probable hearths, two stone-filled features (possibly ovens), numerous small pits, artifact scatters, and soil stains also are identified. In this area, there is negligible vertical separation of Princess Point and Late Archaic/Early Woodland horizons making excavation and interpretation difficult (Smith and Crawford 1997:17). A historic component is evident and, furthermore, due to the shallowness of the archaeological horizons, this area likely received more plough damage than areas A and B. Area C has the lowest number and density of artifacts, with only 14% of the total by number and 7% by weight (Smith and Crawford 1997).

The excavation recovered over 56,000 artifacts (not including bone and plant remains). Smith and Crawford (1997) argue that the site represents three distinct prehistoric occupations, one being Princess Point. The earliest occupation appears to date to the Late Archaic/Early Woodland. The second is Princess Point and the third is historic. Five AMS (accelerator mass spectrometer) dates on maize from this site range from about 1570 to 970 years ago (see Table 1) (Crawford et al. 1997).

Lone Pine Site (AfGx-113)
The Lone Pine site (see Figure 4) is situated at the forks of a tributary of the Grand River, about two kilometres from the river and the same distance from the Grand Banks site. It lies on a low plateau with creek banks surrounding three sides. The site covers about one-half hectare, consisting of about 15 cm clay-loam over a base of heavy Oneida clay. The overburden is thin and, as a result, artifacts have been fragmented by frost and roots. The site has never been ploughed and has been subjected to very little modern cultural disturbance. Artifacts are

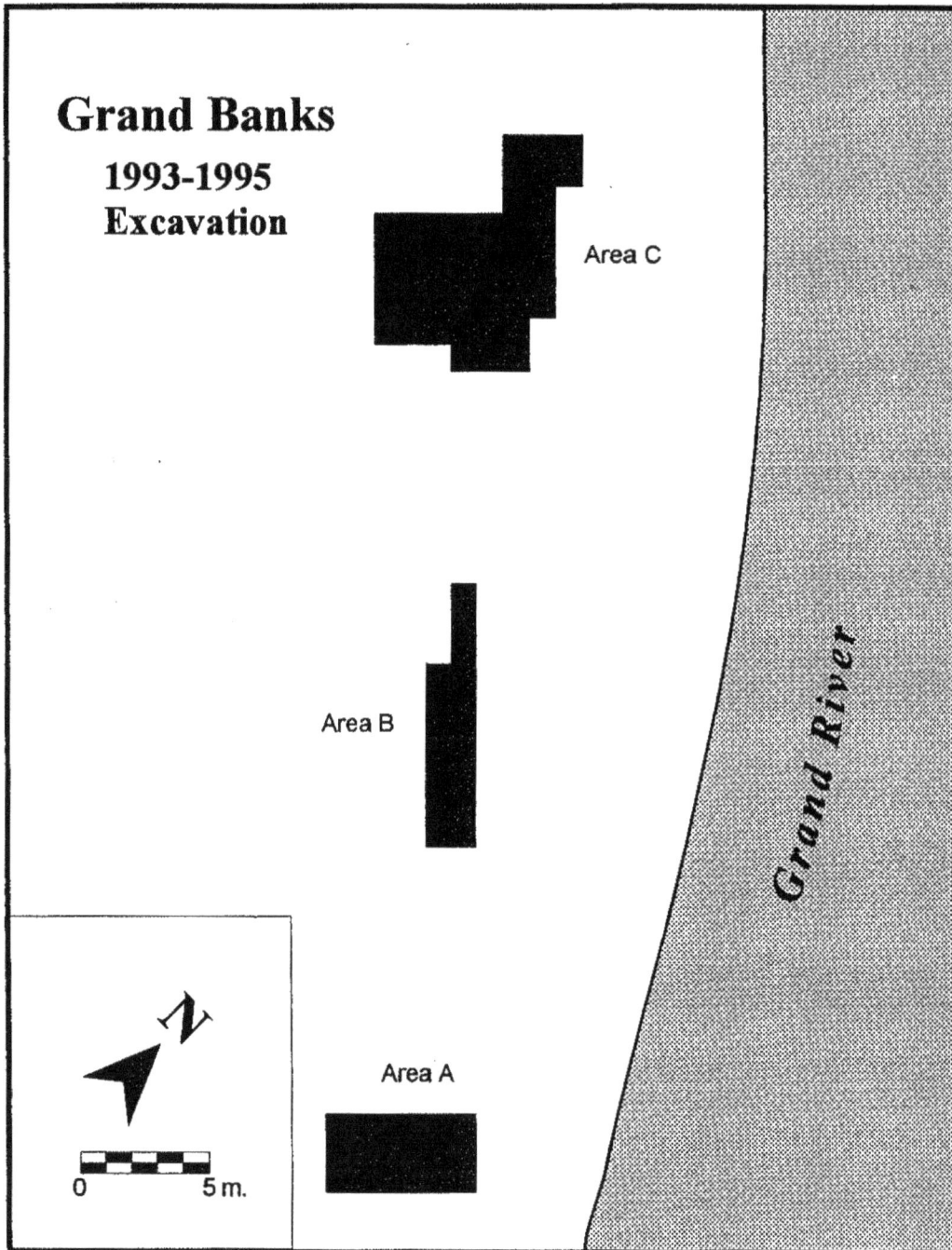

Figure 2 Grand Banks site map

clearly visible on the forest floor (Smith and Crawford 1997).

The surface collection and excavations at Lone Pine yielded pottery and lithics. The pottery is cord-wrapped stick decorated, characteristic of the late part of the Princess Point period (Beckerman 1996). The lithic assemblage is largely comprised of informal flake tools, with a small number of bifaces (Ormerod 1994; Shen 1997). Ceramic smoking pipes were recovered in comparatively large numbers (nine pipe bowls, compared to twenty-six pottery vessels). Settlement features include two hearth floors, but no definite post moulds were identified (Smith and Crawford 1997). Two radiocarbon dates on maize yielded dates from about 1000 to 750 B.P. The latter date is well into the later part of the Early Ontario Iroquoian period (Smith and Crawford 1997:20).

Meyer Site (AfGx-26)
The Meyer site is located on a 20-metre terrace overlooking a river bar on the shores of the Grand River. To date, 111 square metres of the site have been excavated, revealing over 800 post moulds and 70 features. Artifacts include high densities of chipped

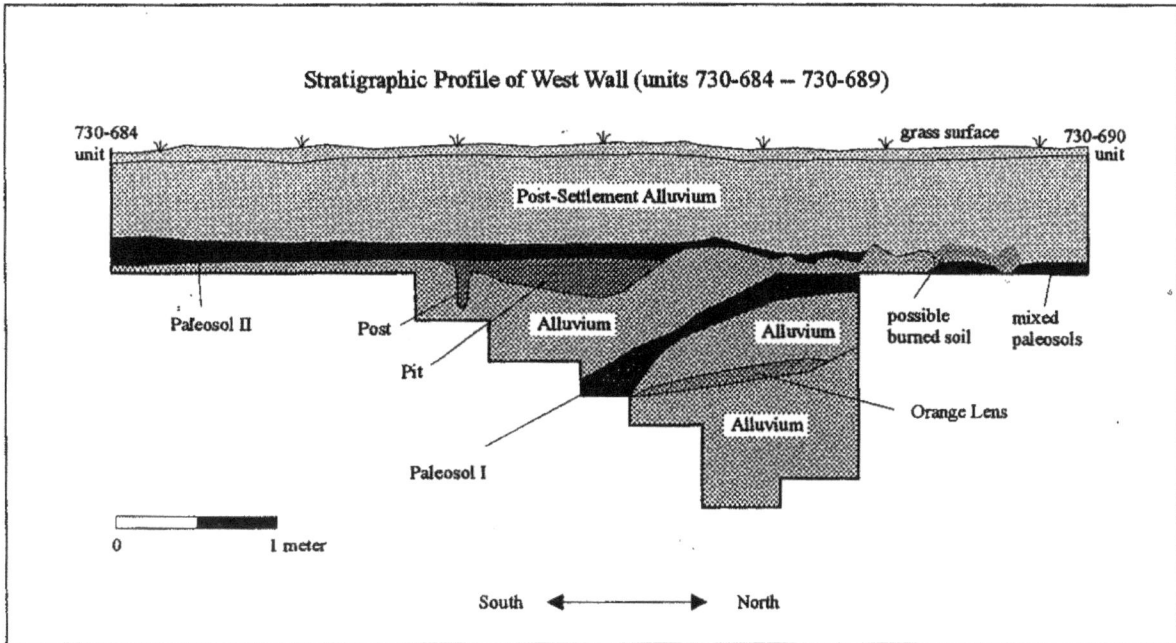

Figure 3 Grand Banks stratigraphy (Area B0

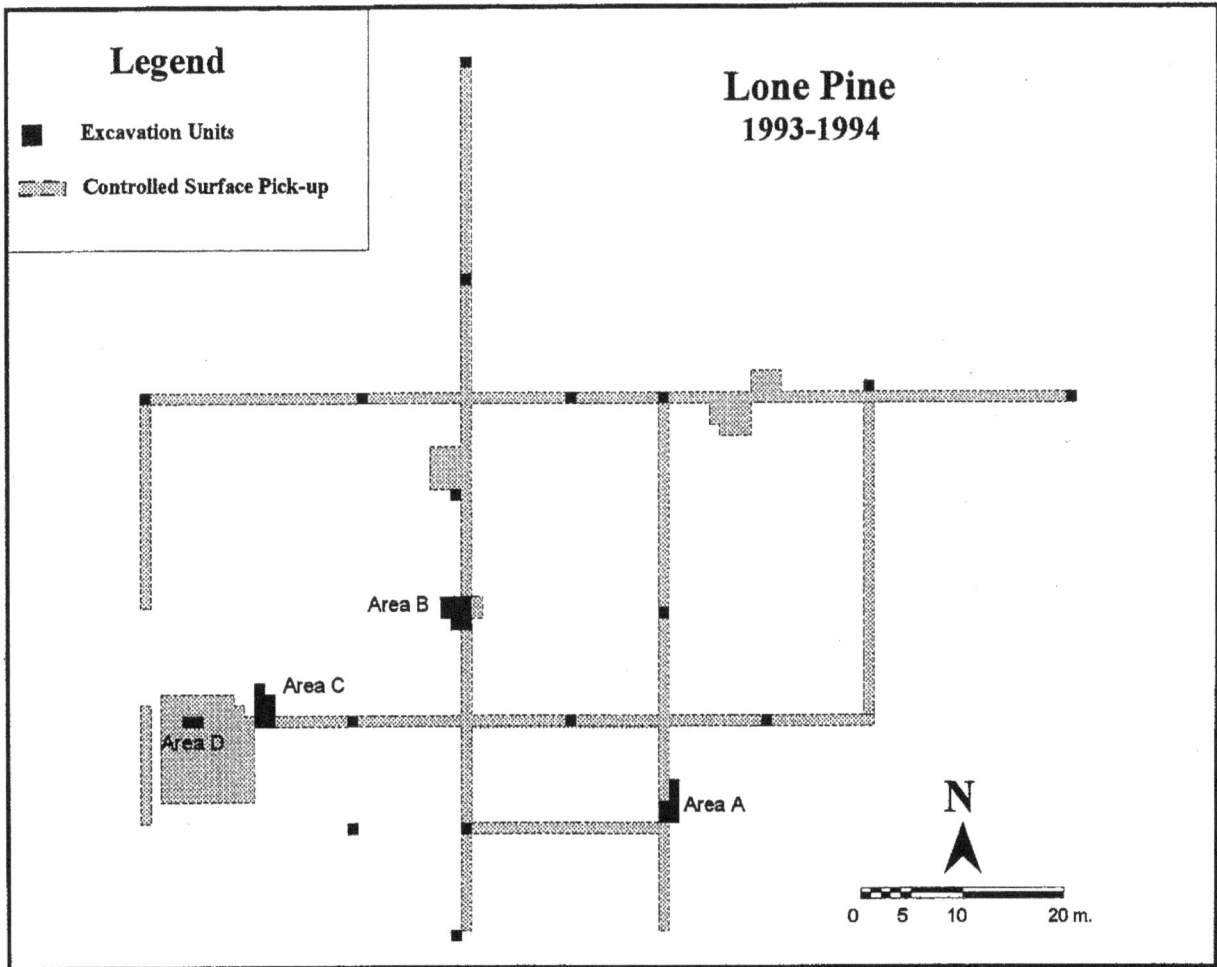

Figure 4 Map of Lone Pine Site (AfGx-113)

lithics, faunal material, and Princess Point cord-wrapped stick pottery. Some artifacts predate Princess Point, and some belong to the Ontario Glen Meyer and Uren stages. At the bottom of Feature 56, an articulated dog skeleton was recovered. One AMS radiocarbon date from the dog produced a date of about 890 B.P.; however, one other date (1270 B.P.) indicates that the occupation of this site spans several centuries (Crawford and Smith n.d.).

Cayuga Bridge Site (AfGx-1)
The Cayuga Bridge site is located on a floodplain of the Grand River. Stothers (1977) excavated the riverbank south of the bridge and, more recently, the University of Toronto excavations were 20 metres north of the bridge and 10 metres from the riverbank. Like Grand Banks, artifacts are abundant in the exposed palaeosol along the riverbank. A 10-by-9-metre area was excavated in one metre squares, exposing a total of 59 posts and 25 other features. The features include historic posts, non-cultural features, ash pits, two probable hearths, and pits with considerable carbonized material. A total of 5914 artifacts have been catalogued. Ceramics are solely cord-wrapped stick decorated pottery diagnostic of Princess Point. Two AMS dates place this site between about 1110 and 980 B.P. (Crawford and Smith n.d.).

Forster Site (AfGx-134)
The Forster site is a multi-component site located on a terrace about 100 metres south of the Grand River. There is substantial material evidence relating to a Princess Point occupation. Feature 1, analyzed in this study, is located within a circular structure about 5 metres in diameter. The feature is interpreted as a large storage pit and measured 90 centimetres in diameter and 65 centimetres in depth. A kernel fragment from the pit was AMS dated to about 1150 B.P.

Cootes Paradise

Bull's Point Site (AhGx-9)
The Bull's Point site is situated on the western side of a peninsula, along the north shore of Cootes Paradise. The site is tucked within the sides of a glacial ravine about 25 metres above the water. The steep banks of the ravine are about 15 to 20 metres wide at the shore, gradually narrowing inland. Archaeologists excavated 34 square metres. The site yielded plant and animal remains, rim sherds from 11 vessels, chipped lithic artifacts (including cores), used flakes and debitage, and fire-cracked rock. All but one of the rim sherds is decorated with Princess Point type cord-wrapped stick motifs. More than 80 post moulds were unearthed, outlining a small structure about 3.5 by 4 metres in size. No interior hearth was evident. Smith and Crawford (1997) conclude that the site may have been used by a small group of people or a single family unit while collecting plant foods in the fall. The location itself provides some shelter and is situated amid an abundance of other food resources, such as fish, shellfish, and waterfowl (Smith *et al.* 1996).

Chapter Three

Sampling and Methods

Introduction

The environment affects cultural development by providing populations with a particular set of resources (Popper and Hastorf 1988:1) and the study of plant remains is essential to understanding cultural change. This chapter provides details on the sampling strategy followed for the analysis of carbonized plant remains, together with methodological information. Challenges specific to the subdiscipline of palaeoethnobotany are explored and the methods of recovery followed in this research are explained.

Macrobotanical Sampling

Preservation

Sampling is part of every archaeological excavation as the archaeologist can only recover that which has been preserved. The challenge of sampling is inherent to the nature of palaeoethnobotany as organic material differentially preserves or deteriorates over time. This topic has been examined by a number of researchers (cf. Adams and Gasser 1980; Schaaf 1981; Toll 1988; Pearsall 1989). To help compensate for variable states of preservation and deterioration, efforts must be made to minimize bias in the recovery and interpretation of materials from flotation samples to mitigate against unavoidable problems (Lennstrom and Hastorf 1995). Detailed collection schemes in the field and careful analysis of specific samples in the laboratory can lead to meaningful contextual interpretations, intrasite variability observations, and the interpretation of feature-specific plant remains (Lennstrom and Hastorf 1995).

Several factors are responsible for the variation in durability of ancient botanical remains. The prehistoric use of plants varied. Often the entire body of a plant was used, while only specific parts (such as leaves, roots, tubers, stalks, flowers, berries, bark, or seeds) of another plant were used. Some plants and some plant parts are physically more robust and more likely to preserve than others. Dense, inedible plant parts, such as nut shells, fruit stones, and maize cobs, tend to have an excellent chance of preservation (Ford 1979; Miksicek 1987:220). Plants with dense but edible structures, such as seeds, grains, and nut meats, may be charred accidentally during preparation and can be well preserved. Plants subjected to heat, and therefore in close proximity to fire and the potential for charring, are more apt to be preserved than those plants that were used fresh. Plant foods that were cooked have a good potential to provide direct information on past human-plant interrelationships. Edible plants with a high moisture content and soft tissue, such as greens, pulpy fruits, or starchy tubers, however, leave little waste, are less likely to be burned, and are not as likely to be preserved (Ford 1979; Miksicek 1987).

The largest amount of plant remains recovered from open archaeological sites in temperate regions like Ontario is in the form of carbon or charcoal (Smith 1985:105). The probability that uncharred material dropped on open soil will become part of the archaeological record is remote; charcoal has a far better chance for survival (Ford 1979). Carbonization is the conversion by heating at high temperatures, in the absence or partial absence of oxygen, of organic carbon to inorganic carbon. Inorganic carbon is less susceptible to attack by decomposing bacteria, and mechanical damage is about the only process that will destroy a completely charred seed (Ford 1979; Miksicek 1987:219). The carbon structure is delicate, however, and may be destroyed by human activities or bioturbation, either during prehistoric times or during excavation (Smith 1985:105).

The activity of soil organisms and geologic processes do impact on archaeological deposits. Ford (1979:299-300) explains that seeds fall down soil cracks, worms displace charred fragments, and burrowing animals relocate objects. The pattern of prehistoric cultural activities, such as the location of plant preparation, consumption, and disposal, also distributes remains on a site. Some of the traditional techniques of archaeological investigations can be harmful to plant remains. Trowel scraping of floors and walking on surfaces can damage plant remains. Botanical material further can be damaged from careless excavation, packing and handling, and recovery.

Sampling Strategy

The value of any analysis depends on the quality of the sample (see Payne 1972; Jarman *et al.* 1972). Soil is ideally sampled on a massive scale since deposits for sampling cannot be rejected on the basis of visual inspection. On this research project (Princess Point Project), Dr. G.W. Crawford ensured that the collection, processing, and storage of soil samples were conducted in a careful and systematic fashion. The sampling method followed by the principal investigators (G.W. Crawford and D.G. Smith, Department of Anthropology, University of Toronto) was geared to highly controlled recovery of fine-grained data.

The emphasis in this project was on "quality over quantity in terms of simple measure of earth moved" (Smith and Crawford 1997:14). A particularist approach to methods and techniques was employed, taking into account local conditions at each site (Smith and Crawford 1997:14). One-square-metre excavation units provided spatial control at each site. All undisturbed deposits were trowel excavated, and, if not collected for flotation, soils routinely were screened through 3 mm mesh (see Smith and Crawford 1997). Palaeosols at Grand Banks were sampled nearly in their entirety. Features and posts were sampled in their entirety for flotation. A minimum of 20% of the soil from all contexts was collected for flotation.

A total of 1670 litres of soil samples from five sites (Grand Banks, Lone Pine, Meyer, Forster, and Bull's Point) was analyzed for this study. This represents 141 individual samples, each sample averaging nearly 12 litres. The number and quantity of samples from individual sites are summarized in Table 3. Tables 8, 19, 30, 45, 56, 67, and 78 delineate volume quantities and gram weight totals of all samples by context and site.

Three pit features are included in the samples from Grand Banks, representing 17% of all samples by volume. Feature 210 stood out for its remarkable preservation and was sampled in its entirety. The samples from Lone Pine include two hearth features, constituting 59% of the sample volume from this site. One feature is represented from Meyer. All samples from Forster derive from one pit feature. No features are represented in the samples from Bull's Point. Nearly one-quarter of the total samples analyzed derive from features, the remaining samples are from site floors.

Method for Recovery of Plant Remains

Flotation was carried out using a modified version (see Crawford 1986) of the SMAP flotation machine (see Watson 1976). Light fractions were recovered using a 0.425 mm geological sieve, and heavy fractions were recovered with 2 mm mesh. All plant remains reported in this project are from light fraction samples. The standardized laboratory procedure follows that of Crawford (1982) and Yarnell (1974) and is explained below.

The raw data for each sample is recorded on individual analysis sheets. The dried light fraction first is weighed and the pre-screened weight is recorded. The sample then is screened through a series of nine Canadian standard geological sieves with mesh sizes of 4.00, 2.80, 2.36, 2.00, 1.40, 1.00, 0.710, 0.425, and 0.212 mm. Sieving into fractions eases the sorting of variable sized material under a microscope. Each resulting individual fraction is weighed and recorded on the analysis sheet. Fractions from the 4.00, 2.80, and 2.36 mm screens are totally sorted into their individual component parts. The components in these upper screens include carbonized plant parts (such as tubers, large seeds, maize kernels, cupules, maize fragments, and nut fragments), wood charcoal, bone, shell, mineral matter, and uncarbonized plant material. These components are weighed; carbonized maize kernels, cupules, and fragments are counted. Fractions below the screen size of 2.36 mm

(lower screens) are examined and all carbonized seeds removed. The components are identified, recorded, and stored separately in gelatin capsules or small tins. The weights of seeds retrieved from these lower screens are negligible, tending to be 0.01 g at the most. The weights of plant parts from the lower screens are not recorded, but their numbers are counted.

Soil samples are sorted under a binocular microscope (stereoscope) of powers 10X to 40X and 10X to 30X. Plant remains are classified into analytical groups categorized by what can be called an ethnobotanical taxonomic system, rather than a botanical taxonomic system. This system classifies plant remains according to ethnographic information and divides plant material by species or genus into groups of cultigens, fleshy fruits, greens and grains, nuts, other taxa, and unknowns and unidentifiables (see Crawford 1983).

Chapter Four

Identification and Quantification of Plant Remains

Introduction

This chapter identifies charred plant remains by species and genus, quantifies the taxa, elucidates patterns, and summarizes data. Quantification of data and descriptive statistics allow comparisons between data sets. The resultant calculations lead to overall observations and summations. Absolute numbers of remains and their ratios are delineated by category and taxa. Standardized density ratios are reviewed by weights, volumes, and numbers, together with the calculated percentages for individual taxa and categories. The frequency of taxa in samples is considered. Detailed numerical information is provided in Tables 5 to 15, representing the numbers for all charred plant remains at all sites, together with percentages and densities that compare these numbers. Graphical representation enhances the data set (see Figures 5 to 18).

Plant Remains Identification

Archaeobotanical remains appear as wood charcoal, seeds, achenes, kernels, nuts, stems, and tubers. In this study, carbonized wood appears most frequently by weight and density. Wood was used for a variety of purposes, including fuel, tools, boats, and shelters. Seeds, crucial for reconstructing subsistence patterns, were an essential component of prehistoric diets, together with fruits. Cultigens, dependent on humans for survival, are important for understanding dynamic cultural patterns. Remains of corn are evidenced by kernels, cupules, fragments, and although not present in this study, cobs. Nuts were used mostly for food and can preserve well but are identifiable to species only if the fragments are large enough to display their surface markings. Tubers can provide important dietary information but these soft, starchy remains often do not preserve (see Hather 1993).

This study used two modern seed identification manuals for northeastern North America, Martin and Barkley (1961) and Montgomery (1977). For comparison with actual plant part specimens (essential to confirm an identification), the reference collections at the palaeoethnobotany lab, University of Toronto, Mississauga; the herbarium, University of Toronto, Mississauga; and the herbarium, Royal Ontario Museum, Toronto were used. Some plant reference specimens were collected in the field. Selected plant remains were photographed using a digital camera interfaced with a microscope and computer (see Plates 1 to 27).

Plant Remains by Taxon and Category

In the category of "Cultigens", maize, sunflower, and possible cucurbit rind were recovered. Kernels, cupules, and fragments provide evidence for maize. Sunflower achenes recovered in this study are placed in this category; however, their domesticated status is yet to be determined. Previous Ontario research (Monckton 1992; Ounjian 1998) categorizes sunflower as a domesticated plant. For consistency and ease of comparison this study follows previous categorization. For a general discussion of the domestication of northeastern North American plants, see Yarnell (1964, 1976), Ford (1985), Keegan (1987), Fritz (1990), Cowan and Watson (1992), Gebauer and Price (1992), Smith (1992, 1995), Scarry (1993), Price and Gebauer (1995), Gremillion (1997), and Hart (1999).

The category of "Fleshy Fruits" includes 11 species and evidence for these plants is by seeds. Plants in the category of "Greens and Grains" generally belong to North American agricultural complexes based on the reliance of oily and starchy seeds (cf. Linton 1924; Jones 1936; Smith 1992). This category includes three plant species and several members of the grass family (Poaceae). Wild rice is identified to the genus level, *Zizania* sp., as its species is not determinable at this time. The morphologies of two species, *Zizania aquatica* and *Z. palustris*, are very similar. Identification to the genus level of *Zizania* sp. follows other recent research conducted on this plant in southern Ontario (Lee *et al.* n.d.). Archaeobotanical specimens of grass remains can be particularly difficult to identify to genus or species as the seeds of different species can be very similar. Those specimens unable to be identified to the species level are identified as Poaceae in general. Ten plant species are represented in the category of "Other Taxa". Seeds, as well as tubers and stem fragments, constitute the evidence for arrowhead.

Evidence for nuts is minimal and fragmented in all samples. Three species are represented (see Table 2). The identification of nut shell and nut meat to individual species is difficult in this study, as the remains are small and fragmented. The nut remains that are not identifiable to species fall under a generic nut category.

Plant seeds and plant parts cannot all be identified. This material is "Unknown or Unidentifiable". Some of the remains could potentially be identified but some material lacks diagnostic characteristics, making identification essentially impossible.

Although the reproductive part of a plant can be known by terms other than "seed", such as grain, kernel, or achene, for the purposes of this study, the term seed is used in a general sense for any propagule. Table 4

Table 2 Common and Scientific Names of Plant Taxa

	Common Name	Scientific Name
Cultigens		
	Corn, Maize	*Zea mays*
	Cucurbit	*Cucurbita pepo*
	Sunflower	*Helianthus annuus*
Fleshy Fruits		
	American Nightshade	*Solanum americanum*
	Blueberry	*Vaccinium myrtiloides*
	Bramble	*Rubus* sp.
	Crowberry	*Empetrum nigrum*
	Dogwood	*Cornus canadensis*
	Elderberry	*Sambucus* sp.
	Grape (wild)	*Vitis* sp.
	Hackberry	*Celtis* sp.
	Hawthorn	*Crataegus* sp.
	Strawberry	*Fragaria* sp.
	Witchhazel	*Hamamelis virginiana*
Greens and Grains		
	Barnyard Grass	*Echinochloa* sp.
	Chenopod	*Chenopodium* sp.
	Erect Knotweed	*Polygonum erectum*
	Grasses	Poaceae, Gramineae
	Little Barley	*Hordeum pusillum*
	Manna Grass	*Glyceria* sp.
	Purslane	*Portulaca oleracea*
	Rye Grass	*Elymus* sp.
	Switch Grass, Panic Grass	*Panicum* sp.
	Wild Rice	*Zizania* sp. (latifolia or palustris)
Other Taxa		
	Arrowhead	*Sagittaria latifolia*
	Cat-tail	*Typha latifolia*
	Cinquefoil	*Potentilla* sp.
	Cleaver, Bedstraw	*Galium* sp.
	Milkvetch	*Astragalus* sp.
	Mint	*Mentha* sp.
	St. Johns Wort	*Hypericum* sp.
	Sassafras	*Sassafras albidum*
	Sumac	*Rhus typhina*
	Wood Sorrel	*Oxalis* sp.
Nut		
	Butternut, Walnut	*Juglans* sp.
	Hickory	*Carya* sp.
	Oak	*Quercus* sp.
Other Plant Species		
	Common Bean	*Phaseolus vulgaris*
	Jerusalem Artichoke	*Helianthus tuberosus*
	Marsh Elder	*Iva Annua*
	Maygrass	*Phalaris caroliniana*
	Pepper-grass	*Lepidium densiflorum*
	Spikenard	*Aralia nudicaulis*
	Sunflower, Common	*Helianthus annuus*
	Sunflower, Woodland	*Helianthus divaricatus*
	Tobacco	*Nicotiana* sp.

displays the presence or absence of plant taxa by individual species (by common and scientific name) and the sites in which particular taxa appear within the samples. Each taxon is marked present or absent only, disregarding the absolute count of a taxon. All sites in this study produced evidence for each of the plant use categories. Not all species within the categories are present, however, at all sites.

Very small numbers represent some samples and categories and, as such, it can be difficult to ascertain whether any differences in the data are meaningful or are by chance. In statistics, the larger the population is, the more reliable the interpretation will be. Palaeoethnobotany is a subdiscipline that inherently deals with preservation (or lack thereof) of organic remains. George Cowgill (1989:74) notes that the quality of archaeological data may be problematic as data can be lacking in quantity. Larger collections give more reliable statistical results. Small samples may under-represent the true diversity of a population. Comparisons between counts or percentages based on data from collections that have only a few objects belonging to categories can be unreliable, as they tend to be biased toward zero. This zero value, however, can indicate the absence of particular variables.

Table 3 Number and Volume of Samples

Site		Litres	
Grand Banks	palaeosol	995.5	
	Fe. 1	26	
	Fe. 210	186	
	Fe. 219	11	
	total	**223**	73.4%
Lone Pine	palaeosol	44.5	
	Fe. B	45	
	Fe. C	16	
	total	**105.5**	6.4%
Meyer	palaeosol	44	
	Fe. 56	18	
	total	**62**	3.7%
Forster, Fe. 1	**total**	**129**	7.8%
Bull's Point	**total**	**144**	8.7%
	total	**1659**	100%

Absolute Numbers and Percentages by Taxon and Category

The first step in identifying and quantifying plant macroremains is to count the number of plant species identified. In this study, 36 plant species are identified and these are classified into five categories (see Table 2). Not all species are present at all sites but evidence for each category is found. Quantification of seeds is essential to evaluating relative contributions of taxa in each sample. The numbers are standardized into percentages of categories and taxa. This exercise focuses on identifying the features and sites that individual taxa and categories are found. By comparing and standardizing the data, information is culled regarding the uniformity of deposition, preservation, and recovery rates.

A total of 2958 seeds are identified in this study: 1671 greens and grains, 667 fleshy fruits, 346 other taxa, 75 cultigens, and 199 unknowns/unidentifiables. The most common taxa by absolute count is grasses, followed by purslane, American nightshade, chenopod, and bramble. Table 5 summarizes the number of seeds, as well as other plant remains by category and site.

The samples from Feature 210 at Grand Banks stand out for their exceptional preservation and for their greater numbers in comparison to other samples from this study. For this reason, Grand Banks is examined with and

without Feature 210, and Feature 210 is explored on its own merit. This section reviews the absolute numbers and percentages of categories and individual plant taxa identified from individual sites by citing species that are particularly noteworthy, either for their commonality or scarcity. Tables supporting all data for individual sites are noted below.

Grand Banks produced a total of 2646 seeds (see Tables 8.1 to 8.11). The majority of these seeds are from Feature 210: 2386 seeds (260 seeds from the rest of the site). Ninety percent of the seed count derives from Feature 210. Grand Banks produced the greatest number of maize kernels, cupules, and fragments. Of all sites, Grand Banks has the greatest diversity of fleshy fruit species. Bramble seeds are most common. The greens and grains category constitutes over half of all seeds. However, most of these seeds are from Feature 210. The most common taxon is grasses, followed by purslane, American nightshade, and chenopod.

A small percentage of the total remains from Feature 210 are maize kernels (39 kernels) but most of the cultigens (including cupules) retrieved from Grand Banks are from Feature 210 (see Tables 9.1 to 9.15). Greens and grains is the most common category and the most common taxon is purslane, followed by grasses, American nightshade, and chenopod. The category of other taxa is third most common. Milkvetch, cleaver, cat-tail, wood sorrel, and St. Johns wort are identified. One arrowhead seed is identified, together with five arrowhead tubers, and over 100 stems in varying states of preservation. Some are minute fragments; others, as long as 16 mm.

Lone Pine produced 39 seeds. In the cultigens category, maize kernels, cupules, and fragments are identified (see Tables 10.1 to 10.11). The fleshy fruit category accounts for most seeds and the most common seed is bramble. The only other fleshy fruit is American nightshade. The greens and grains category is comprised of chenopod, together with one knotweed. Cleaver and sumac are present from the other taxa category.

Fifty seeds were recovered from the Meyer site (see Tables 11.1 to 11.11). Meyer produced maize kernels and cupules. The most common category is fleshy fruits, mostly consisting of bramble, strawberry seeds, and American nightshade. Chenopod and knotweed are identified from the greens and grains category, and, from other taxa, St. John's wort and cat-tail.

A total of 150 seeds are identified from Forster, mostly from the fleshy fruit category (bramble and one blueberry) (see Tables 12.1 to 12.11). Several maize cupules and a few kernels are present. Chenopod and knotweed represent the greens and grains category. Cleaver milkvetch, and arrowhead are present from the other taxa category.

Table 4 Plant Remains - Presence/Absence

Scientific Name	Common Name	Bull's Point	Forster	GrandBanks	G.B.Fe210	LonePine	Meyer
Cultigens							
Cucurbita pepo	Cucurbit	*					
Helianthus annuus	Sunflower				*		
Zea mays	Maize	*	*	*	*	*	*
Fleshy Fruits							
Celtis sp.	Hackberry			*			
Cornus canadensis	Dogwood				*		
Crataegus sp.	Hawthorn			*			
Empetrum nigrum	Crowberry	*					
Fragaria sp.	Strawberry	*					*
Hamamelis virginiana	Witchhazel	*					
Rubus sp.	Bramble	*	*	*	*	*	*
Sambucus sp.	Elderberry	*					
Solanum americanum	American Nightshade	*		*	*	*	*
Vaccinium myrtiloides	Blueberry	*	*	*	*		
Vitis sp.	Grape				*		
Greens/Grains							
Chenopodium sp.	Chenopod	*	*	*	*	*	*
Poaceae (Gramineae)	Grasses	*		*	*		*
Polygonum erectum	Knotweed			*	*	*	*
Portulaca oleracea	Purslane	*		*	*		
Other Taxa							
Astragalus sp.	Milkvetch		*	*	*		
Galium sp.	Cleaver, Bedstraw	*	*		*	*	
Hypericum perforatum	St.Johns Wort	*		*	*		*
Mentha sp.	Mint			*			
Oxalis sp.	Wood Sorrel	*		*	*		
Potentilla sp.	Cinquefoil				*		
Rhus typhina	Sumac	*		*			
Sagittaria latifolia	Arrowhead		*		*		
Sassafras sp.	Sassafras	*					
Typha latifolia	Cat-tail	*			*		*
Nuts		*	*	*	*	*	*
Unknown/ Unidentifiable		*	*	*	*	*	*

Table 5

Princess Point Sites
Absolute Numbers - Categories and Taxa

Site	Maize Kernels	Maize Cupules	Maize Frags.	Helianthus	Total Cultigens	Celtis	Cornus	Crataegus	Empetrum	Fragaria	Hamamelis	Rubus	Sambucus	Solanum	Vaccinium	Vitis	Total Fleshy Fruits	Chenopod	Grasses	Polygonum	Portulaca	Total Greens/Grains	Astragalus	Galium	Hypericum	Mentha	Oxalis	Potentilla	Rhus	Sagittaria seed	Sagittaria tuber	Sassafras	Typha	Total Other Taxa	TOTAL
Grand Banks	55	70	397	3	525	1	3	2		1		68		388	4	2	469	270	665	11	681	1627	89	73	50	2	27	14	6	1	5	0	54	316	2937
Lone Pine	8	15	82		93							8		3			11	7		1		8		2					3					5	117
Meyer	6	12	17		35					5		6		1			12	2	5	4		11			6								5	11	69
Forster	3	39	39		81							133			1		134	5	1	1		7	1	1						1				3	225
Bull's Point			15		15		2		2	4	2	5	2	22	2		41	2	15	1	1	18	1	4	1		2		2			1	1	11	85
Totals	72	136	550	3	749	1	5	2	2	10	2	220	2	414	7	2	667	286	686	17	682	1671	90	80	57	2	29	14	11	2	5	1	60	346	3433

27

Table 6 Absolute Numbers Percentages

Site	Total Cultigens	Total Fleshy Fruits	Total Greens/Grains	Total Other Taxa	Unknown/Unidentify
Grand Banks	2.19	17.7	61.45	8.2	10.47
Lone Pine	20.51	28.2	20.51	13	17.77
Meyer	12	24	22	22	20
Forster	2	89.3	4	2	2.67
Bull's Point	0	56.2	24.66	13.7	5.48
Totals	2.5	22.6	56.5	11.71	6.74

Table 7 Absolute Numbers per Litre

	Total Seeds	Maize Kernel	Cultigen Remains	Fleshy Fruits	Greens/Grains	Other Taxa
Grand Banks	2.17	0.05	0.43	0.38	1.33	0.26
Lone Pine	0.37	0.08	1	0.1	0.08	0.05
Meyer	0.61	0.1	0.56	0.19	0.18	0.18
Forster	0.93	0.02	0.50	0.83	0.04	0.02
Bull's Point	0.47	0	0.10	0.26	0.12	0.07
Average	0.91	0.05	0.52	0.35	0.35	0.12

Table 8.1 Grand Banks - Absolute Numbers and Weights

	X-Y Provenience	Feature	Cultural Level	(cm) Below Surface	(litres) Volume	(g) Wood Charcoal	(g/L) Wood Charcoal	(g) Maize Kernel	(no.) Maize Kernel	(g) Cupule	(no.) Cupule	(g) Maize Frags.	(no.) Maize Frags.	(g) Total Maize	(g) Quercus	(g) Juglans	(g) Carya	(g) Total Nut	(g) Sagittaria tuber	(g) Sagittaria rhizome	(g) Shell	(g) Bone
1	725-669		3	75	39	10.3	0.53	0.03	2	0.02	2	0.13	5	0.18	0.42			0.42			1.69	0.01
2	725-670		3	75	40	8.06	0.40	0.02	1	0.01	1	0.18	13	0.21	0.31			0.31			1.37	
3	725-671		3	75	20	0.45	0.02								0.04		0.04			0.08		
4	726-669		3	75	18	9.02	0.50	0.04	2	0.05	2	0.06	5	0.15	0.55			0.55			0.46	0.14
5	726-671		3	75	40	1.75	0.09	0.02	1	0.01	1	0.03	5	0.06	0.02			0.02			0.27	
6	726-699		3	75	19	9.30	0.49					0.23	12	0.23	0.36			0.36			0.43	
7	727-669		3	75	53	15.33	0.86	0.03	2	0.02	2	0.33	31	0.38	1.12			1.12			2.33	0.81
8	727-671		3	75	35	1.26	0.07								0.02			0.02			0.11	
9	728-669		3	75	37	11.08	0.59			0.07	3	0.29	32	0.36	0.81			0.81			1.53	
10	728-671		3	75	18	2.75	0.15					0.18	25	0.18	0.44			0.44			0.46	
11	729-670		8	50-79	73	1.59	0.16			0.01	1	0.01	2	0.02	0.05			0.05			0.57	
12	729-670		12	120-147	108.5	8.12	0.92			0.01	1	0.25	23	0.26	0.19			0.19			3.21	
13	729-670		13	153-175	20	0.18	0.02														9.72	
14	729-671		8	60-85	87.5	11.33	1.27			0.01	1	0.09	15	0.1			0.03	0.03			2.23	23.8
15	729-680		3	46-60	85	5.06	0.26	0.02	1	0.06	1	0.03	6	0.11	0.23	0.06		0.29			1.34	
16	730-680	210		50-100	186	193.31	0.96	0.88	39	0.62	46	1.4	175	2.9	0.71		0.02	0.71	1.11	1.54	24.19	0.78
17	730-684			45	17	0.75	0.04					0.15	17	0.15	0.31			0.31			0.24	
18	730-685			45	79	3.74	0.19	0.14	7	0.13	7	0.02	3	0.29	0.37	0.29		0.66			0.21	0.17
19	730-686			57	39	4.00	0.21			0.04	2	0.26	21	0.30	0.41			0.41			0.25	
20	730-698		3	25-43	40	0.35	0.03								0.03			0.03			7.46	
21	730-699		3	20-35	16	0.09	0.01														5.37	
22	731-698		3	22-44	28	3.45	0.36														1.92	
23	731-699		3	25-60	83.5	4.66	0.60					0.04	5	0.04	0.12	0.03	0.18	0.33			7.45	0.03
24	731-699	1	3	50-65	26	2	0.23					0.01	2	0.01							11.44	0.04
25	733-705	219		44	11	2.20	0.20							0.30				0.30			13.43	
Totals					1218.5	310.13	0.25 av. g/L	1.18	55	1.06	70	397	397	5.93 av. total 0.04	6.77	0.42	0.23	7.40	1.11	1.54	88.75	1.98

28

Table 8.1 continued

X-Y Provenience	Seeds (no.)	Astragalus	Celtis	Chenopod	Cornus	Crataegus	Empetrum	Fragaria	Galium	Grass (Poaceae)	cf. Elymus	cf. Echinochloa	cf. Glyceria	cf. Hordeum	cf. Panicum	Zizania	Hamamelis	Helianthus	Hypericum	Maize Kernel	Mentha	Oxalis
1 725-669				3						1										2		
2 725-670				6						1											1	
3 725-671										1												
4 726-669																				2		
5 726-671																					1	
6 726-699																						
7 727-669													.							2		
8 727-671				2																		
9 728-669																						
10 728-671																						
11 729-670																						
12 729-670																						
13 729-670																						
14 729-671								1														
15 729-680						1				1									1		1	
16 730-680		86	1	232	3				70	13	6	24	2	207	349			3	43	39		25
17 730-684																						
18 730-685		3		13		1				10	2			1	11	1			7	7		2
19 730-686				13						14	8				10							
20 730-698																						
21 730-699																						
22 731-698																						
23 731-699									2													
24 731-699									1	3												
25 733-705																						
Totals		89	1	270	3	2		1	73	44	16	24	2	208	370	1		3	50	55	2	27
		3.36%	0.04%	10.2%	0.11%	0.08%		0.04%	2.76%	1.66%	0.6%	0.91%	0.08%	7.86%	13.98%	0.04%		0.11%	1.89%	2.08%	0.08%	1.02%

X-Y Provenience	Polygonum	Portulaca	Potentilla	Rhus	Rubus	Sagittaria	Sambucus	Sassafras	Solanum	Typha	Vaccinium	Vitis	Unidentified	Unknown	Total Seeds
1 725-669	2													5	13
2 725-670		2			1				1						12
3 725-671															1
4 726-669															2
5 726-671														1	3
6 726-699			.												
7 727-669									.						2
8 727-671				3										1	6
9 728-669															
10 728-671															
11 729-670															
12 729-670															
13 729-670															
14 729-671					2								6		9
15 729-680		2												7	13
16 730-680	8	671	14		62	1			387	54	2	2	38	44	2386
17 730-684															
18 730-685	1	3			2									19	83
19 730-686		5			1						2			36	89
20 730-698															
21 730-699															
22 731-698															
23 731-699													6	1	10
24 731-699				1									12	7	17
25 733-705															
Totals	11	681	14	6	68	1			388	54	4	2	56	120	2646
	0.42%	25.74%	0.53%	0.23%	2.57%	0.04%			14.66%	2.04%	0.15%	0.08%	2.12%	4.54%	

total 2646
/liter 2.17
/gram 8.53

Table 8.2 - Absolute Numbers – Cultigens

	X-Y Provenience	Feature	Maize Kernel	Maize Cupule	Maize Frags.	Helianthus	Total Cultigens
1	725-669		2	2	5		9
2	725-670		1	1	13		16
3	725-671						
4	726-669		2	2	5		9
5	726-671		1	1	5		7
6	726-699				12		12
7	727-669		2	2	31		35
8	727-671						
9	728-669			3	32		35
10	728-671				25		25
11	729-670			1	2		3
12	729-670			1	23		24
13	729-670						
14	729-671			1	15		16
15	729-680		1	1	6		8
16	729-681	210	39	46	175	4	264
17	730-684				17		17
18	730-685		7	7	3		17
19	730-686			2	21		23
20	730-698						
21	730-699						
22	731-698						
23	731-699				5		5
24	731-699				2		2
25	733-705						
	Totals		55	70	397	4	526

Table 8.3 - Fleshy Fruits

	X-Y Provenience	Feature	Celtis	Cornus	Crataegus	Empetrum	Fragaria	Hamamelis	Rubus	Sambucus	Solanum	Vaccinium	Vitis	Total Fleshy Fruits
1	725-669													
2	725-670								1	1				2
3	725-671													
4	726-669													
5	726-671													
6	726-699													
7	727-669													
8	727-671													
9	728-669													
10	728-671													
11	729-670													
12	729-670													
13	729-670													
14	729-671						1		2					3
15	729-680				1									1
16	729-681	210	1	3					62	387	2	2		457
17	730-684													
18	730-685								2					2
19	730-686								1		2			3
20	730-698													
21	730-699													
22	731-698													
23	731-699													
24	731-699	1												
25	733-705	219												
	Totals		1	3	1		1		68	388	4	2		468

Table 8.4 - Greens/Grains

	X-Y Provenience	Feature	Chenopod	Grasses	Polygonum	Portulaca	Total Greens/Grains
1	725-669		3	1	2		6
2	725-670		6	1			7
3	725-671			1			1
4	726-669						
5	726-671						
6	726-699						
7	727-669						
8	727-671		2				2
9	728-669						
10	728-671						
11	729-670						
12	729-670						
13	729-670						
14	729-671						
15	729-680			1		2	3
16	729-681	210	232	601	8	671	1512
17	730-684						
18	730-685		13	25		3	41
19	730-686		14	32		5	51
20	730-698						
21	730-699						
22	731-698						
23	731-699		1				1
24	731-699	1		3			3
25	733-705	219					
	Totals		271	665	10	681	1627

Table 8.5 - Other Taxa

	X-Y Provenience	Feature	Astragalus	Galium	Hypericum	Mentha	Oxalis	Potentilla	Rhus	Sagittaria seed	Sagittaria tuber	Sassafras	Typha	Total Other Taxa
1	725-669													
2	725-670								2					2
3	725-671													
4	726-669													
5	726-671					1								1
6	726-699													
7	727-669													
8	727-671								3					3
9	728-669													
10	728-671													
11	729-670													
12	729-670													
13	729-670													
14	729-671													
15	729-680					1								1
16	729-681	210	86	70	43		25	14		1	_5_		54	293
17	730-684													
18	730-685		3		7		2							12
19	730-686													
20	730-698													
21	730-699													
22	731-698													
23	731-699			2										2
24	731-699	1		1										1
25	733-705	219												
	Totals		89	73	50	2	27	0	5	0			1	315

Table 8.6- Charcoal, Maize, Nut - Percentage of Weights and Ratios

	X-Y Provenience	Feature	Wood Charcoal	Maize Kernel	Maize Cupule	Maize Frags.	Total Maize	Quercus	Juglans	Carya	Total Nut	Charcoal/Maize	Charcoal/Nut	Char/Maize/Nut
1	725-669		94.66%	0.58%	0.35%	1.17%	1.63%	3.72%			3.72%	64	71	19.68%
2	725-670		94.35%	0.53%	0.26%	3.76%	2.28%	3.37%			3.37%	74	45	12.36%
3	725-671		91.84%						8.16%		8.16%		11	2.06%
4	726-669		92.80%	0.41%	0.51%	0.62%	1.54%	5.66%			5.66%	60	16	25.15%
5	726-671		95.92%	3.17%	0.83%	2.50%	3.25%	1.67%			1.67%	.30	57	7.35%
6	726-699		94.03%			2.33%	2.33%	3.64%			3.64%	40	26	21.56%
7	727-669		91.34%	0.48%	0.32%	2.65%	3.05%	6.63%			6.63%	43	16	19.91%
8	727-671		98.57%					2.86%			2.86%		34	5.20%
9	728-669		88.17%		0.83%	3.40%	3.82%	8.02%			8.02%	38	15	20.28%
10	728-671		81.60%			5.34%	5.34%	13.06%			13.06%	15	6	16.23%
11	729-670		96.14%		3.57%	3.85%	3.71%	19.23%			19.23%	23.50	4	13.90%
12	729-670		97.66%		2.33%	8.50%	9.50%	4.55%			4.55%	21	41	11.48%
13	729-670		100%											2.05%
14	729-671		97.85%		0.34%	4.52%	36.84%			0.87%	0.87%	211	114	13.59%
15	729-680		89.65%	2.06%	6.19%	0.93%	4.58%	13.57%	1.85%		10.64%	57	26	7.42%
16	730-680	210	96.59%	1.66%	1.46%	2.98%	4.05%	0.47%		0.15%	0.36%	58	272	15.47%
17	730-684		61.98%			12.40%	12.40%	25.62%			25.62%	5	2	4.50%
18	730-685		80.90%	4.90%	4.55%	4.17%	7.68%	11.00%	20.28%		13.34%	13	9	3.25%
19	730-686		87.07%		2.50%	5.09%	6.34%	13.18%			13.18%	14	6	5.91%
20	730-698		94.88%					10.24%			10.24%		10	1.35%
21	730-699		100%											0.38%
22	731-698		100%											9.80%
23	731-699		91.86%			3.00%	3.00%	6.80%	5.66%	10.98%	10.77%	67	26	5.55%
24	731-699	1	99.3%			1.69%	1.69%						58	10.00%
25	733-705	219	88.00%					12.00%			12.00%		7	8.16%
	Totals		95.88%	0.36%	0.33%	1.14%	1.83%	2.09%	0.13%	0.07%	2.29%	52	42	16.40%

Table 8.7- Absolute Numbers per Litre - Cultigens

	X-Y Provenience	Feature	Volume (L)	Maize Kernel	Maize Cupule	Maize Frags.	Helianthus	Cultigens
1	725-669		39	0.11	0.10	0.25		0.23
2	725-670		40	0.05	0.05	0.65		0.38
3	725-671		20					
4	726-669		18	0.11	0.11	0.28		0.00
5	726-671		40	0.06	0.05	0.23		0.17
6	726-699		19			0.63		0.00
7	727-669		53	0.10	0.10	0.90		0.66
8	727-671		35					
9	728-669		37		0.16	0.88		0.95
10	728-671		18			1.39		0.00
11	729-670		73		0.10	0.11		0.03
12	729-670		108.5		0.13	1.19		0.21
13	729-670		20					
14	729-671		87.5		0.11	0.39		0.19
15	729-680		85	0.05	0.05	0.27		0.16
16	729-681	210	186	0.21	0.26	0.94	0.02	1.41
17	730-684		17			1.00		1.00
18	730-685		79	0.08	0.08	0.04		0.21
19	730-686		39		0.10	0.55		0.60
20	730-698		40					
21	730-699		16					
22	731-698		28					
23	731-699		83.5			0.06		0.06
24	731-699	1	26			0.22		0.22
25	733-705	219	11					
	Totals		1218.5	0.05	0.06	0.33	0.003	0.43

Table 8.8- Percentage of Absolute Numbers - Cultigens

	X-Y Provenience	Feature	Maize	Helianthus	Total Cultigens
1	725-669		18.18%		18.18%
2	725-670		8.33%		8.33%
3	725-671				
4	726-669		100%		100%
5	726-671		100%		100%
6	726-699				
7	727-669		100%		100%
8	727-671				
9	728-669				
10	728-671				
11	729-670				
12	729-670				
13	729-670				
14	729-671				
15	729-680		100%		100%
16	730-680	210	1.63%	0.13%	1.76%
17	730-684				
18	730-685		13.84%		13.84%
19	730-686				
20	730-698				
21	730-699				
22	731-698				
23	731-699				
24	731-699	1			
25	733-705	219			
	Totals		2.08%	0.11%	2.19%

Table 8.9- Fleshy Fruits

	X-Y Provenience	Feature	Celtis	Cornus	Crataegus	Empetrum	Fragaria	Hamamelis	Rubus	Sambucus	Solanum	Vaccinium	Vitis	Total Fleshy Fruits
1	725-669													
2	725-670								8.33%		8.33%			16.67%
3	725-671													
4	726-669													
5	726-671													
6	726-699													
7	727-669													
8	727-671													
9	728-669													
10	728-671													
11	729-670													
12	729-670													
13	729-670													
14	729-671						12.50%		56.25%					62.50%
15	729-680				50.00%									50.00%
16	730-680	210	1.32%	0.85%					2.30%		17.45%	0.25%	0.25%	15.60%
17	730-684													
18	730-685								4.40%					4.50%
19	730-686								4.17%			2.85%		5.00%
20	730-698													
21	730-699													
22	731-698													
23	731-699													
24	731-699	1												
25	733-705	219												
	Totals		0.04%	0.11%	0.04%	0.04%			2.57%		14.66%	0.15%	0.08%	17.69%

Table 8.10- Greens/Grains

	X-Y Provenience	Feature	Chenopod	Grasses	Polygonum	Portulaca	Total Greens/Grains
1	725-669		27.27%	9.09%	100%		68.18%
2	725-670		50.00%	8.33%			58.33%
3	725-671			100%			100%
4	726-669						
5	726-671						
6	726-699						
7	727-669						
8	727-671		60.00%				60.00%
9	728-669						
10	728-671						
11	729-670						
12	729-670						
13	729-670						
14	729-671						
15	729-680			50.00%		28.57%	39.29%
16	730-680	210	19.02%	35.03%	0.78%	14.08%	51.16%
17	730-684						
18	730-685		20.10%	32.65%		7.69%	49.64%
19			11.32%	31.18%		7.69%	46.35%
20	730-698						
21	730-699						
22	731-698						
23	731-699		100%				100%
24	731-699	1		35.90%			35.90%
25	733-705	219					
	Totals		10.20%	25.13%	0.38%	25.74%	61.45%

Table 8.11- Other Taxa

	X-Y Provenience	Feature	Astragalus	Galium	Hypericum	Mentha	Oxalis	Rhus	Sagittaria	Sassafras	Typha	Total Other Taxa
1	725-669											
2	725-670							16.67%				16.67%
3	725-671											
4	726-669											
5	726-671					50.00%						50.00%
6	726-699											
7	727-669											
8	727-671							60.00%				60.00%
9	728-669											
10	728-671											
11	729-670											
12	729-670											
13	729-670											
14	729-671											
15	729-680					14.29%						14.29%
16	729-680	210	26.78%	12.09%	3.32%		2.30%		0.06%		3.70%	25.20%
17	730-684											
18	730-685		15.00%		13.94%		10.00%					17.63%
19	730-686											
20	730-698											
21	730-699											
22	731-698											
23	731-699			41.66%								41.66%
24	731-699	1		50.00%								50.00%
25	733-705	219										
	Totals		3.36%	2.76%	1.89%	0.08%	1.02%	0.19%			2.04%	8.20%

33

Table 9.1 Grand Banks (Fe. 210) - Absolute Numbers and Weights

	Totals	%	%	%
X-y Provenience				
Feature	210			
(cm) Below Surface	50-100			
Volume (litres)	186			
Wood Charcoal (g)	193.31			
Wood Charcoal (g/L)	1.04 av. g/L			
Maize Kernel (g)	0.88			
Maize Kernel (no.)	39			
Cupule (g)	0.62			
Cupule (no.)	46			
Maize Frags. (g)	1.40			
Maize Frags. (no.)	175			
Total Maize (g)	2.90 av. total maize 0.27			
Quercus (g)	0.71			
Juglans (g)				
Carya (g)	0.02			
Total Nut (g)	0.71			
Sagittaria tuber (g)	1.11			
Sagittaria stem (g)	1.54			
Shell (g)	24.2			
Bone (g)	0.78			
Seeds (no.)		3.6%		
Astragalus	86			
Celtis	1		0.04%	
Chenopod	232			9.72%
Cornus	3			0.13%
Crataegus				
Empetrum				
Fragaria				
Gallium	70			2.93%

	total	%	%	%	%
Grass (Poaceae)	13				
cf. Elymus	6	0.54% 0.25%			
cf. Echinochloa	24		1.01%		
cf. Glyceria	2			0.08%	
cf. Hordeum	207			8.67%	
cf. Panicum	349				14.61%
Zizania					
Hamamelis					
Helianthus	3	0.13%			
Hypericum	43		1.8%		
Maize Kernel	39			1.63%	
Mentha					
Oxalis	25	1.05%			
Polygonum	8		0.34%		
Portulaca	671			28.1%	
Potentilla	14			0.6%	
Rhus					
Rubus	62				2.6% 0.04%
Sagittaria	1				
Sambucus					
Sassafras					
Solanum	387	16.21%			
Typha	54		2.26%		
Vaccinium	2			0.1%	
Vitis	2			0.1%	
Unidentified	38				1.6%
Unknown	44				1.84%
Total Seeds	2388	/litre 12.84 /gram 12.35			

Table 9.2- Absolute Numbers - Cultigens

X-Y Provenience	Feature	Maize Kernels	Maize Cupules	Maize Frags.	Helianthus	Total Cultigens	Total Seeds
	Totals 210	39	46	175	3	263	2386

Table 9.3- Fleshy Fruits

X-Y Provenience	Feature	Celtis	Cornus	Crataegus	Empetrum	Fragaria	Hamamelis	Rubus	Sambucus	Solanum	Vaccinium	Vitis	Total Fleshy Fruits	Total Seeds
	Totals 210	1	3					62		387	2	2	457	2386

Table 9.4- Greens/Grains Table

X-Y Provenience	Feature	Chenopod	Grasses	Polygonum	Portulaca	Total Greens/Grains	Total Seeds
	Totals 210	232	601	8	671	1512	2386

9.5- Other Taxa

X-Y Provenience	Feature	Astragalus	Galium	Hypericum	Mentha	Oxalis	Potentilla	Rhus	Sagittaria seed	Sagittaria tuber	Sassafras	Typha	Total Other Taxa	Total Seeds
	Totals 210	86	70	43		25	14		1	5		54	293	2386

Table 9.6- Charcoal, Maize, Nut - Percentage of Weights and Ratios

Feature	Wood Charcoal	Maize Kernel	Maize Cupule	Maize Frags.	Total Maize	Quercus	Juglans	Carya	Total Nut	Maize/Charcoal	Nut/Charcoal	Char/Maize/Nut
Totals 210	98.17%	0.45%	0.31%	0.71%	1.47%	0.36%		0.01%	0.36%	67	272	27.01%

Table 9.7- Absolute Numbers per Litre – Cultigens (all remains)

Feature	Volume (L)	Maize Kernel	Cupule	Maize Frags.	Helianthus	Cultigens
Totals 210	186	0.21	0.25	0.94	0.02	1.41

Table 9.8- Cultigens (seeds only)

Feature	Volume (L)	Maize Kernel	Helianthus	Cultigens
Totals 210	186	0.21	0.02	0.23

Table 9.9- Fleshy Fruits

Feature	Volume (L)	Celtis	Cornus	Crataegus	Empetrum	Fragaria	Hamamelis	Rubus	Sambucus	Solanum	Vaccinium	Vitis	Fleshy Fruits
Totals 210	186	0.01	0.02					0.33		2.08	0.01	0.01	2.46

Table 9.10- Greens/Grains

Feature	Volume (L)	Chenopod	Grasses	Polygonum	Portulaca	Greens/Grains
Totals	210	186	1.25	3.23	0.04	3.61	8.13

Table 9.11- Other Taxa

Feature	Volume (L)	Astragalus	Galium	Hypericum	Mentha	Oxalis	Potentilla	Rhus	Sagittaria	Sassafras	Typha	Other Taxa
Totals	210	186	0.46	0.38	0.23		0.13	0.08		0.01		0.29	1.58

Table 9.12- Percentage of Absolute Numbers - Cultigens

Feature	Maize	Helianthus	Total Cultigens
Totals	210	1.63%	0.13%	1.76%

Table 9.13- Fleshy Fruits

Feature	Celtis	Cornus	Crataegus	Empetrum	Fragaria	Hamamelis	Rubus	Sambucus	Solanum	Vaccinium	Vitis	Total Fleshy Fruits
Totals	210	0.04%	0.13%					2.60%		16.22%	0.08%	0.08%	19.15%

Table 9.14- Greens/Grains

Feature	Chenopod	Grasses	Polygonum	Portulaca	Total Greens/Grains
Totals	210	15.34%	39.75%	0.34%	28.12%	63.37%

Table 9.15- Other Taxa

Feature	Astragalus	Galium	Hypericum	Mentha	Oxalis	Potentilla	Rhus	Sagittaria	Sassafras	Typha	Total Other Taxa
Totals	210	3.6%	2.93%	1.8%		1.05%	0.59%		0.04%		2.26%	12.28%

Table 10.1 Lone Pine - Absolute Numbers and Weights

Provenience X-Y	Feature	Below Surface (cm)	Volume (litres)	Wood Charcoal (g)	Wood Charcoal (g/L)	Maize Kernel (g)	Maize Kernel (no.)	Cupule (g)	Cupule (no.)	Maize Frags. (g)	Maize Frags. (no.)	Total Maize (g)	Quercus (g)	Juglans (g)	Carya (g)	Total Nut (g)	Sagittaria tuber (g)	Sagittaria rhizome (g)	Shell (g)	Bone (g)	Seeds (no.)	Astragalus	Celtis	Chenopod	Cornus	Crataegus	Empetrum	Fragaria	Gallium
1 460-499	C hearth	7 to 14	7	1.68	0.24	0.15	6	0.23	15	0.06	12	0.06												5					
2 460-500	C hearth	5 to 10	31	12.86	1.20	0.05	2			0.02	5	0.4																	
3 461-501	C hearth	7 to 14	7	13.32	1.90							0.05	1.83			1.83													2
4 469-489	area C	7 to 14	10	0.54	0.05					0.01	3	0.01							0.01										
5 478-509	B hearth	7 to 14	8	3.34	0.42					0.07	8	0.07																	
6 479-508	B hearth	7 to 14	8	3.60	0.45					0.17	26	0.17	0.01			0.01								2					
7 479-510	area B	5 to 10	15	14.92	3.01																								
8 480-508	area B	7 to 14	10.5	1.2	0.47					0.05	7	0.05																	
9 480-510	area B	7 to 14	9	18.05	2.01					0.14	21	0.14	0.23			0.23													
Totals			105.50	69.51	0.66 average g/L	0.20	8	0.23	15	0.52	82	0.95 / average total maize 0.07	2.07			2.07			0.01		7			7					2
																								17.95%					5.13%

Provenience X-Y	Grass (Poaceae)	cf. Elymus	cf. Echinochloa	cf. Glyceria	cf. Hordeum	cf. Panicum	Zizania	Hamamelis	Helianthus	Hypericum	Maize Kernel	Mentha	Oxalis	Polygonum	Portulaca	Potentilla	Rhus	Rubus	Sagittaria	Sambucus	Sassafras	Solanum	Typha	Vaccinium	Vitis (no.)	Unidentified	Unknown	Total Seeds
1 460-499																												5
2 460-500											6						3	6				3					4	22
3 461-501											2																2	4
4 469-489																												2
5 478-509																		2										5
6 479-508																											1	
7 479-510																												
8 480-508																												
9 480-510														1														1
Totals											8			1			3	8				3					7	39 total
											20.51%			2.56%			7.69%	20.51%				7.69%					17.95%	/liter 0.37
																												/gram 0.56

Table 10.2 Absolute Numbers - Cultigens

	X-Y Provenience	Feature	Maize Kernels	Maize Cupules	Maize Frags.	Helianthus	Total Cultigens	Total Seeds
1	460-499	C hearth			12			5
2	460-500	C hearth	6	15	5		26	22
3	461-501	C hearth	2				2	4
4	469-489	area C			3		3	
5	478-509	B hearth			8		8	2
6	479-508	B hearth			26		26	5
7	479-510	area B						
8	480-508	area B			7		7	
9	480-510	area B			21		21	1
	Totals		8	15	82		93	39

Table 10.3- Fleshy Fruits

	X-Y Provenience	Feature	Celtis	Cornus	Crataegus	Empetrum	Fragaria	Hamamelis	Rubus	Sambucus	Solanum	Vaccinium	Vitis	Total Fleshy Fruits	Total Seeds
1	460-499	C hearth													5
2	460-500	C hearth							6		3			9	22
3	461-501	C hearth													4
4	469-489	area C													
5	478-509	B hearth													2
6	479-508	B hearth							2					2	5
7	479-510	area B													
8	480-508	area B													
9	480-510	area B													1
	Totals								8		3			11	39

Table 10.4- Greens/Grains

	X-Y Provenience	Feature	Chenopod	Grasses	Polygonum	Portulaca	Total Greens/Grains	Total Seeds
1	460-499	C hearth	5				5	5
2	460-500	C hearth						22
3	461-501	C hearth						4
4	469-489	area C						
5	478-509	B hearth						2
6	479-508	B hearth	2				2	5
7	479-510	area B						
8	480-508	area B						
9	480-510	area B			1		1	1
	Totals		7		1		8	39

Table 10.5- Other Taxa

	X-Y Provenience	Feature	Astragalus	Galium	Hypericum	Mentha	Oxalis	Potentilla	Rhus	Sagittaria seed	Sagittaria tuber	Sassafras	Typha	Total Other Taxa	Total Seeds
1	460-499	C hearth													5
2	460-500	C hearth							3					3	22
3	461-501	C hearth													4
4	469-489	area C													
5	478-509	B hearth		2										2	2
6	479-508	B hearth													5
7	479-510	area B													
8	480-508	area B													
9	480-510	area B													1
	Totals			2					3					5	39

Table 10.6- Charcoal, Maize, Nut - Percentage of Weights and Ratios

	X-Y Provenience	Feature	Wood Charcoal	Maize Kernel	Maize Cupule	Maize Frags.	Total Maize	Quercus	Juglans	Carya	Total Nut	Maize/Charcoal	Nut/Charcoal	Char/Maize/Nut
1	460-499	hearthC	4.17%			0.15%	0.15%					28		4.32%
2	460-500	hearthC	4.10%	0.07%	0.11%	0.12%	0.16%					70		4.26%
3	461-501	hearthC	9.51%	0.04%			0.04%	1.31%			1.31%	266	7	10.85%
4	469-489	area C	1.56%			0.03%	0.03%					54		1.59%
5	478-509	hearthB	4.84%			0.10%	0.10%					48		4.95%
6	479-508	hearthB	7.27%			0.34%	0.34%	0.02%			0.02%	21	360	7.63%
7	479-510	area B	13.36%											13.36%
8	480-508	area B	2.35%			0.20%	0.20%					23		2.45%
9	480-510	area B	21.96%			0.17%	0.17%	0.28%			0.28%	129	78	22.41%
	Totals		95.84%	0.02%	0.03%	0.06%	1.31%	0.24%			2.85%	73	34	8.35%

Table 10.7- Absolute Numbers per Litre - Cultigens

	X-Y Provenience	Feature	Volume (L)	Maize Kernel	Maize Cupule	Maize Frags.	Helianthus	Cultigens
1	460-499	hearthC	7			1.71		1.71
2	460-500	hearthC	31	0.29	0.67	1		0.83
3	461-501	hearthC	7	0.29				
4	469-489	area C	10			0.30		
5	478-509	hearthB	8			1.00		1.00
6	479-508	hearthB	8			3.25		3.25
7	479-510	area B	15					
8	480-508	area B	10.5			2.80		2.80
9	480-510	area B	9			2.33		2.33
	Totals		105.5	0.08	0.14	0.78		1.00

Table 10.8- Percentage of Absolute Numbers - Cultigens

	X-Y Provenience	Feature	Maize Kernels	Helianthus	Total Cultigens
1	460-499	hearthC			
2	460-500	hearthC	23.81%		23.81%
3	461-501	hearthC	50.00%		50.00%
4	469-489	area C			
5	478-509	hearthB			
6	479-508	hearthB			
7	479-510	area B			
8	480-508	area B			
9	480-510	area B			
	Totals		20.51%		20.51%

39

Table 10.9- Fleshy Fruits

#	X-Y Provenience	Feature	Celtis	Cornus	Crataegus	Empetrum	Fragaria	Hamamelis	Rubus	Sambucus	Solanum	Vaccinium	Vitis	Total Fleshy Fruits
1	460-499	hearthC												
2	460-500	hearthC							35.24%		20.00%			45.24%
3	461-501	hearthC												
4	469-489	area C												
5	478-509	hearthB												
6	479-508	hearthB							40.00%					40.00%
7	479-510	area B												
8	480-508	area B												
9	480-510	area B												
	Totals								20.51%		7.69%			28.21%

Table 10.10- Greens/Grains

#	X-Y Provenience	Feature	Chenopod	Grasses	Polygonum	Portulaca	Total Greens/Grains
1	460-499	hearthC	100%				100%
2	460-500	hearthC					
3	461-501	hearthC					
4	469-489	area C					
5	478-509	hearthB					
6	479-508	hearthB	40.00%				40.00%
7	479-510	area B					
8	480-508	area B					
9	480-510	area B			100%		100%
	Totals		17.95%		2.56%		20.51%

Table 10.11- Other Taxa

#	X-Y Provenience	Feature	Astragalus	Galium	Hypericum	Mentha	Oxalis	Potentilla	Rhus	Sagittaria	Sassafras	Typha	Total Other Taxa
1	460-499	hearthC											
2	460-500	hearthC							13.81%				13.81%
3	461-501	hearthC											
4	469-489	area C											
5	478-509	hearthB		100%									100%
6	479-508	hearthB											
7	479-510	area B											
8	480-508	area B											
9	480-510	area B											
	Totals			5.13%					7.69%				13.00%

Table 11.1 Meyer - Absolute Numbers and Weights

Provenience X-Y	Feature	Below Surface (cm)	Volume (litres)	Wood Charcoal (g)	Charcoal (g/L)	Maize Kernel (g)	Maize Kernel (no.)	Cupule (g)	Cupule (no.)	Maize Frags. (g)	Maize Frags. (no.)	Total Maize (g)	Quercus (g)	Juglans (g)	Carya (g)	Total Nut (g)	Sagittaria tuber (g)	Sagittaria stem (g)	Shell (g)	Bone (g)
1 571-508	56	15 to 35	18	12.73	0.71	0.14	5	0.02	3	0.02	6	0.18	0.01			0.01			0.01	0.04
2 573-513			15	0.79	0.11	0.01	1	0.02	2	0.03	6	0.06								0.84
3 574-514		10 to 30	29	2.52	0.27			0.03	7	0.02	5	0.05	0.05			0.05				
Totals			62	16.04	0.26	0.15	6	0.07	12	0.07	17	0.29	0.06			0.06			0.01	0.88

average g/L 0.26

average total maize 0.05

Provenience X-Y	Seeds (no.)	Astragalus	Celtis	Chenopod	Cornus	Crataegus	Empetrum	Fragaria	Galium	Grass (Poaceae)	cf. Elymus	cf. Echinochloa	cf. Glyceria	cf. Hordeum	cf. Panicum	Zizania	Hamamelis	Helianthus	Hypericum	Maize Kernel	Mentha	Oxalis	Polygonum	Portulaca	Potentilla	Rhus	Rubus	Sagittaria seed	Sagittaria tuber	Sambucus	Sassafras	Solanum	Typha	Vaccinium	Vitis	Unidentified	Unknown	Total Seeds
1 571-508								5		1										5			4				4					1	5			2		27
2 573-513				1							1								3	1																	1	7
3 574-514				1						2	1								3								2										7	16
Totals				2				5		3	2								6	6			4				6					1	5			2	8	50
%				4%				10%		6%	4%								12%	12%			8%				12%					2%	10%			4%	16%	

seeds/liter 0.81

seeds/gram 3.12

Table 11.2- Absolute Numbers – Cultigens

	X-Y Provenience	Feature	Maize Kernels	Maize Cupules	Maize Frags.	Helianthus	Total Cultigens	Total Seeds
1	571-508	56	5	3	6		14	27
2	573-513		1	2	6		9	6
3	574-514			7	5		12	17
	Totals		6	12	17		35	50

Table 11.3 - Fleshy Fruits

	X-Y Provenience	Feature	Celtis	Cornus	Crataegus	Empetrum	Fragaria	Hamamelis	Rubus	Sambucus	Solanum	Vaccinium	Vitis	Total Fleshy Fruits	Total Seeds
1	571-508	56							5	4	1			10	27
2	573-513														6
3	574-514								2					2	17
	Totals								5	6	1			12	50

Table 11.4- Greens/Grains

	X-Y Provenience	Feature	Chenopod	Grasses	Polygonum	Portulaca	Total Greens/Grains	Total Seeds
1	571-508	56		1	4		5	27
2	573-513			1			1	6
3	574-514		2	3			5	17
	Totals		2	5	4		11	50

Table 11.5- Other Taxa

	X-Y Provenience	Feature	Astragalus	Galium	Hypericum	Mentha	Oxalis	Potentilla	Rhus	Sagittaria seed	Sagittaria tuber	Sassafras	Typha	Total Other Taxa	Total Seeds
1	571-508	56											5	5	27
2	573-513				3									3	6
3	574-514				3									3	17
	Totals				6								5	11	50

Table 11.6- Charcoal, Maize, Nut - Percentage of Weights and Ratios

	X-Y Provenience	Feature	Wood Charcoal	Maize Kernel	Maize Cupule	Maize Frags.	Total Maize	Quercus	Juglans	Carya	Total Nut	Charcoal-Maize	Charcoal-Nut	Char/Maize/Nut
1	571-508	56	98.53%	1.08%	0.15%	0.15%	1.39%	0.08%			0.08%	71	1273	14.93%
2	573-513		93.76%	1.85%	3.23%	2.54%	6.25%					40		2.15%
3	574-514		96.22%			1.14%	1.89%	1.90%			2.00%	157	105	3.60%
	Totals		97.86%	0.92%	0.43%	0.43%	1.77%	0.37%			0.37%	55	267	6.41%

Table 11.7- Absolute Numbers per Litre - Cultigens

	X-Y Provenience	Feature	Volume (L)	Maize Kernel	Maize Cupule	Maize Frags.	Helianthus	Cultigens
1	571-508	56	18	0.28	0.17	0.33		0.78
2	573-513		15	0.1	0.27	0.86		1.27
3	574-514		29		0.77	0.50		1.23
	Totals		62	0.10	0.19	0.27		0.56

Table 11.8- Percentage of Absolute Numbers – Cultigens

	X-Y Provenience	Feature	Maize Kernel	Helianthus	Total Cultigens
1	571-508	56	18.52%		18.52%
2	573-513		50.00%		50.00%
3	574-514				
	Totals		12.00%		12.00%

Table 11.9- Fleshy Fruits

	X-Y Provenience	Feature	Celtis	Cornus	Crataegus	Empetrum	Fragaria	Hamamelis	Rubus	Sambucus	Solanum	Vaccinium	Total FleshyFruits
1	571-508	56					18.52%		14.81%	3.70%	3.70%		37.04%
2	573-513												
3	574-514								12.88%				12.88%
	Totals						10.00%		12.00%		2.00%		24.00%

Table 11.10- Greens/Grains

	X-Y Provenience	Feature	Chenopod	Grasses	Polygonum	Portulaca	Total Greens/Grains
1	571-508	56		3.70%	14.81%		18.52%
2	573-513			25.00%			25.00%
3	574-514		12.88%	17.43%			30.30%
	Totals		4.00%	10.00%	8.00%		22.00%

Table 11.11- Other Taxa

	X-Y Provenience	Feature	Astragalus	Galium	Hypericum	Mentha	Oxalis	Potentilla	Rhus	Sagittaria	Sassafras	Typha	Total OtherTaxa
1	571-508	56										18.52%	18.52%
2	573-513			75.00%									75.00%
3	574-514			27.27%									27.27%
	Totals			12.00%								10.00%	22.00%

Table 12.1 Forster - Absolute Numbers and Weights

Feature	Volume (litres)	Wood Charcoal (g)	Wood Charcoal (g/L)	Maize Kernel (g)	Maize Kernel (no.)	Cupule (g)	Cupule (no.)	Maize Frags. (g)	Maize Frags. (no.)	Total Maize (g)	Quercus (g)	Juglans (g)	Carya (g)	Total Nut (g)	Sagittaria tuber (g)	Sagittaria stem (g)	Shell (g)	Bone (g)
Pit 1	161	28.37	0.18	0.04	3	0.35	39	0.23	39	0.62	0.42	0.20		0.62			0.01	0.22

(Total: 1) — average g/L 0.18 — average total maize 0.06

Taxon	Seeds (no.)	%
Astragalus	1	0.67%
Celtis		
Chenopod	5	3.33%
Cornus		
Crataegus		
Empetrum		
Fragaria		
Galium	1	0.67%
Grass (Poaceae)	1	0.67%
cf. Elymus		
cf. Echinochloa		
cf. Glyceria		
cf. Hordeum		
cf. Panicum		
Zizania		
Hamamelis		
Helianthus		
Hypericum		
Maize Kernel	3	2%
Mentha		
Oxalis		
Polygonum	1	0.67%
Portulaca		
Potentilla		
Rhus		
Rubus	133	88.67%
Sagittaria	1	0.67%
Sambucus		
Sassafras		
Solanum		
Typha		
Vaccinium	1	0.67%
Vitis		
Unidentified		
Unknown	3	2%
Total Seeds	150	

3 total — /liter 0.93 — /gram 5.29

Table 12.2- Absolute Numbers – Cultigens

Feature	Maize Kernels	Maize Cupules	Maize Frags.	Helianthus	Total Cultigens	Total Seeds
Totals Pit 1	3	39	39		81	150

Table 12.3- Fleshy Fruits

Feature	Celtis	Cornus	Crataegus	Empetrum	Fragaria	Hamamelis	Rubus	Sambucus	Solanum	Vaccinium	Vitis	Total Fleshy Fruits	Total Seeds
Totals Pit 1							133			1		134	150

Table 12.4- Greens/Grains

Feature	Chenopod	Grasses	Polygonum	Portulaca	Total Greens/Grains	Total Seeds
Totals Pit 1	5	1	1		7	150

Table 12.5- Other Taxa

Feature	Astragalus	Galium	Hypericum	Mentha	Oxalis	Potentilla	Rhus	Sagittaria seed	Sagittaria tuber	Sassafras	Typha	Total Other Taxa	Total Seeds
Totals Pit 1	1	1							1			3	150

Table 12.6- Charcoal, Maize, Nut - Percentage of Weights and Ratios

Feature	Wood Charcoal	Maize Kernel	Maize Cupule	Maize Frags.	Total Maize	Quercus	Juglans	Carya	Total Nut	Maize/Charcoal	Nut/Charcoal	Char/Maize/Nut
Totals Pit 1	93.11%	0.22%	1.72%	1.22%	3.44%	2.33%	1.11%		3.44%	27	27	6.73%

Table 12.7- Absolute Numbers per Litre – Cultigens

Feature	Volume (L)	Maize Kernel	Maize Cupules	Maize Frags.	Helianthus	Cultigens
Totals Pit 1	149	0.02	0.23	0.24		0.49

Table 12.8- Percentage of Absolute Numbers - Cultigens

Feature	Maize Kernels	Helianthus	Total Cultigens
Totals Pit 1	2.00%		2.00%

Table 12.9- Fleshy Fruits Table

Feature	Celtis	Cornus	Crataegus	Empetrum	Fragaria	Hamamelis	Rubus	Sambucus	Solanum	Vaccinium	Vitis	Total Fleshy Fruits
Totals Pit 1							88.67%			0.67%		89.33%

12.10- Greens/Grains

Feature	Chenopod	Grasses	Polygonum	Portulaca	Total Greens/Grains
Totals Pit 1	3.33%	0.67%	0.67%		4.00%

Table 12.11- Other Taxa

Feature	Astragalus	Galium	Hypericum	Mentha	Oxalis	Potentilla	Rhus	Sagittaria	Sassafras	Typha	Total Other Taxa
Totals Pit 1	0.67%	0.67%						0.67%			2.00%

Table 13.1 Bull's Point - Absolute Numbers and Weights

Part 1

Provenience X-Y	(cm) Below Surface	Volume (litres)	Wood Charcoal (g)	Wood Charcoal (g/L)	Maize Frags. (g)	Maize Frags. (no.)	Total Maize (g)	Quercus (g)	Total Nut (g)	Chenopod	Cornus	Empetrum	Fragaria	Gallium
1 501-495	15	19	1.31	0.07				0.02	0.02	1	2		1	1
2 501-497	15	9											1	1
3 502-496	15	16	4.01	0.25	0.02	11	0.02		0.01			2		
4 502-497	15	10												
5 502-498	15	8	0.02	0.03	0.01	4	0.01			1			3	3
6 502-500	15	10	0.29	0.02										
7 503-495	15	10	0.21											
8 503-497	15	9												
9 504-496	15	9	1.08	0.12										
10 504-499	15	10	0.33	0.04										
11 505-495	15	10	0.61	0.06										
12 505-496	15	9	0.82	0.08										
13 505-497	15	10												
14 505-499	15	10	0.11	0.01										
15 506-498	15	7	0.20	0.03										
Totals		155	8.99	0.06 average	0.03	15	0.03	0.02	0.03	2	2	2	4	4
%							average total maize (g) 0.001			2.74%	2.74%	2.74%	5.48%	5.48%

Part 2

Provenience X-Y	Grass (Poaceae)	Hamamelis	Hypericum	Oxalis	Portulaca	Rhus	Rubus	Sambucus	Sassafras	Solanum	Typha	Vaccinium	Unknown	Total Seeds
1 501-495	1											1		2
2 501-497														6
3 502-496						2	2	1		12		1		19
4 502-497														
5 502-498														
6 502-500	7	2		1						3	1		3	16
7 503-495														5
8 503-497														
9 504-496														
10 504-499			1				3	1	1	3				11
11 505-495				1						1				3
12 505-496														
13 505-497														
14 505-499	4				1					2				6
15 506-498	3									1	1			5
Totals	15	2	1	2	1	2	5	2	1	22	1	2	3	73
%	20.55%	2.74%	1.37%	2.74%	1.37%	2.74%	6.85%	2.74%	1.37%	30.14%	1.37%	2.74%	4.11%	seeds /liter 0.47 /gram 8.12

Table 13.2- Absolute Numbers - Cultigens

	X-Y Provenience	Maize Kernels	Maize Cupules	Maize Frags.	Helianthus	Total Cultigens	Total Seeds
1	501-495						2
2	501-497						6
3	502-496			11		11	19
4	502-497						
5	502-498			4		4	
6	502-500						16
7	503-495						5
8	503-497						
9	504-496						
10	504-499						11
11	505-495						3
12	505-496						
13	505-497						
14	505-499						6
15	506-498						5
	Totals			15		15	73

Table 13.3- Fleshy Fruits

	X-Y Provenience	Celtis	Cornus	Crataegus	Empetrum	Fragaria	Hamamelis	Rubus	Sambucus	Solanum	Vaccinium	Vitis	Total Fleshy Fruits	Total Seeds
1	501-495										1		1	2
2	501-497	2						2	1				5	6
3	502-496			2	1					12	1		16	19
4	502-497													
5	502-498													
6	502-500					2							2	16
7	503-495									3			3	5
8	503-497													
9	504-496													
10	504-499				3			3		3			9	11
11	505-495								1	1			2	3
12	505-496													
13	505-497													
14	505-499									2			2	6
15	506-498									1			1	5
	Totals	2		2	4	2		5	2	22	2		41	73

Table 13.4- Greens/Grains Table

	X-Y Provenience	Chenopod	Grasses	Polygonum	Portulaca	Greens/Grains	Total Seeds
1	501-495		1			1	2
2	501-497	1				1	6
3	502-496						19
4	502-497						
5	502-498						
6	502-500		7			7	16
7	503-495	1				1	5
8	503-497						
9	504-496						
10	504-499						11
11	505-495						3
12	505-496						
13	505-497						
14	505-499		4			4	6
15	506-498		3	1		4	5
	Totals	2	15	1		18	73

13.5- Other Taxa

	X-Y Provenience	Astragalus	Galium	Hypericum	Mentha	Oxalis	Potentilla	Rhus	Sagittaria seed	Sagittaria tuber	Sassafras	Typha	Total Other Taxa	Total Seeds
1	501-495													2
2	501-497													6
3	502-496	1					2						3	19
4	502-497													
5	502-498													
6	502-500	3										1	4	16
7	503-495					1							1	5
8	503-497													
9	504-496													
10	504-499		1								1		2	11
11	505-495					1							1	3
12	505-496													
13	505-497													
14	505-499													6
15	506-498													5
	Totals	4	1			2	2				1	1	11	73

Table 13.6- Charcoal, Maize, Nut - Percentage of Weights and Ratios

	X-Y Provenience	Wood Charcoal	Maize Kernel	Maize Cupule	Maize Frags.	Total Maize	Quercus	Juglans	Carya	Total Nut	Charcoal-Maize	Charcoal-Nut	Char/Maize/Nut
1	501-495	96.66%					6.67%			6.67%		14	0.52%
2	501-497												
3	502-496	98.70%			0.73%	0.73%				1.14%	401	86	1.89%
4	502-497												
5	502-498	66.67%			33.33%	33.33%						2	0.40%
6	502-500	100%											0.25%
7	503-495	100%											0.72%
8	503-497												
9	504-496	100%											1.30%
10	504-499	100%											0.43%
11	505-495	100%											0.58%
12	505-496	100%											0.83%
13	505-497	100%											
14	505-499	100%											0.21%
15	506-498	100%											1.07%
	Totals	99.34%		0.33%	0.33%	0.22%				0.33%	300	300	0.69%

Table 13.7- Absolute Number per Litre- Cultigens

	X-Y Provenience	Volume (L)	Maize Kernel	Maize Cupule	Maize Frags.	Helianthus	Cultigens
1	501-495	19					
2	501-497	9					
3	502-496	16			0.69		0.69
4	502-497	10					
5	502-498	8			0.50		0.50
6	502-500	10					
7	503-495	10					
8	503-497	9					
9	504-496	9					
10	504-499	9					
11	505-495	10					
12	505-496	10					
13	505-497	9					
14	505-499	10					
15	506-498	7					
	Totals	155			0.10		0.10

Table 13.8- Percentage of Absolute Numbers – Cultigens

	X-Y Provenience	Maize Kernel	Helianthus	Total Cultigens
1	501-495			
2	501-497			
3	502-496			
4	502-497			
5	502-498			
6	502-500			
7	503-495			
8	503-497			
9	504-496			
10	504-499			
11	505-495			
12	505-496			
13	505-497			
14	505-499			
15	506-498			
	Totals			

Table 13.9- Fleshy Fruits

	X-Y Provenience	Celtis	Cornus	Crataegus	Empetrum	Fragaria	Hamamelis	Rubus	Sambucus	Solanum	Vaccinium	Vitis	Total Fleshy Fruits
1	501-495											50.00%	50.00%
2	501-497	33.33%						33.33%	16.67%				83.33%
3	502-496			22.22%	11.11%					62.78%	10.00%		84.45%
4	502-497												
5	502-498												
6	502-500						12.50%						12.50%
7	503-495									60.00%			60.00%
8	503-497												
9	504-496												
10	504-499					27.27%		27.27%		27.27%			81.82%
11	505-495								33.33%	33.33%			66.67%
12	505-496												
13	505-497												
14	505-499									33.33%			33.33%
15	506-498									20.00%			20.00%
	Totals	2.74%	2.74%	5.48%	2.74%	6.85%	2.74%			30.14%		2.74%	56.16%

Table 13.10- Greens/Grains

	X-Y Provenience	Chenopod	Grasses	Polygonum	Portulaca	Total Greens/Grains
1	501-495		50.00%			50.00%
2	501-497	16.67%				16.67%
3	502-496					
4	502-497					
5	502-498					
6	502-500		43.75%			43.75%
7	503-495	20.00%				20.00%
8	503-497					
9	504-496					
10	504-499					
11	505-495					
12	505-496					
13	505-497					
14	505-499		66.67%			66.67%
15	506-498		60.00%	20.00%		80.00%
	Totals	2.74%	20.55%	1.37%		24.66%

Table 13.11- Other Taxa

	X-Y Provenience	Astragalus	Galium	Hypericum	Mentha	Oxalis	Potentilla	Rhus	Sagittaria	Sassafras	Typha	Total Other Taxa
1	501-495											
2	501-497											
3	502-496							20.00%				20.00%
4	502-497											
5	502-498											
6	502-500	18.75%									6.25%	25.00%
7	503-495					20.00%						20.00%
8	503-497											
9	504-496											
10	504-499			9.09%						9.09%		18.18%
11	505-495					33.33%						33.33%
12	505-496											
13	505-497											
14	505-499											
15	506-498											
	Totals	4.11%	1.37%	2.74%		2.74%				1.37%	1.37%	13.70%

Small maize fragments were recovered from Bull's Point (see Tables 13.1 to 13.11). Most seeds are from the fleshy fruit category. Other than Grand Banks, Bull's Point has the greatest diversity of species in this category (seven species): American nightshade, bramble, blueberry, crowberry, elderberry, strawberry, and witchhazel. Grasses, chenopod, and purslane are identified. Cat-tail, cleaver, St. John's wort, sassafras, sumac, and wood sorrel comprise the other taxa category.

Density Ratios by Weight and Volume

A simple method of standardizing data is through the use of ratios. One of the most basic ratios in palaeoethnobotany is density (Miller 1988:73; also see Crawford 1983), using the total volume of the sediment sample as the denominator. Density can be expressed as the number of charred items or the weight of the charred material per litre of soil sample. A number of different comparisons can be made, depending on the standard and the sample. Density values are one of the most important and basic measures for interpreting depositional and preservational variability (Miller 1988:83). Density values are particularly useful in this study as they allow for the comparison of not only Princess Point samples but of Princess Point to Glen Meyer samples by reducing the complexity of the data and isolating factors. This exercise allows for the standardization of data despite the variability of deposition, preservation, and recovery rates.

The total number of seeds per litre of soil sample is used as a variable in this study. The total number of cultigens per litre is used, taking into account maize kernels, cupules, and fragments, and sunflower seeds. The calculation of individual taxa of seeds per litre is conducted only on Feature 210 from Grand Banks. The samples from other sites and features are represented by insufficient numbers to provide meaningful results. Densities are provided for total counts of categories at all sites.

Densities are also calculated from the weight (by gram) of wood charcoal. For each gram of charcoal recovered, the weight of maize remains and the total number of seeds per site are calculated. The weights of seeds are not determined as these weights are minimal, being no more than 0.01 g per sample at the maximum. The total weights of wood charcoal, maize, and nuts are calculated and the relative percentages of each component are provided.

Wood charcoal is a standard used against which to compare maize and seed preservation with the assumption that charcoal represents domestic fuel use, thus providing a control for the likelihood of preservation. For example, Johannessen (1988) measured varying rates of nut shell deposition relative to wood charcoal deposition in southern Illinois. Asch and Asch Sidell (1988) report sequences of stratified plant remains in southern Illinois, from the Archaic to Woodland, by examining wood charcoal variation within closely separated levels of occupational layers. Greater evidence for botanical remains, in comparison to wood charcoal evidence, should signify greater use of that particular plant and of plant material in general. Fire likely was used for numerous purposes, including cooking and warmth. Kadane (1988) notes that this type of measurement has limitations as one must make assumptions about relative preservation rates of wood charcoal and other plant material.

The average density for Princess Point is nearly one seed per litre, ranging from 2.17 for Grand Banks to 0.37 for Lone Pine. The fleshy fruits category has the highest density (0.354), closely followed by greens and grains (0.35), then other taxa (0.12), and cultigens (0.05). Densities for Feature 210 are higher: an average of 3.1 (greens/grains, 8.13; fleshy fruits, 2.46; other taxa, 1.58; and cultigens, 0.23). The density for greens and grains is considerably more than that for fleshy fruits in this feature. Tables supporting all data are noted below for individual sites.

The density from the Grand Banks sheet midden (palaeosol, see Figure 3) (not including Feature 210) is 0.25 seed per litre. The density level for maize at Grand Banks is 0.05; Feature 210 is slightly higher, 0.21. Grand Banks produced about 0.25 g wood charcoal per litre. For each gram of charcoal, there are about eight seeds. As in all samples, wood charcoal accounts for most of the carbonized material from Grand Banks; maize and nuts account for minor amounts. Less than one seed per litre is identified from Feature 1, and nearly nine seeds per gram of wood charcoal. No seeds are identified from Feature 219. There is over one gram of wood charcoal per litre at Feature 210, with an average of nearly 12 seeds per gram of charcoal (see Tables 8.6 and 8.7 for Grand Banks, and Tables 9.6 to 9.11 for Feature 210).

Lone Pine produced less than one seed per litre. Nearly 70 g of wood charcoal were recovered (over half a gram per litre), representing less than one seed per gram of charcoal. For each gram of charcoal, there is a minimal amount of maize (see Tables 10.6 and 10.7). At Meyer, 50 seeds are identified; 27 from Feature 56. This represents nearly one seed per litre for the entire site and 1.5 seeds per litre for Feature 56. The cultigen density is 0.56. There are about three seeds per gram of wood charcoal (see Tables 11.6 and 11.7).

Forster produced nearly one seed per litre. A low cultigen density (0.02) and about five seeds per gram of wood charcoal are calculated (see Tables 12.6 and 12.7). The density for Bull's Point is 0.47. Per gram of charcoal, there are about eight seeds. There was 300 times more wood charcoal than maize recovered, accounting for nearly all carbonized material by weight (see Tables 13.6 and 13.7).

Frequency of Taxa by Sample and Site

Taxa frequency, or ubiquity, provides some comparison

between samples but, mostly, ubiquity is simply the first step towards more sophisticated analyses (Popper 1988). Ubiquity depends on volume and the probability that each sample has the same preservation, which is unlikely. Ubiquity also depends on the improbable likelihood that each sample location had the same presence of the taxon when the site was in use. Therefore, the importance of different categories or taxa cannot be compared directly by frequency or ubiquity and this method of analysis has been criticized (see Kadane 1988).

The frequency score of a category is the number of samples in which the category or taxon is present, expressed as a percentage of the total number of samples at each site. The use of percentages allows the comparison of categories by standardizing each sample. The analysis considers the category or taxon present in a sample whether the sample contains one remain or 100 (see Table 14 for the percentage of each category; Table 15 for the percentage of each taxon) (also see Figures 5 and 6).

Table 14 Ubiquity of Samples - Categories by Site

Plant Category	Bull's Point	Forster	Grand Banks	Lone Pine	Meyer
Cultigens	9.5%	29.7%	21.9%	34.8%	25.0%
Fleshy Fruits	33.3%	32.4%	11.0%	8.7%	15.0%
Greens/Grains	16.7%	8.1%	22.8%	13.0%	15.0%
Other Taxa	16.7%	8.1%	15.1%	13.0%	15.0%
Nuts	4.8%	16.2%	19.2%	13.0%	15.0%
Unknown/ Unidentifiable	19.0%	5.4%	10.0%	17.4%	15.0%
Totals	100%	100%	100%	100%	100%

Lone Pine has the largest percentage of samples containing the category of cultigens (maize only). Forster has the second largest percentage of samples containing cultigens. Cultigens appear in a quarter of Meyer samples. Bull's Point has the smallest percentage of samples containing cultigens. Bull's Point has the largest percentage of samples with fleshy fruits; Forster has the second largest percentage. Grand Banks and Lone Pine have the smallest percentages of samples with fleshy fruits. The fleshy fruit category is present in nearly twice as many samples from Feature 210 than from the remainder of Grand Banks (see Figures 7 and 8).

The greens and grains category appears in more samples from Grand Banks than any other site. This is the most common category identified in samples from that site.

This category appears least often in samples from Forster. The other taxa category is found in the most samples from Bull's Point and in the least from Forster. Grand Banks has the most samples with nut and Bull's Point, the lowest. Feature 210 has fewer samples containing nuts than the remainder of samples from Grand Banks. At the other three sites, the amount of nuts is relatively similar. Unknowns and unidentifiables are present at all sites, and in the highest percentage of samples from Bull's Point and Lone Pine, and in the lowest percentage from Forster.

Table 15 Ubiquity of Samples - Taxa by Site

Scientific Name	Common	Bull's Point	Forster	Grand Banks	Lone Pine	Meyer
Cultigens						
Cucurbita pepo	Cucurbit	2.4%				
Helianthus annuus	Sunflower			2.3%		
Zea mays	Maize	7.1%	29.7%	19.6%	34.8%	25.0%
Fleshy Fruits						
Celtis sp.	Hackberry			0.5%		
Cornus canadensis	Dogwood			0.9%		
Crataegus sp.	Hawthorn			0.5%		
Empetrum nigrum	Crowberry	2.4%				
Fragaria sp.	Strawberry	4.8%		0.5%		5.0%
Hamamelis virginiana	Witchhazel	2.4%				
Rubus sp.	Bramble	2.4%	29.7%	4.1%	4.3%	10.0%
Sambucus sp.	Elderberry	2.4%				
Solanum americanum	American Nightshade	14.3%		1.8%	4.3%	5.0%
Vaccinium myrtilloides	Blueberry	4.8%	2.7%	1.8%		
Vitis sp.	Grape			0.9%		
Greens/Grains						
Chenopodium sp.	Chenopod	4.8%	5.4%	7.3%	8.7%	5.0%
Poaceae	Grasses	9.5%	2.7%	9.6%		10.0%
Polygonum sp.	Knotweed			1.8%	4.3%	5.0%
Portulaca oleracea	Purslane	2.4%		4.1%		
Other Taxa						
Astragalus sp.	Vetch		2.7%	1.4%		
Galium sp.	Cleaver	2.4%	2.7%	2.7%	4.3%	
Hypericum perforatum	St.Johns Wort	2.4%		2.7%		5.0%
Mentha sp.	Mint			0.9%		
Oxalis sp.	Wood Sorrel	4.8%		1.4%		
Potentilla sp.	Cinquefoil			0.9%		
Rhus typhina	Sumac	2.4%		1.4%	8.7%	
Sagittaria latifolia	Arrowhead		2.7%	2.7%		
Sassafras sp.	Sassafras	2.4%				
Typha latifolia	Cat-tail	2.4%		0.9%		
Nuts		4.8%	16.2%	19.2%	13.0%	15.0%
Unknown/ Unidentifiable		19.0%	5.4%	10.0%	17.4%	15.0%
Totals		100%	100%	100%	100%	100%

Table 16 Descending Counts of Taxa - Princess Point and Glen Meyer

	Princess Point			Glen Meyer
1.	Grasses		1.	Cat-tail
2.	Purslane		2.	Maize (kernels only)
3.	American Nightshade		3.	Tobacco
4.	Chenopod		4.	Bramble
5.	Bramble		5.	Sumac
6.	Milkvetch		6.	Strawberry
7.	Cleavers		7.	Elderberry
8.	Maize (kernels only)		8.	American Nightshade
9.	Cat-tail		9.	Purslane
10.	St. John's Wort		10.	Grasses
11.	Wood Sorrel		11.	Cucurbit
12.	Erect Knotweed		12.	Chenopod
13.	Cinquefoil		13.	Cleavers
14.	Sumac		14.	Erect Knotweed

Table 17 Descending Seed Density - Princess Point and Glen Meyer

	Princess Point (Fe. 210, Grand Banks site)			Glen Meyer
1.	Purslane		1.	Cat-tail
2.	Grasses		2.	Maize (kernels only)
3.	American Nightshade		3.	Bramble
4.	Maize (kernels only)		4.	Elderberry
5.	Chenopod		5.	Sumac
6.	Milkvetch		6.	Tobacco
7.	Cleavers		7.	Strawberry
8.	Bramble		8.	American Nightshade
9.	Cat-tail		9.	Purslane
10.	St. John's Wort		10.	Grasses
11.	Wood sorrel		11.	Erect Knotweed
12.	Cinquefoil		12.	Cucurbit
13.	Erect Knotweed		13.	Cleavers
14.	Sumac		14.	Chenopod

Table 18 Percentages of Categories by Absolute Numbers - Princess Point and Glen Meyer

	Princess Point	Glen Meyer
Greens/Grains	56%	9%
Fleshy Fruits	23%	27%
Other Taxa	12%	32%
Unknowns/Unidentified	7%	7%
Cultigens	3%	25%

Table 19 Absolute Numbers per Litre - Princess Point and Glen Meyer

	Princess Point	Glen Meyer
Fleshy Fruits	0.352	2.13
Greens/Grains	0.35	0.15
Other Taxa	0.12	3.39
Cultigens	0.05	1.76

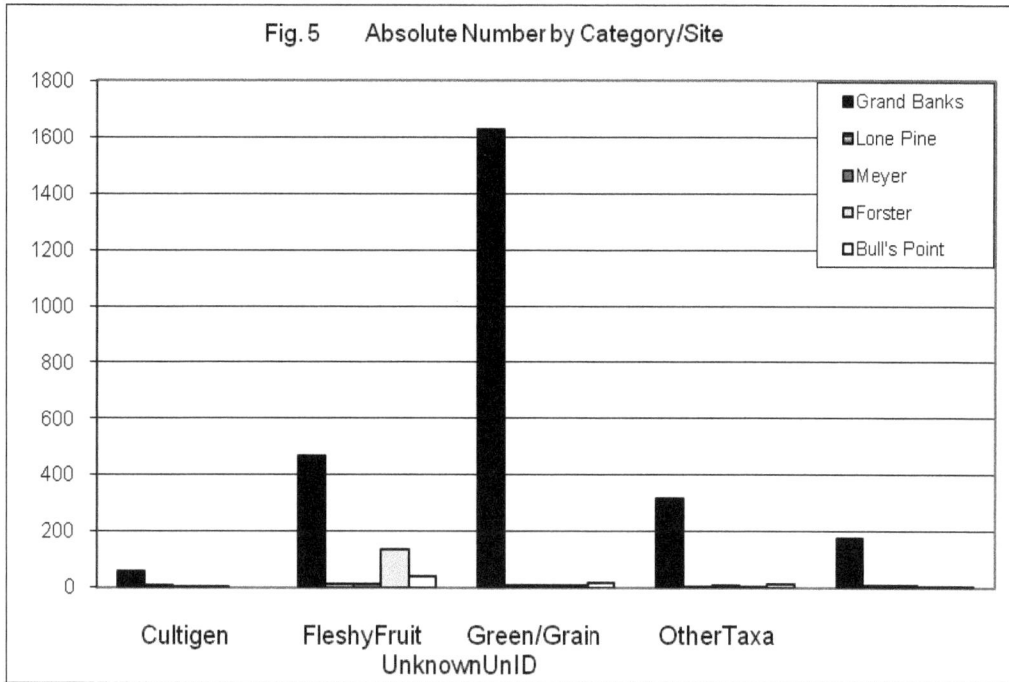

Fig. 5   Absolute Number by Category/Site

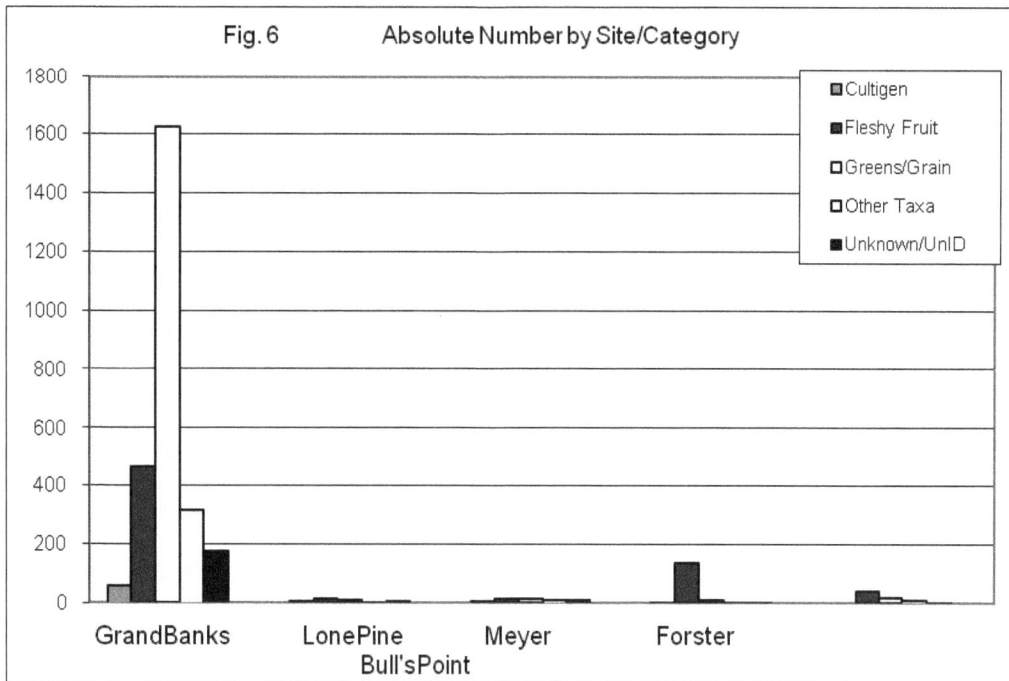

Fig. 6   Absolute Number by Site/Category

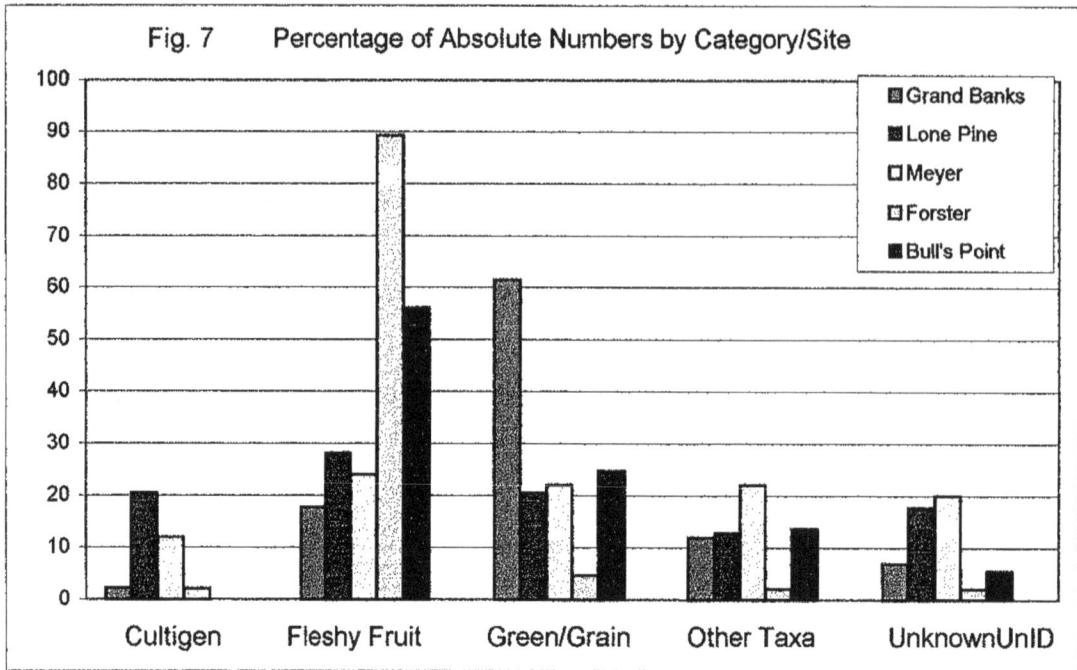

Fig. 7   Percentage of Absolute Numbers by Category/Site

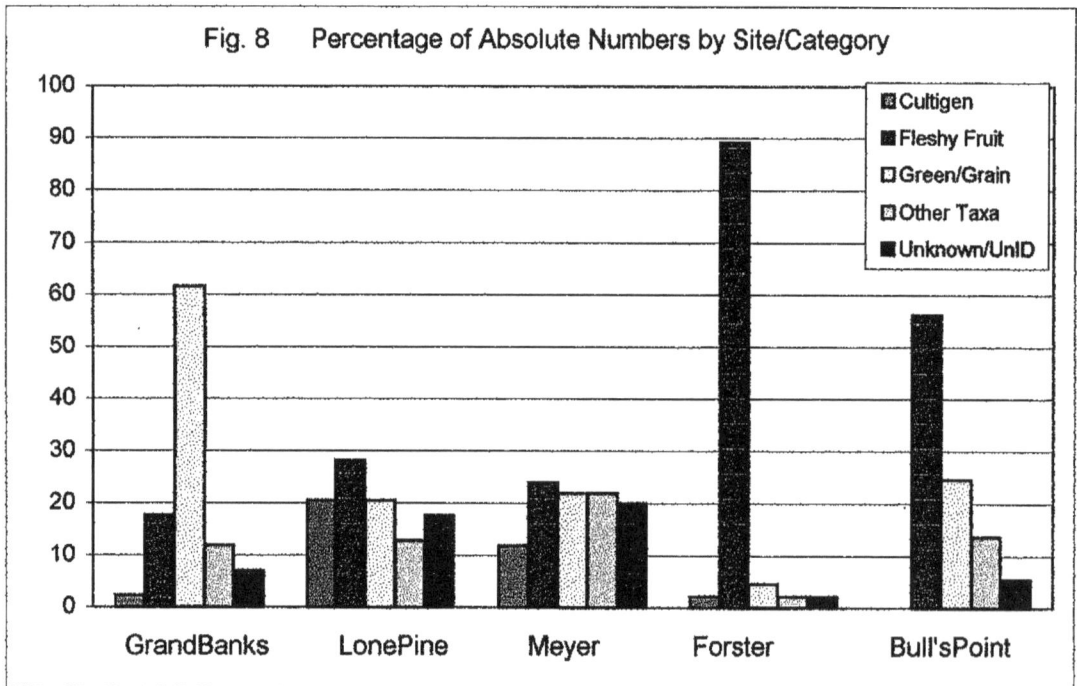

Fig. 8   Percentage of Absolute Numbers by Site/Category

Correspondence Analysis

Correspondence analysis has the potential to compare assemblages with low sample sizes. It analyzes data that consist of frequencies (Shennan 1990:283), such as the frequency of occurrence of a taxon. The relationships between sites can then be analyzed and represented by scattergram to see which cases are most alike. Common techniques, such as correlation analysis, are only satisfactory measures of association when data are numeric and the distributions of individual variable are relatively normal (Shennan 1990:283). Correspondence analysis does not have this constraint and accounts for problems that arise when the variables in an analysis are not normally distributed numeric ones. The variables in this study are skewed as a result of small sample sizes and zero values.

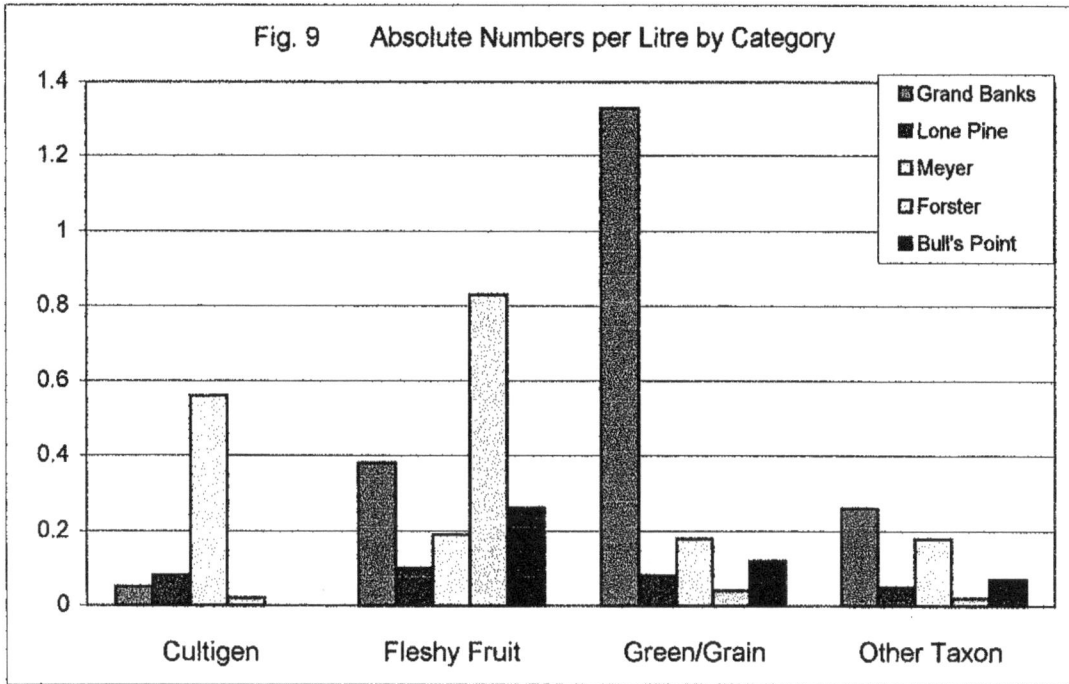

Fig. 9   Absolute Numbers per Litre by Category

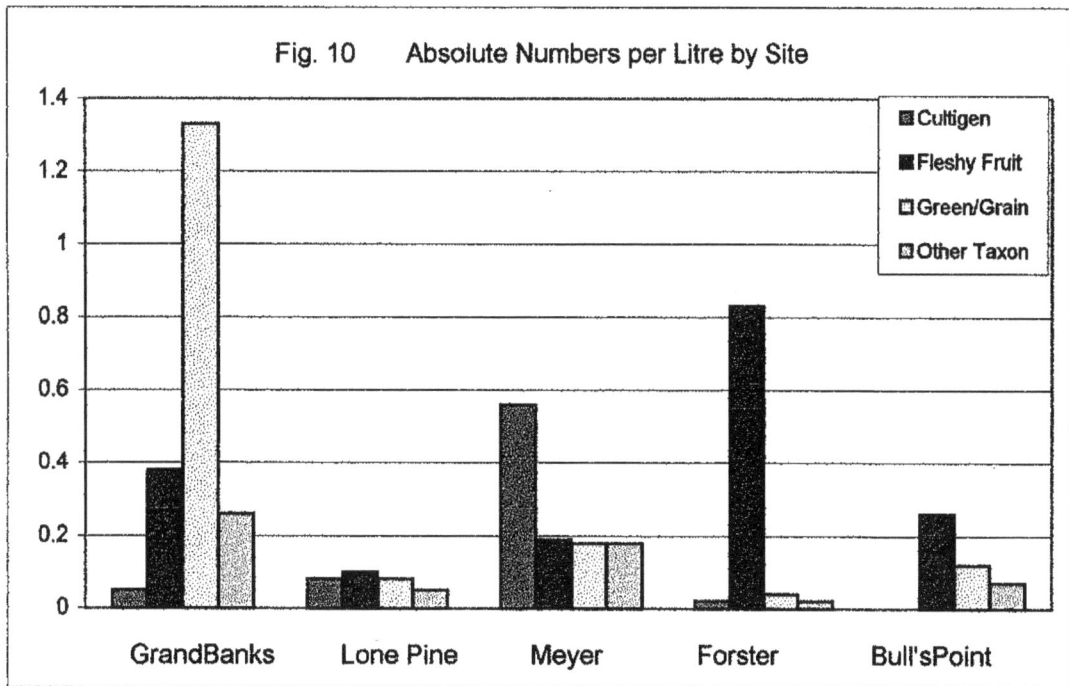

Fig. 10   Absolute Numbers per Litre by Site

Fig. 11 Total Absolute Numbers by Category

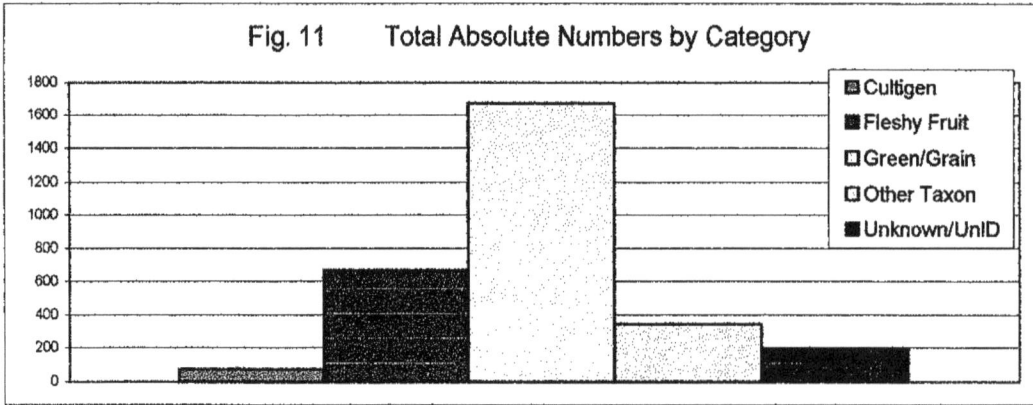

Legend: Cultigen, Fleshy Fruit, Green/Grain, Other Taxon, Unknown/UnID

Fig. 12 Total Percentage of Absolute Numbers by Category

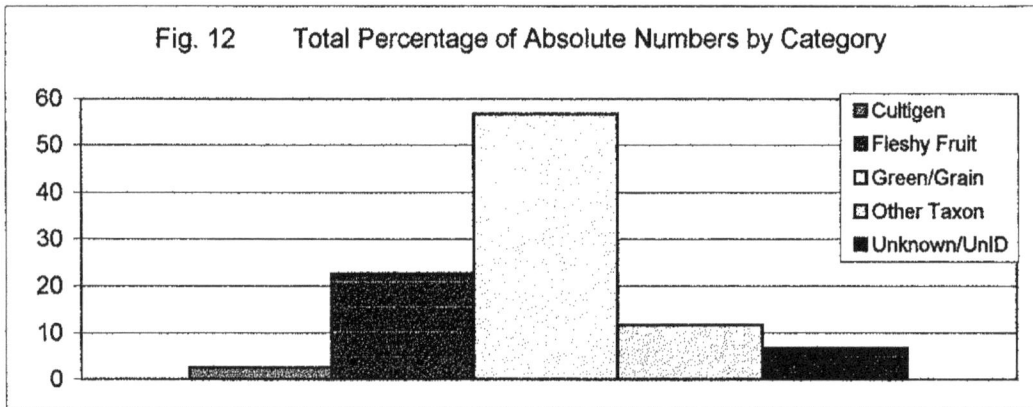

Legend: Cultigen, Fleshy Fruit, Green/Grain, Other Taxon, Unknown/UnID

Fig. 13 Absolute Numbers per Litre by Category - All Sites

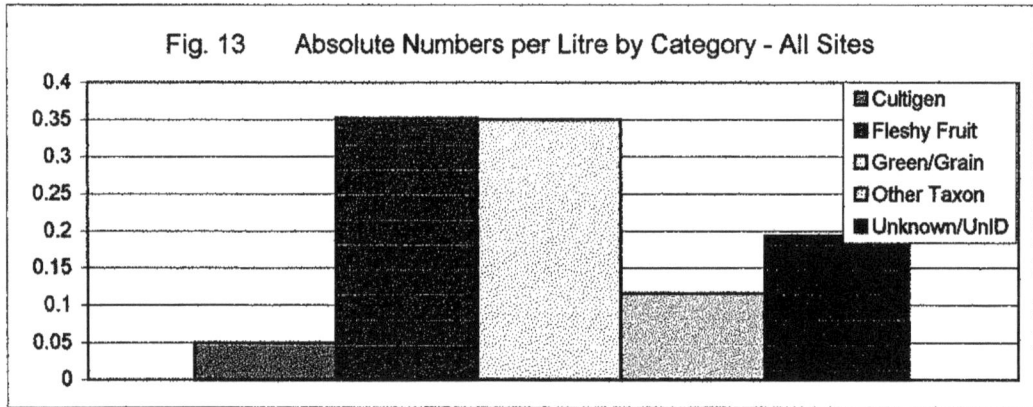

Legend: Cultigen, Fleshy Fruit, Green/Grain, Other Taxon, Unknown/UnID

Fig. 14 Absolute Numbers per Litre by Category, Fe. 210

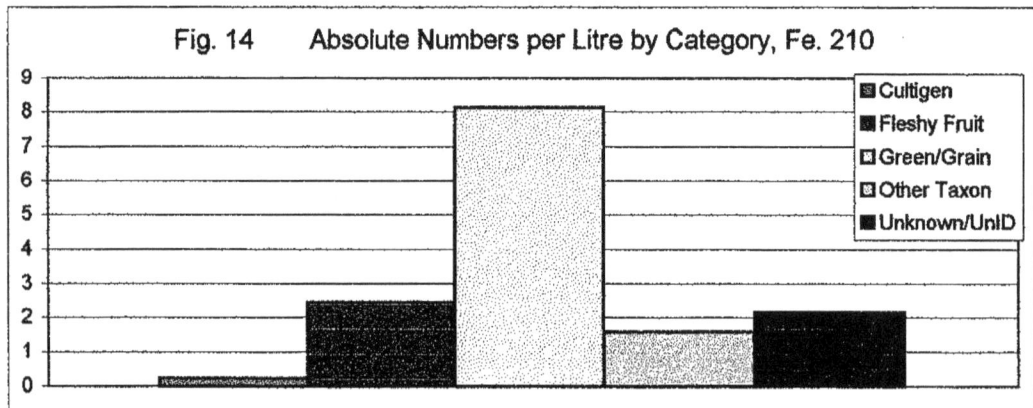

Legend: Cultigen, Fleshy Fruit, Green/Grain, Other Taxon, Unknown/UnID

Fig. 15   Maize & Nut Percentages - All Sites by Weight

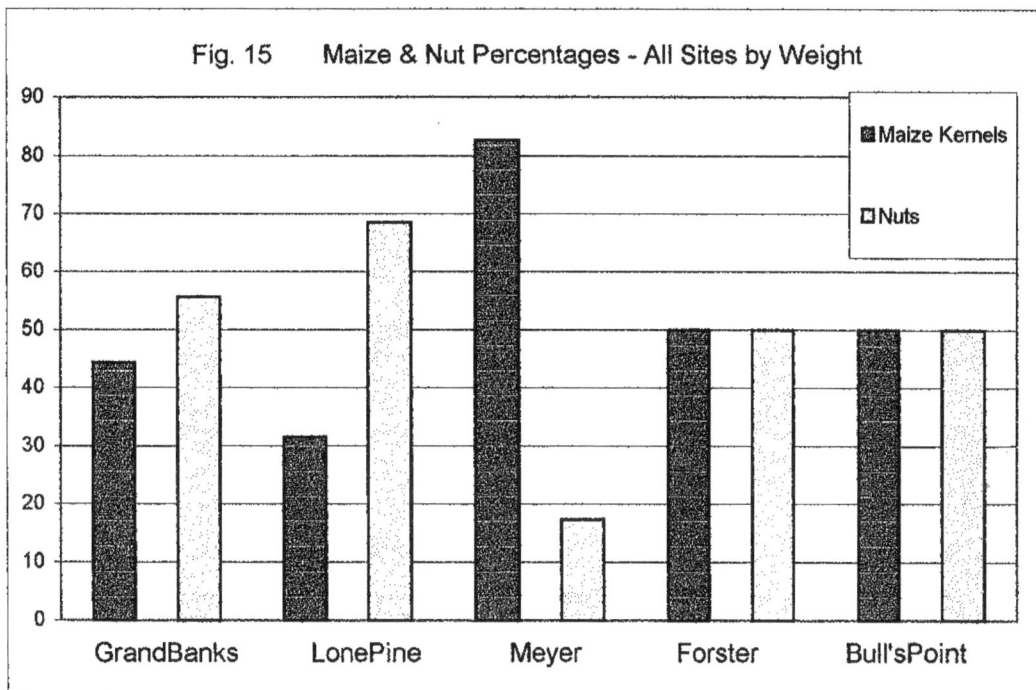

Fig. 16   Maize & Nut Percentages: Princess Point & Glen Meyer

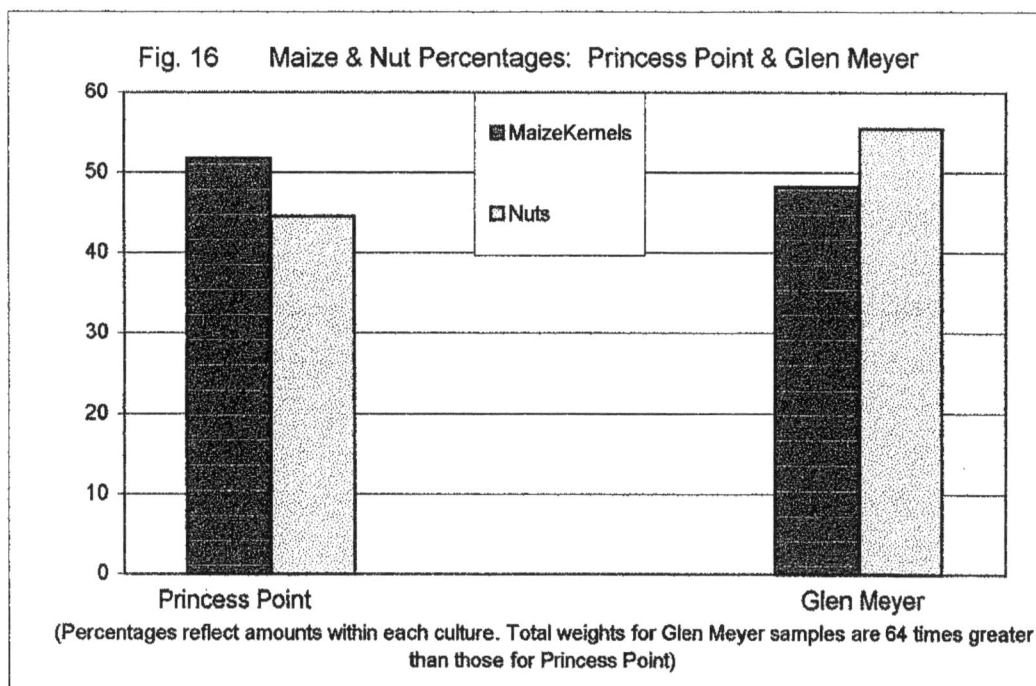

(Percentages reflect amounts within each culture. Total weights for Glen Meyer samples are 64 times greater than those for Princess Point)

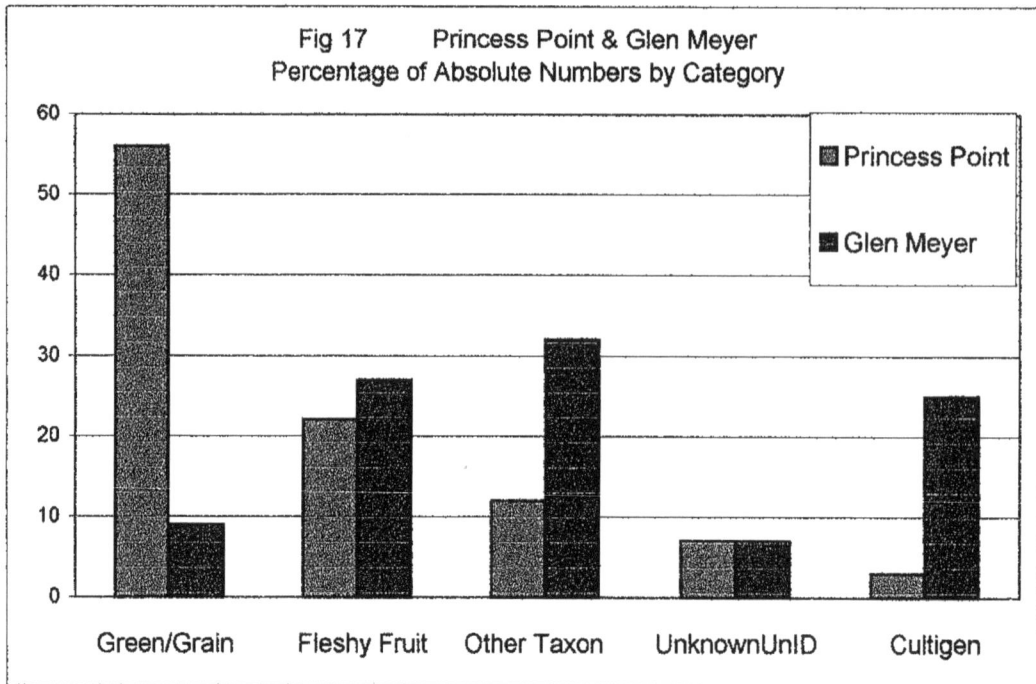

Fig 17 Princess Point & Glen Meyer
Percentage of Absolute Numbers by Category

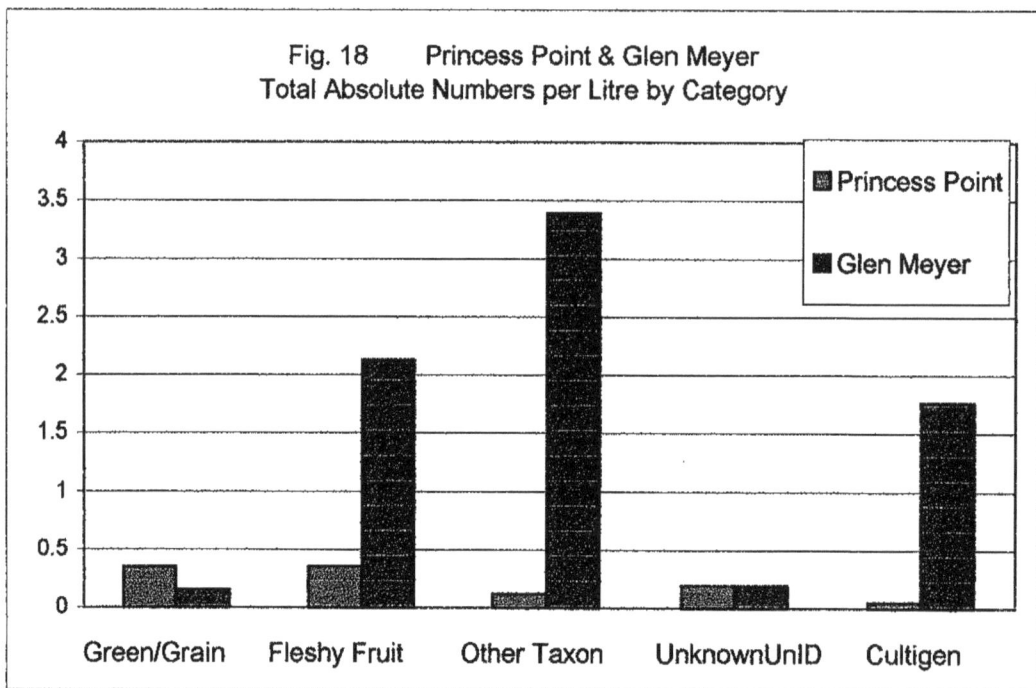

Fig. 18 Princess Point & Glen Meyer
Total Absolute Numbers per Litre by Category

Preliminary correspondence analysis suggests that Lone Pine, Meyer, and Grand Banks are most similar to each other. Forster and Bull's Point are least similar to the other three and to each other (see Figure 19). This analysis includes all categories (cultigens, fleshy fruits, greens/grains, other taxa, nuts, and unknowns/unidentifiables) and considers their levels of similarity for each site by absolute numbers. The categories of greens/grains and other taxa are most similar in their distribution at the five sites. Cultigens, fleshy fruits, nuts, and unknown/unidentifiables exhibit less similarity in their distribution across the sites (see Figure 20).

The scattergrams reflect what intuitively can be seen in the bar graphs (see Figures 9 and 10) depicting the

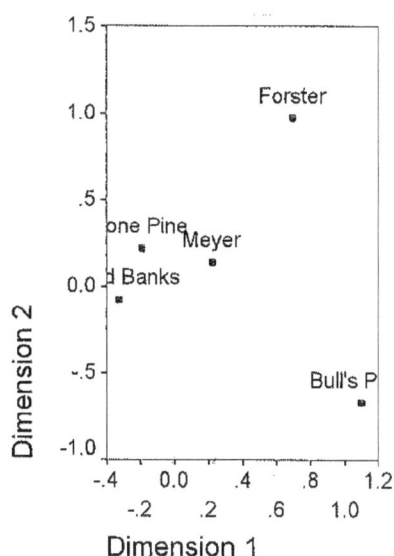

Figure 19 Graph - Correspondence Analysis - Sites

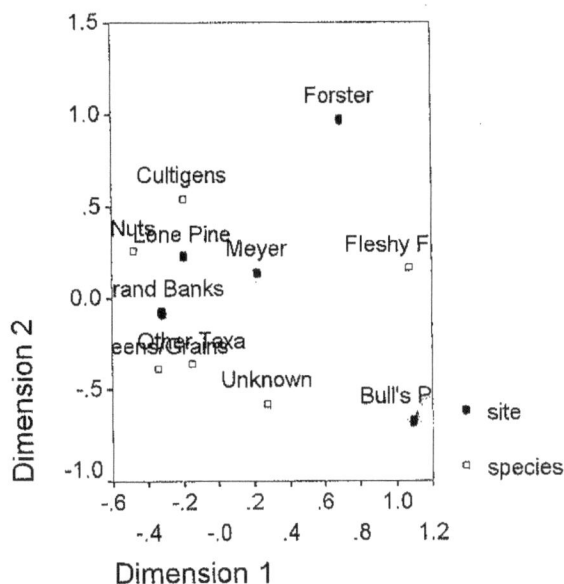

Figure 20 Graph - Correspondence Analysis - Categories

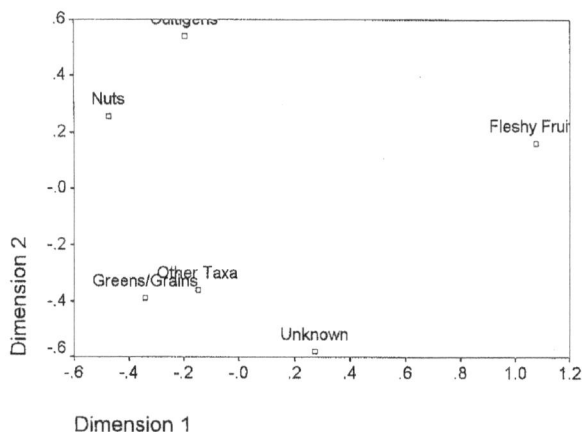

Figure 21 Graph - Correspondence Analysis - Sites and Categories

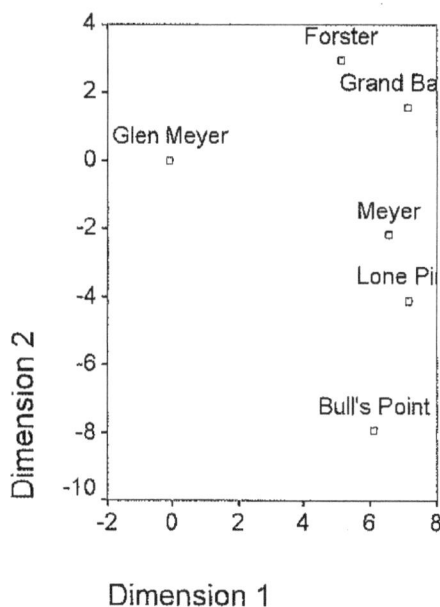

Figure 22 Graph - Correspondence Analysis - Princess Point & Glen Meyer

absolute numbers of categories. Grand Banks, Lone Pine, and Meyer are most similar; and the greens/grains category bears the most similarity across all sites (see Figure 21). A comparison of the total seed counts of Glen Meyer sites (Ounjian 1998) to the five Princess Point sites resulted in Princess Point sites exhibiting more similarity to one another than to Glen Meyer sites (see Figure 22).

This analysis is preliminary. Continued analysis of varied combinations of factors would examine the similarities or differences between various elements. For example, as Ounjian (1998) notes, a large quantity of cat-tail at one Glen Meyer site skews the distribution of the other taxa category upwards. Correspondence analysis eliminating cat-tail from both Princess Point and Glen Meyer would factor out this anomaly. Another suggestion is to change the categories under which seeds presently are categorized, that is, from an ethnobotanical perspective to an ecological one.

Alternative ways of displaying data would explore the distribution of other combinations, such as wetland

plants. Similarities and differences in the information can be teased out of the raw data by alternating the inclusion of certain taxa, changing categories, and varying sites to compare with one another. It may be possible to see some relationship between activity patterns and archaeological deposition. Relationships among factors (such as, sites and categories), however, will be discernible.

Measurements and Domestication Markers

The transition from wild to domesticated plant occurs when plants undergo genetic alteration resulting in morphological changes. These genetic and morphological changes are the result of selective pressures within the human-made habitat and reflect adaptation to a human-manipulated environment. Domesticated species, unlike their wild varieties, cannot survive without continued human attention and intervention (Smith 1992). The main morphological marker for domestication in archaeology is an increase in seed size. Seed size determined the status of marsh elder and sunflower as prehistoric domesticates in the Eastern Woodlands (Yarnell 1978; Asch and Asch 1978). A number of morphological changes indicate the process of domestication of chenopod (Smith 1992) and these are reviewed in this section. The documentation of seed sizes and seed characteristics from assemblages from different regions will result in a better understanding of domestication and of prehistoric plant use generally.

Many of the plant remains in this study tend to have preserved in an extremely fragmented condition, undoubtedly due to processing, charring, and post-depositional events. However, maize kernels, maize cupules, sunflower, and chenopod seeds that did preserve in a fairly complete state are measured (see Tables 20 to 24). The maximum size of each intact plant part is determined to the nearest 0.1 mm using a calibrated glass microscope slide.

This study compares these measurements to those from the Glen Meyer and prehistoric Neutral sites (Ounjian 1998). Ounjian notes that the morphological variability seen in the Glen Meyer plant assemblages may reflect the proximity in time of that culture to the introduction of agriculture. When agriculture begins, the growth and morphology of crop plants are not uniform because plants are responding to a period of human interference with their growth habits and some varieties respond better to change and to the local environment than others (Smith 1992). This morphological variability can be reflected in archaeological remains. With time, after plants have adapted to the stress factors of change and crop selection has improved, plants become more uniform. Uniformity in morphology is seen in the prehistoric Neutral assemblages. The morphology of plant remains from Glen Meyer tends to be more variable than prehistoric Neutral suggesting that cultigens were still adapting to southwestern Ontario.

The uniformity or variation of plant remains is reflected in the standard deviation of a measurement. The standard deviation for maize kernels from the Princess Point Grand Banks site is over three times that calculated for Glen Meyer maize kernels (see Table 24). There is little morphological difference between those kernels recovered from the palaeosol and from pits. The average

Table 20 Maize Kernel Dimensions

Site measurements/mm	X-Y	Feature	Kernel Width	Kernel Length	Kernel Thickness	Kernel W/L Ratio	Kernel W/T Ratio
Grand Banks	730-680	210	5.2	3.4	2.3	1.53	2.26
n=6	730-680	210	8.2	6.0	4.6	1.37	1.78
	730-680	210	6.6	5.3	3.4	1.25	1.94
	730-680	210	8.4	6.5	5.2	1.29	1.62
	730-680	210	5.2	4.8	3.4	1.08	1.53
	730-680	210	9.2	6.9	4.3	1.33	2.14
		mean	7.13	5.48	3.87	1.30	1.84
		range	5.2- 9.2 1.5	3.4- 6.9	2.3-5.2	1.08- 1.53	1.53- 2.26
		stand.dev.	7	1.17	0.95	0.13	0.26
Grand Banks	730-685		4.0	3.1	3.4	1.29	1.18
n=3	730-685		4.0	3.1	2.5	1.29	1.60
	731-699		7.6	5.4	3.6	1.41	2.11
		mean	5.20	3.87	3.17	1.34	1.64
		range	4.0- 7.6	3.1- 5.4	2.5-3.6	1.29- 1.41	1.60- 2.11
		stand.dev.	1.70	1.08	0.48	0.06	0.38
Lone Pine	460-500		8.4	5.2	5.4	1.62	1.56
n=1		mean	8.4	5.2	5.4	1.62	1.56
		range	8.4	5.2	5.4	1.62	1.56
		stand.dev.	0	0	0	0	0
Forster	710- 390W	1	5.8	5.5	3.4	1.05	1.71
n=1		mean	5.8	5.5	3.4	1.05	1.71
		range	5.8	5.5	3.4	1.05	1.71
		stand.dev.	0	0	0	0	0

Table 21 Maize Cupule Dimensions

Site measurements in mm		Cupule Width	Cupule Thickness	Cupule Ratio
Grand Banks	mean	7.02	2.55	2.76
n=29	range	2.2-9.1	1.3-4.3	1.47-4.68
	stand.dev.	1.81	0.66	0.75
Lone Pine	mean	5.34	2.36	2.26
n=8	range	3.5-8.7	2.0-3.0	1.33-3.15
	stand.dev.	1.87	0.38	0.59
Meyer	mean	5.60	2.60	2.15
n=3	range	5.1-6.2	2.2-3.0	1.70-2.50
	stand.dev.	0.45	0.33	0.35
Forster	mean	6.86	2.76	2.49
n=7	range	5.0-9.7	1.8-3.7	2.09-2.82
	stand.dev.	1.43	0.66	0.23

Table 23 Sunflower Dimensions

Site measurements in mm		Seed Diameter
Grand Banks	mean	1.22
(entire site)	range	0.9-1.6
n=54	stand.dev.	0.16
Feature 210	mean	1.26
Grand Banks	range	1.0-1.6
n=30	stand.dev.	0.16

Table 22 Chenopod Dimensions

Site measurements in mm*		Seed length	Seed width	Seed ratio l/w
Grand Banks	mean	4.3	1.59	4.3-1.59
n=3	range	4.3-4.3	1.52-1.65	2.73-3.39
	stand.dev.	0	0.05	0.10
*corrected following Yarnell (1978:296)				

size of Princess Point kernels is slightly smaller than Glen Meyer kernels. The standard deviation calculated on Grand Banks Princess Point maize cupules is five times that calculated for Glen Meyer cupules. Because of poor preservation, kernels could be measured only from the Grand Banks site. Cupules, however, were measured from Grand Banks, Lone Pine, Meyer, and Forster. The standard deviation calculated on cupules from the Meyer site is three times less than that calculated for the other sites. Although there is less morphological variation in cupules from the Meyer site, the average size of cupules from all sites and features is similar, but somewhat smaller than those from Glen Meyer sites.

There is little morphological variation in chenopod seeds recovered from both Princess Point sites and Glen Meyer sites. Although slight, the standard deviation calculated on seeds from Princess Point is about twice that calculated on Glen Meyer seeds. The average size of all seeds is similar, whether they come from pits or the palaeosol. The standard deviations calculated on sunflower seeds from Princess Point (Grand Banks site) and from the Glen Meyer Calvert assemblage are low, but there is slightly more morphological variation with Princess Point. Glen Meyer seeds, however, are larger than Princess Point seeds.

Maize

Archaeobotanists have recovered large quantities of maize remains from southern Ontario sites, and corn often comprises the majority of the plant food remains by weight (Crawford 1985, 1986; Monckton 1990, 1992; Ounjian 1998; Monckton 1999). Archaeological corn throughout the Northeast is generally Eastern eight-row (Eastern complex or Northern flint/flour); this is the only archaeological corn confirmed in pre-contact Ontario (Crawford and Smith 2001). Measurements of cupules and kernels from the Lone Pine and Grand Banks sites fall within the range of Eastern eight-row maize (Bowyer 1995).

Although most specimens recovered in this study are fragmented and distorted, the kernels and cupules measured represent those that are well preserved and in a relatively intact state. Dependable measurements on archaeobotanical remains of corn are difficult to attain because of the fragmentary nature of the remains and because of differential affects of heating on kernels and cupules (King 1994:36). Cob row number, cupule width, degree of cupule pairing, and kernel width provide the attributes to identify Eastern eight-row corn (Bird 1994; King 1994). Maize kernels are measured in three dimensions: length, width, and thickness. Ratios of width/thickness and width/length illustrate size variation. Eastern eight-row corn typically exhibits four rows of cupules, each cupule containing two crescent-shaped kernels (Yarnell 1964:107). This variety of corn tolerates cool weather, a longer day length, and produces within a short growing season (Yarnell 1964; Mangelsdorf 1974).

Nine kernels were measured from Grand Banks. The mean width is 6.49 mm, mean length is 4.94 mm, and mean thickness, 3.63 mm. The mean ratio of kernel width/length is 1.31 and width/thickness is 1.79. For Feature 210, the mean ratio of kernel width/length is 1.30 and width/thickness is 1.84 (see Table 20).

Table 24   T-test Results of Maize Kernel Dimensions

Kernel Width

(9 Princess Point and 5 Glen Meyer measurements)

t-Test: Two-Sample Assuming Equal Variances

	5.2	9.26
Mean	6.65	8.575
Variance	4.145714286	0.06923333
Observations	8	4
Pooled Variance	2.92277	
Hypothesized Mean Difference	0	
df	10	
t Stat	-1.838729228	
P(T<=t) one-tail	0.047898857	
t Critical one-tail	1.812461505	
P(T<=t) two-tail	0.095797713	
t Critical two-tail	2.228139238	

Kernel Length

(9 Princess Point and 5 Glen Meyer measurements)

t-Test: Two-Sample Assuming Equal Variances

	3.4	6.62
Mean	5.1375	6.6175
Variance	2.03125	0.097291667
Observations	8	4
Pooled Variance	1.4510625	
Hypothesized Mean Difference	0	
df	10	
t Stat	-2.006333026	
P(T<=t) one-tail	0.036308701	
t Critical one-tail	1.812461505	
P(T<=t) two-tail	0.072617402	
t Critical two-tail	2.228139238	

Kernel Thickness

(9 Princess Point and 5 Glen Meyer measurements)

t-Test: Two-Sample Assuming Equal Variances

	2.3	6.3
Mean	3.8	5.3725
Variance	0.722857143	0.078891667
Observations	8	4
Pooled Variance	0.5296675	
Hypothesized Mean Difference	0	
df	10	
t Stat	-3.528363797	
P(T<=t) one-tail	0.002730846	
t Critical one-tail	1.812461505	
P(T<=t) two-tail	0.005461693	
t Critical two-tail	2.228139238	

Ounjian's (1998) measurements for the mean of maize kernels at Glen Meyer sites are larger: width, 8.83 mm, length, 6.64 mm, and thickness, 5.31 mm. The width/length ratio is 1.31 and the width/thickness mean ratio is 1.65. Ounjian's (1998) measurements for the mean of maize kernels at prehistoric Neutral sites are also larger: width, 9.82 mm, length, 7.50 mm, and thickness, 5.93 mm. The width/length ratio is 1.32 and the width/thickness ratio is 1.68. Ounjian's calculations derive from a total of 638 kernels measured from five Glen Meyer sites. A comparison of measurements between Princess Point and Glen Meyer found that there was a significant difference in the size of kernels by their width, length, and thickness (see Table 24).

Twenty-nine cupules from Grand Banks produced a mean width of 7.02 mm; mean thickness, 2.55 mm; and width/thickness ratio of 2.76. Feature 210 (n=20) cupules produced a mean width of 6.97 mm; mean thickness, 2.55 mm; and width/thickness ratio of 2.73. At Lone Pine, the mean cupule width is 5.34 mm (n=8); mean thickness, 2.36 mm; and the mean width/thickness ratio is 2.26. At Meyer, the mean width is 5.60 mm (n=3); mean thickness, 2.60 mm; and the mean width/thickness ratio is 2.15. At Forster, the mean width is 6.86 mm (n=7); mean thickness, 2.76 mm; and the mean width/thickness ratio is 2.49 (see Table 21). The mean width of cupules in the Glen Meyer assemblages is 7.00 mm and the mean width for prehistoric Neutral cupules is 7.39 mm (Ounjian 1998).

Chenopod

Almost all prehistoric chenopod from the Northeast are recognized as belonging to subsection *Cellulata* of section *Chenopodia* (Smith 1995a). There are two wild species of *Cellulata*: *Chenopodium bushianum* and *C. berlandieri*. Both grow eastward from the Atlantic coast to Missouri and North Dakota; a major distinction between the seeds of these taxa is size (Asch and Asch 1977; Wilson 1980; Smith 1995a; see also Monckton 1992:46). *Chenopodium bushianum* seeds tend to be slightly larger in diameter (1.5 to 2.0 mm) than *C. berlandieri* seeds (1.2 to 1.6 mm).

A characteristic feature of the species belonging to *Cellulata* is the prominent reticulations of the pericarp. In prehistoric collections of chenopod, the thin pericarp that encloses the seed often is not preserved. Nondomesticated *Cellulata* seeds, if well preserved, are identifiable as nondomesticated as the seed coats have a distinctive, alveolate surface. When the pericarp is missing, seed diameter is the only criterion by which *C. bushianum* can be distinguished from *C. berlandieri*. The two species, however, are interfertile and morphological intergrades occur (Asch and Asch 1985:173).

Chenopod seeds measured from Grand Banks range from 0.9 to 1.6 mm, with a standard deviation of 0.16. The mean diameter measures 1.22 mm. Seeds from Feature

210 at Grand Banks range from 1.0 to 1.6 mm, with a standard deviation of 0.16. The mean diameter of chenopod seeds at Feature 210 is 1.26 mm. Chenopod seeds from the Grand Banks palaeosol tend to be somewhat smaller, with a mean of 1.22 mm, a range of 0.9 to 1.5, and a standard deviation of 0.14 (see Table 22). Based on these measurements, the species of chenopod recovered from Grand Banks is within the range of *Chenopodium berlandieri*. Plate 15 displays some of the morphological variety of this seed, together with its tendency to easily fragment, as seen by the small bits of seeds in the photograph.

Ounjian's (1998) mean diameter for chenopod seeds in the Glen Meyer assemblages is 1.21 mm, and for what she calls "large chenopod", the mean is 1.60 mm. The mean diameter for chenopod seeds at prehistoric Neutral sites is 1.21 mm and the mean diameter for the larger seeds is 1.52 mm.

The identification of prehistoric chenopod for morphological indicators is important for assessing the harvest potential of this plant. Smith (1995:125) encourages the scrutiny of chenopod assemblages to better understand the timing and geographical location of chenopod domestication and plant management. Indepth, continued research on the remains recovered in this study and in Ounjian's (1998) study would be helpful to better understand the standing of chenopod as a wild or domesticated plant during Princess Point times and subsequent periods. Studies provide evidence for the presence of domesticated chenopod by 2500 B.P. in central Kentucky (Salts Cave), and both west-central Illinois (Smiling Dan) and northeastern Alabama (Russell Cave) by 2000 B.P. Smith (1995:125) makes the assumption that this crop was a component of early plant husbandry systems over a broad area of the Eastern Woodlands.

Comparison of the external diameter of modern wild and domesticated varieties of *Chenopodium* does not indicate a significantly larger size for domesticates. However, in domesticated varieties, Smith (1992:113) notes that there is a shift to a rectanguloid cross section and flattening or "truncation" of the seed coat margin. There is also a change in the cross section of the cotyledons from the thick, round cross section typical of wild forms to a more elliptical shape present in domesticates. Domesticated seeds also exhibit a distinctive radiating elongated-alveolate pattern on their ventral surface.

These factors, together with increased internal fruit volume, perisperm food reserves, and a reduction in the thickness of the outer epiderm or testa represent clear indicators of domesticated chenopod that can be observed on individual seeds within archaeobotanical assemblages (see Smith 1992:111-115). A number of outer epiderm thickness measurements on the Russell Cave chenopod assemblage were found to have thinner outer seed coats than wild counterparts, ranging in thickness from 7 to 16 microns. The outer epiderm thickness values for modern wild species ranged from 40 to 57 microns (Smith 1992). The seed coat thickness of chenopod seeds recovered from Late Woodland Memorial Park features in Pennsylvania falls within the range of that for cultigens (Hart and Asch Sidell 1996).

Sunflower

Intentional human propagation of sunflower may not have been essential for the common sunflower to persist prehistorically as there are weedy varieties of this taxa (Heiser 1985). In the Northeast, however, sunflower generally is conceded to have required some degree of cultivation (Asch and Asch 1985:165). Achene dimensions are the most common source of information about prehistoric sunflower domestication and from the Archaic through to the Late Woodland and Mississippian, the average seed size increases (Yarnell 1978; Asch and Asch 1985). The actual measurements (that is, uncorrected for pericarp loss and carbonization) of sunflower seeds from west-central Illinois during the early Late Woodland are larger (with a range of 6.0 x 6.6 to 2.0 x 4.1, length by width in mm) (Asch and Asch 1985:168) than those from this study. Princess Point sunflower achenes are also smaller than the Glen Meyer samples (see Table 23).

If any, or all, Princess Point seeds are *Helianthus annuus* (common sunflower), rather than an indigenous species, such as *H. tuberosus* (Jerusalem artichoke) or *H. divaricatus* (woodland sunflower) is difficult to determine. Both species are native to Ontario. The achenes of the woodland sunflower average 4.2 x 2.3 mm and those of the Jerusalem artichoke, 4.5 mm x 1.12 mm. Sunflower can exhibit considerable variation within single periods of time and over geographic areas (Asch and Asch 1995). Achene size even varies within a single disk.

The achenes found at Ontario sites tend to be typically smaller than those from sites to the south and the smaller size may be an indicator of varietal diversity or may be the result of local growing conditions (Crawford and Smith 2001). Although there are numerous factors that affect the size of seeds, size is probably the most important one for identifying sunflower variety within an archaeological context (Crawford and Smith 2001) and is a topic worth pursuing for a better understanding of this plant within a palaeoethnobotanical context. Further research is needed on the prehistoric use of sunflower. Genetic testing, together with substantial measurement criteria, would be a worthwhile route to follow in tracing the origins of sunflower in Ontario.

Measurements are corrected to compensate for shrinkage due to carbonization and for loss of pericarp, following the recommendations of Yarnell (1978:296). The achene lengths and widths are increased by 11% and 27%, respectively. The three sunflower seeds from Grand Banks (Feature 210) measured 4.3 mm in length. ne measured 1.52 mm in width and the other two, 1.65 mm. The average measurement is length 4.3 mm and width, 1.59 mm (see Table 23). These measurements are larger than the mean measurements of the "small sunflower seeds" recorded by Ounjian (1998) for the Glen Meyer: length, 3.21 mm and width, 1.26 mm. The measurements are smaller than the "large sunflower seeds" (length 7.85 mm and 3.90 width) from Glen Meyer.

Chapter Five

Princess Point Plant Use

Ethnobotanical Discussion

Palaeoethnobotany refers to the analysis and interpretation of ancient botanical remains to elucidate past interaction between people and plants (Hastorf and Popper 1988:ix). The dynamic interaction between people and plants relates to the subsistence pattern of a population. The term "subsistence pattern", however, does not refer only to the production of the basic survival resource, food energy, but to numerous other uses. Most cultures classify plants into a unified taxonomy that includes both foods and medicines (Ford 1979). Plants also are indispensable to ritual and religion, symbolizing a connection with gods and even "transporting" the believer into the spiritual world itself (Gow 1995).

Plants symbolize and create new social relationships. Sharing food, drinking beverages, or smoking together reinforces relationships (Ford 1979). Social identity, both individual and group, is tied to food preferences and changes in food can indicate an alteration in self-definition (Hastorf and Johannessen 1994:435). What people eat, drink, and smoke expresses who and what they are socially. Yarnell (1964), the first to explore the palaeoethnobotany of the Upper Great Lakes, compiled the uses of over 300 cultigens, nuts, seeds, and fruits. He categorized plants as foods, beverages and flavourings, medicinal teas, other medicines, charms and ceremonial, dyes, smoking, and utilitarian uses.

Although the archaeological evidence for many of these plants is incomplete, Yarnell (1964) contends that there is little doubt that prehistoric peoples developed close ecological interrelationships with many plant species. Plant use is affected by human biological factors, as well as by culture (Ford 1979). Plant biology also imposes constraints on a culture. A culture defines appropriate plant resources and the behavioural consequences of plant use modify, more or less, the structure and composition of local plant communities. Plant remains are indispensable for reconstructing cultural adaptation and change. This chapter explores diet and nutrition, provides ethnographic details about Iroquoian food preparation and plant use, and summarizes some medicinal and pharmacological properties of plants. The chapter reviews possible uses of the plant taxa recovered in this study.

There is an extensive ethnographic record of plant use by the Iroquois (cf. Waugh 1916; Parker 1912, edited by Fenton 1968; Densmore 1928; Arnason *et al.* 1981; Moerman 1982; 1998; Dickason 1991). As the Iroquoian may be descendant to the Princess Point, their ethnographic material may indicate, by way of analogy, how particular plants may have been used by the Princess

Point. However, there is a significant lapse of time between the time of Princess Point and when these ethnographic details were recorded. The applicability of these details to the Princess Point is unknown and impossible to determine.

An extensive review of ethnographic information on Ontario plants is provided by Ounjian (1998). She provides a comprehensive table (Ounjian 1998:697-701) listing plants and their importance ethnobotanically as recorded in the Jesuit Relations during the 1600s. Ounjian (1998) also relies upon information from a number of other ethnobotanical and ethnohistorical sources (e.g., Jenks 1900; Speck 1915; Waugh 1916; Smith, H. 1923, 1928, 1933; Densmore 1928; Yarnell 1964; Kalm 1966; Heiser 1969; Herrick 1977; Moerman 1986), providing both Native and European uses of plants commonly used prehistorically within the Great Lakes area.

This study refers to these works, as well as that of Arthur C. Parker (Parker 1912, edited by Fenton 1968). Parker, an anthropologist, was of Seneca Iroquoian ancestry through his father. From the late 1800s to the mid-1900s, Parker lived with the Seneca of New York State and learned Iroquoian culture first-hand. His formal ethnographic work, which was conducted from 1904 to 1912, appears as an edited volume (edited by William N. Fenton, 1968) with three distinct sections: Iroquois Uses of Maize and Other Food Plants; The Code of Handsome Lake, the Seneca Prophet; and The Constitution of the Five Nations.

Diet

Humans are omnivores and opportunistic consumers of various plant and animal products. A tremendous range of variability within omnivorous habits is exhibited by hunter-gatherers and horticulturalists, and the relative proportions of plant and animal products consumed in various cultures (Johns 1996:215). The optimum amounts of various food constituents that should be included in a proper diet can only be broadly estimated (Johns 1996:231). Nutrient requirements vary under different conditions and stages of life history but, always, a varied diet is necessary for health. Essential nutrients are divided into five categories: carbohydrates, fat, protein, vitamins, and minerals.

When exploring prehistoric plant use, the biological needs of humans and how the local environment can satisfy these needs should be considered (Ford 1979:287). However, as Monckton (1992:83) notes, the reconstruction of prehistoric diets often is a set of inferences made solely from the archaeobotanical evidence for certain plants, and plant morphology, chemistry, and nutrition. Hastorf (1988:120) explains that plants found at an archaeological site may relate to diet, as well as may reflect a wide range of other activities. Some activities may be more visible than others in archaeobotanical data.

Furthermore, with differential preservation, the reconstruction of the relative contribution of each plant class is difficult (Johannessen 1988:155; see Chapter 3). Pearsall (1989:228) explains that plants associated with activities involving fire (that is, heating or cooking) are more likely to be charred than those plants not exposed to fire. Equal exposure to fire does not necessarily lead to equal chances of preservation, however. For example, boiling tubers and parching corn kernels both involve the use of fire but the chances of preservation of recognizable charred remains are different for these two foods.

Various parts of a plant can be used for food. Leaves may be used because they are readily available, easily collected, and easy to process for use. Leaves often provide little in the way of carbohydrates but can be an excellent source of vitamins and minerals. Roots and tubers are an excellent food source as they act as storage for secondary metabolites. There are some 60 species that produce underground plant parts in southern Ontario (Elliott 1995). Roots and tubers have a higher proportion of extractable material per unit weight than bark. The vegetative parts of plants, that is, stems, roots, and tubers, are more predictable than leaves and fruits in the time and place of their occurrence. Vegetative parts can be relied upon during periods of seasonal and unpredicted shortage, and to meet regular nutritional needs. Seeds provide an abundant energy source and often can be exploited in quantity.

These plant parts, together with buds, flowers, shoots, fruits, berries, nuts, bulbs, rhizomes, inner bark, and sap, were incorporated into the Iroquoian diet (Arnason *et al.*1981; Johns 1996; Moerman 1998). Early spring plants would have been exploited for their buds, sap, and young shoots. Vegetative parts would have been gathered from early summer through to the fall. Fruits, berries, nuts, seeds, and grains were late summer or fall plant resources. Yarnell (1964) lists plants that were prepared and stored for use over the winter months and plants that were available for food from early spring through autumn.

A diet that includes meat is one way to ensure protein consumption and good all-round nourishment (Johns 1996:214-244), and meat would have been available fresh year-round. An increase in protein consumption actually enables more variety in the consumption of plants as protein increases the physiological tolerance to toxic plant chemicals (Johns 1996:244). With the consumption of meat, however, there is the risk of parasitic and bacterial infection but plants with toxins that have advantageous medicinal qualities can be consumed with

some impunity to rid the body of such infections (Johns 1996:258, 275). A healthy diet with sufficient protein and other nutrients is essential to enable people to tolerate potential toxic effects from plants (Johns 1996:214-244).

Food Preparation

Although many plants are edible fresh and without any type of preparation, some plants are made more digestible through processing, such as boiling, heating, leaching, and grinding. While some plant toxins are destroyed by various processing techniques, preparation methods have a variable effect on reducing toxicity.

Parker (1912) provides ethnographic information regarding food preparation methods of the Iroquois. The Iroquois boiled foods with water in pots made of clay or in vessels made of tree bark. Foods also were heated by being placed directly over fire or in hot coals. Foodstuffs were contained in clay pots and bark vessels or wrapped in large leaves and then heated. Ethnographic accounts by Sagard and the Jesuits (Sagard 1939:95-106) describe soups made with water, corn, and fish or meat, cooked in clay pots, as the most common foodstuff.

Parker (1912:46) also describes large clay vessels used to cook corn. The clay vessels were placed directly over the fire and supported by three or four stones. Although evidence for pottery use is ubiquitous throughout Princess Point sites, pottery may not routinely have been used for food preparation. Biochemical analyses of Princess Point potsherds found many potsherds produced minimal or no evidence of ancient organic residues (Saunders 1994). Evidence for the presence of plants was found in some potsherds but no evidence to suggest that meat was cooked in vessels was found. Clay pots may have been used primarily for storing plant foods and water, or foods were not routinely cooked in vessels.

A number of cooking methods do not involve the use of clay pots. For example, the Iroquois baked under hot ashes unleavened bread that was made from cornmeal (Parker 1912:69; Sagard 1939:99-102). Dried fruits and pieces of meat were sometimes mixed into the dough which was then made into small cakes and the cakes were wrapped in fresh corn leaves or placed directly into the hot ashes. Corn cobs, fish, and meat also were roasted directly over an open fire or in hot ashes. Parker (1912:51) describes vessels made from tree bark peeled in the spring or early summer and bent into a bowl shape. Bark bowls were used for mixing corn meal and for holding corn bread. The vessels were used also for cooking by heated stones being thrown into the liquid in the bowl. Bark vessels can be put over an open fire and will not burn if direct flames are kept away.

Difficult to digest foods, such as tough grains, can be processed by grinding and then further processed by cooking. Parker (1912:48) notes that the Iroquois ground foods by stone mortar and pestle or in a mortar hollowed out of a tree trunk and ground with a long pole (Parker 1912:47). Green corn kernels were removed from the cob by scraping them with a deer mandible (Parker 1912:53). Often the kernels first were mashed with a milling stone and then scraped. Dried corn was milled in a similar fashion (Parker 1912:54). Ethnohistoric accounts describe corn stored in pits that were about 100 cm in diameter and 125 cm deep, lined with bark and grass and covered with earth (Sagard 1939:94-96). The corn was stored fresh or was burned and charred. Often the entire pit was burned, including the corn, any other contents, and the grass lining (Parker 1912:35). Corn was also stored inside pots suspended from two poles, thus keeping the pots and its contents safe from rodents.

Medicine

Many plants consumed as food are recognized as having pharmacological properties, in addition to nutritional value, and Johns (1996:282) explains that cultures often do not make a strong distinction between food and medicine. People may interpret food and medicine in combination and are more concerned with what they see as the "power of plants" (Johns 1996:282). Food, beverage, medicine, and stimulant form an overlapping continuum. The array of chemical compounds found in plants is complex and these chemicals have been indispensable to human survival and evolution.

The chemical structure of a plant might suggest how a plant was used. For example, the roots of nightshade contain a compound effective in eradicating intestinal and stomach worms but consumption in excess can cause illness (Perez et al. 1998). Moerman (1998:635) states the Ojibwa did use American nightshade for eradicating worms. Evidence for American nightshade is found in this study and perhaps the Princess Point used the plant for medicinal purposes. Many plants contain toxins that can be deadly if ingested in large quantities but, ironically, these same toxins, if administered in controlled quantities, may provide medicinal benefits (Johns 1996; Moerman 1998; Plotkin 2000).

The distinction between teas consumed as a beverage and teas used as a medicinal tonic is ambiguous. Teas are often the preferred way of consuming medicines but also provide nutritional value and necessary liquids. Stimulants, ingested through eating, drinking, or smoking, are used by shamans to dream and envision an appropriate cure for fellow group members (Johns 1996:283).

Medical knowledge of the efficacy of plants usually exists within a particular cultural context and present day hunter-gatherers tend to have a well-developed herbal pharmacopoeia (Johns 1996:261). Much of this knowledge probably has great time depth. Commonly, small-scale, non-industrialized tribal peoples use herbal medicines that treat ailments such as skin problems, wounds, pain, parasites, diarrhea, headache, fever, colds, and reproductive and menstrual problems (Johns 1996:261). Shamans and medicine societies generally are the keepers of medical knowledge (Herrick 1995; Johns 1996:281; Plotkin 2000).

These same individuals are used as a conduit to the spirit world and the spirit world is tied intimately to medicine and healing. Plants play an important role in ritual and not only may symbolize a connection with the supernatural but may metaphorically transport the believer into the spiritual world through the use of mind-altering plant material (Gow 1995:62-93). Medicine is a complex component of tribal cultures, such as the Iroquoian, and is closely interwoven with aspects of the supernatural or magic (Herrick 1995:29; Moerman 1998:13-14). The mind and the body, the psychological and the physical are not separated (Herrick 1995:29, see also pp. 16-23 and 28-31).

Plant Taxa

This section reviews the plant remains for which there is archaeological evidence in this study, taking into consideration the possible uses of plants as foods and medicines. The Agricultural Research Service of the United States conducts chemical and nutritional research on plants that currently are agriculturally important.

The chemical ecology of many wild fruits and their seeds has not been widely studied in natural habitats and we are dependent on the observations of ecologists studying other aspects of vegetation for much information about wild plants (Harbourne 1997:354). Numerous wild plants await analysis and with recent advances in analytical technology, information about wild plants is improving. In this section, chemical and nutritional information is provided only on plants that have been tested and analyzed by other agencies and for which that information is available. Plants for which there is evidence are divided into the categories of cultigens, fleshy fruits, greens and grains, other taxa, and nuts.

Cultigens

Maize
Evidence for Princess Point maize use at Grand Banks, Lone Pine, Meyer, Forster, and Bull's Point is by carbonized kernels and cupules (see Plates 1 to 4). The most frequent cultigen recovered in Ounjian's (1998) Glen Meyer study is maize. Archaeobotanists have recovered large quantities of maize remains from southern Ontario sites and indeed, corn often comprises the majority of the plant food remains by weight (Crawford 1985; Crawford 1986; Monckton 1992; Ounjian 1998; Monckton 1999). Most early maize remains are in the form of carbonized kernels and cupules. Throughout the Northeast, remains are generally of the Eastern eight-row variety (Eastern Complex or Northern Flint/Flour), which is the only archaeological corn present in Ontario (Crawford and Smith 2001). The

identification of this variety is discussed previously in Chapter Four.

Maize was an integral component of the Iroquoian lifeway and was used not only as a food resource but various parts of the plant (the stock, husk or leaves) provided the material for making such items as ropes, baskets, trays, mats, masks, baby hammocks, and dolls (see Parker 1912). There were also ceremonial and symbolic uses for the plant (Parker 1912; Dickason 1991). Parker (1912) details a number of ways that the Iroquois prepared maize for food. He explains that the Iroquois used maize, green or ripened, often prepared in the form of soup, gruel or bread, and pounded, mashed or ground. Kernels also were boiled or roasted. The ashes of burned cobs produced lye that was used to induce vomiting (Parker 1912:87). In small quantities, the ashes killed stomach worms and prevented dyspepsia (Parker 1912:87). Oil extracted from kernels was an ingredient in poultices; the kernels, dried and pulverized, were believed to have healing powers (Dickason 1991:24).

Taking into account that the material remains for the earliest-dated corn is small and fragmented, Hastorf and Johannessen (1994:434) suggest that corn may not have been adopted first solely on the basis of its potential as a staple food but perhaps only as a seasonal food. Furthermore, early corn production may have been based on social needs and symbolic values. Corn may have spread in trade as an item of value and, like tobacco, may have been associated with a set of symbolic traditions (Hastorf and Johannessen 1994:434). Hastorf and Johannessen (1994:434) argue that the unique cultural importance of corn did not stem entirely from any dietary prominence. In eastern North America, some of the early occurrences of maize are in symbolic contexts, such as burials (Johannessen 1993:73).

In southern Ontario, corn plays a prominent role in Iroquoian mythology (see Parker 1912; Herrick 1995). It likely took several generations before corn moved from a peripheral role to become a staple, with the extra labour and scheduling that producing it entailed (Hastorf and Johannessen 1994:442). In general, maize was regarded as a nutritious, utilitarian, and symbolic plant by the Iroquois (Dickason 1991).

Due to its current importance agriculturally, considerable research has been conducted on the phytochemistry and nutritional value of maize. Maize is high in essential fatty acids and also contains significant nutritive value by way of compounds such as ascorbic acid, carbohydrates, iodine, iron, magnesium, and niacin (Beckstrom-Sternberg and Duke 1994, 2000).

The niacin from corn is not released readily through digestion and a diet rich in corn can result in a niacin deficiency. This deficiency can result in pellagra, an illness which can cause severe skin problems and, ultimately, serious mental disorders. To combat pellagra

in diets where maize is a staple food, maize should be consumed or cooked with an alkaline compound, such as calcium or lye (FAO 1992). Nicotinic acid also can release the niacin in maize (FAO 1992). Nicotinic acid is found in cleaver (Beckstrom-Sternberg and Duke 1994, 2000) and cleaver is found at all sites in this study except at Meyer. Tobacco also contains nicotinic acid (Beckstrom-Sternberg and Duke 1994, 2000) and although no evidence for tobacco was found in this study, tobacco is recognized as being extremely important to the later Iroquoian culture. There may be a cultural connection between the use of corn and tobacco in concert.

Sunflower and Jerusalem Artichoke
Sunflower and Jerusalem artichoke belong to the same family and have many botanical similarities. Sunflower is identified from Feature 210 at the Grand Banks site (see Plate 5). Sunflower is common archaeologically in southern Ontario (see Monckton 1990, 1992; Ounjian 1998). Ounjian (1998) identifies sunflower as the third most frequent cultigen in her samples; corn and tobacco are the two most common. Later Huron samples analyzed by Monckton (1990, 1992) also produced a number of sunflower seeds and achenes. Sunflower was present at two Glen Meyer sites and, from her sample population, Ounjian concludes that the achenes increased in size from Glen Meyer through to prehistoric Neutral times.

This trend of larger achene size over time is seen generally throughout the Northeast (Asch and Asch 1985; Crawford and Smith 2001). The achenes identified in this Princess Point study are smaller than those recovered by Ounjian 1998. Sunflower can exhibit considerable variation within single periods of time and over geographic areas (Asch and Asch 1995). Achene size even varies within a single disk. Achenes found at Ontario sites tend to be typically smaller than those from sites to the south and the smaller size may be an indicator of varietal diversity or may be the result of local growing conditions (Crawford and Smith 2001). Although there are factors that effect the size of seeds, size is probably the most important factor for identifying the variety of carbonized sunflower (Crawford and Smith 2001).

Some unidentifiable or questionable tubers may be Jerusalem artichoke. However, the identification of many tubers to species is routinely difficult, if not impossible, as a multitude of plants produce very similar looking tuberous parts. This problem is exacerbated over time with archaeological remains through shrinking, biodegradation, and charring (see Hather 1993).

Iroquoian ethnographic reference for either sunflower (Monckton 1992:39; Herrick 1995:20) or Jerusalem artichoke (Arnason *et al.* 1981) is uncommon. Herrick (1995:20) argues that the importance of the sunflower to the Iroquois is revealed by its mention in their creation stories and that the seeds of sunflower and the tubers of Jerusalem artichoke were food resources for the Iroquois.

Parker (1912:102) notes that sunflower oil was used in quantity by the Iroquois. It was prepared by grinding the seed in a mortar, heating the mass, and then adding it to boiling water to separate the oil from the pulp. The water was then strained and the oil skimmed.

Jerusalem artichoke tubers were eaten raw, as well as cooked (Parker 1912:105).The plant grew wild in cornfields and women commonly gathered and ate the tubers as they worked in the fields (Parker 1912:105). Together with being rich in fatty acids, the seeds of sunflower and Jerusalem artichoke contain citric acid, serine, and threonine, which are all antioxidants. Antioxidants are known to help maintain health generally and, specifically, help prevent the growth of cancerous tumors. The tubers are rich in carbohydrates and inulin (Beckstrom-Sternberg and Duke 1994, 2000; Elliott 1995).

Cucurbit
The identification of cucurbit rind at Bull's Point is tentative. However, cucurbit is an easily grown plant and may have been used. The Iroquois cultivated many varieties of cucurbit and they could be stored fresh or dried (Parker 1912). Ounjian (1998) notes that cucurbit is well represented in her study of Glen Meyer and prehistoric Neutral, identifying the species as *Cucurbita pepo*. Most of her evidence derives from seeds but there is one instance of cucurbit rind from the Glen Meyer Boisclair site. She recovered 98 cucurbit seeds from two Glen Meyer sites.

Princess Point peoples may have used cucurbit for food and medicines, as well as for making containers, floats for fishing, and rattles (Herrick 1995:20). Parker (1912) recorded that boiled cucurbit flowers were eaten and that squash was one of the principal foods of the Iroquois. Squash usually was roasted whole in hot embers and was preserved by first being cut into thin sections and then hung to dry. Cucurbit is rich in alanine, an antioxidant, and potassium, an essential mineral (Beckstrom-Sternberg and Duke 1994, 2000).

Fleshy Fruits

American Nightshade
American nightshade, a member of the Solanaceae family, is found at all sites except Forster (see Plates 25 to 27). A common weedy herb, it grows abundantly in open fields. Ounjian (1998) reports the commonality of this plant as well. Plants in the Solanaceae family are particularly rich in alkaloids (Alexander and Paredes 1998) and the chemicals solasodine, solasonine, and solanidine have been isolated from the fruit (Perez *et al.* 1998). These alkaloids make the unripe fruit toxic but the levels of alkaloid in the pulp decrease significantly as the fruit ripens, making the fruit edible. The alkaloids tend to be concentrated in the seed of the ripe fruit. The alkaloids can cause significant reduction in spontaneous locomotor activity, induce sleep, and are relaxants (Harbourne

1997:357). The roots of the plant contain tigogenin which can provide an effective infusion to get rid of intestinal and stomach worms (Alexander and Paredes 1998; Moerman 1998) and, combined with other plants, can be used for external ailments (Herrick 1995). The berry contains essential fatty acids (Beckstrom-Sternberg and Duke 1994, 2000).

Blueberry
As is typical for Ontario sites (see Ounjian 1998), few blueberry seeds were recovered in this study but some are identified from Grand Banks, Forster, and Bull's Point. *Vaccinium* species (such as blueberry and cranberry) seeds tend to be similar morphologically and difficult to distinguish. The berries from blueberry and cranberry bushes are edible and both can be dried but cranberry has the added advantage that it can be stored for several months without significant loss in quality (Smith *et al.* 2000).

Blueberries and other types of berries were gathered in season by the Iroquoian (Parker 1912:96-97). Some berries, such as blueberries and cranberries, were dried whole for later use but soft berries, such as strawberries and raspberries, were mashed before drying. All berries also were eaten fresh or were added to cornbread and soup. Per 140 g, blueberries provide 80 calories, 19 g carbohydrates, and 1 g protein. One 140 g serving of blueberries provides 15% of the recommended daily value of Vitamin C and 2% of the recommended value of iron (Health Canada 1999). Berries and fruits were an important source of energy, vitamins, and minerals throughout prehistoric North America (Ford 1979).

The chemical content of blueberries and cranberries parallels other berries. However, recent evidence shows that *Vaccinium* species contain especially high levels of antioxidants (Smith *et al.* 2000). The primary organic acid in blueberries is citric acid, while cranberries exhibit high levels of quinic acid. *Vaccinium* species are also rich in tannins (Beckstrom-Sternberg and Duke 1994, 2000; Caruso and Ramsdell 1995:4). Tannins have well-defined astringency characteristics that can help relieve sore throats, and heal cuts and burns. However, extreme astringency can be a deterrent to the consumption of foodstuffs and the absorption of essential compounds. For example, high tannin diets can lead to a serious decrease in the availability of iron and lead to anemia (Robbins *et al.* 1997:250-255).

Bramble
Bramble is the most common seed recovered and is present at every site in this study (see Plate 19). In Ounjian's (1998) study, bramble also is common. A 125 g serving of raspberries contains 50 calories, 1.7 g carbohydrates, 8 g fiber, 12 g sugar, and 1 g protein. A daily serving of 125 g fulfills 40% of the recommended daily value of vitamin C, 2% of iron, 10% of folic acid, and 2% of calcium. Blackberries contain 50 calories, 1 g fat, 12 g carbohydrates, 6 g fiber, 11 g sugar, and 1 g

protein per 144 g. One 144 g serving of blackberries has 50% of the recommended daily value of vitamin C, 10% of the recommended value of folic acid, and is a good source of potassium, calcium, and iron (Health Canada 1999). Berries can be eaten fresh or added to a tea or tonic made with bramble leaves and twigs (Herrick 1995). The berries contain two antioxidants, chlorogenic acid and ferulic acid. The leaves are rich in tannins (Beckstrom-Sternberg and Duke 1994, 2000).

Crowberry
Evidence for this plant was found at Bull's Point. The berry of crowberry is a juicy black edible fruit and this low, mat-forming plant is commonly found in wet, peaty soils (Peterson 1977:168). Its fruits are ripe late summer to early fall.

Dogwood
This fleshy fruit is recovered from Grand Banks, Feature 210. Ounjian's (1998) research also produced evidence for this plant. The fruit of dogwood is high in calcium, magnesium, and potassium (Beckstrom-Sternberg and Duke 1994, 2000). Herrick (1995:177) notes that dogwood was used by the Iroquois medicinally as a tonic to relieve fever or a cough. Its fruits ripen from late summer through the early fall and can be eaten raw or cooked (Peterson 1977:20).

Elderberry
Elderberry seeds are identified from Bull's Point. Elderberry is one of the most common seeds recovered in Ounjian's (1998) study but is much less common with the Princess Point. A 100 g serving of elderberry has 72 calories (Health Canada 1999) and the small berries are an excellent source of Vitamin C, essential fatty acids, and together with the compounds histidine, leucine, and threonine promote a healthy heart (Beckstrom-Sternberg and Duke 1994, 2000). The bark of elderberry can be steeped in water and drank to relieve headaches and is an effective laxative. The bark can also be used as a poultice for cuts and burns (Herrick 1995:223-224). Tryptophan, found in elderberries, is an antidepressant and sedative. Elderberry is also rich in tannins (Beckstrom-Sternberg and Duke 1994, 2000). Elderberries ripen mid to late summer (Peterson 1977:172).

Grape
Evidence for wild grape is found only at Grand Banks, Feature 210 (see Plate 13). Ounjian (1998) also reports little evidence for this plant. Grape is high in essential fatty acids (Beckstrom-Sternberg and Duke 1994, 2000) and provides 90 calories per 138 g serving, 1 g fat, 24 g carbohydrates, 1 g fiber, 23 g sugar, and 25% of the recommended daily value of Vitamin C (Health Canada 1999). The stems, leaves, and fruit of the plant can be soaked in water and the decoction used to help with kidney or stomach problems (Herrick 1995:184). Grape contains ascorbic acid and resveratrol, a bactericide and fungicide (Beckstrom-Sternberg and Duke 1994, 2000).

Hackberry
Evidence for this plant is found at Grand Banks, Feature 210. The bark of hackberry may have been used to make a tea and this decoction may relieve menstrual problems (Herrick 1995:130). Hackberry fruit can be used to flavour foods, such as corn or meat. A chemical assay is not available for this plant; however, it is a good source of calcium (Arnason *et al.* 1981). The fruit is available from early to late fall (Peterson 1977:194).

Hawthorn
Grand Banks produced evidence for hawthorn. Ounjian (1998) also found evidence for this plant. Parker (1912:95) notes that the hawthorn fruit generally was eaten raw but also was boiled for sauce or baked in hot embers. The fruit was stored in bark barrels and buried in pits or cut in thin slices and dried. Hawthorn berry, resembling a tiny apple or rose hip, contains calcium, potassium, and quercetin (an antioxidant), and is rich in tannins. The leaf of the hawthorn contains rutin, an antioxidant (Beckstrom-Sternberg and Duke 1994, 2000).

Strawberry
Strawberry seeds are identified only from the Meyer and Bull's Point sites. Strawberry tends to be common in archaeobotanical samples and was one of the most common fruits found by Ounjian (1998). Eight medium-sized strawberries (147 g) contain 45 calories, 12 g carbohydrates, and provide a full daily value of vitamin C, together with 20% of the requirement of folic acid, 2% of calcium, and 4% of iron (Health Canada 1999). Strawberries are one of the first berries to ripen after winter and their arrival was likely a welcome sign of summer. Their importance is reflected by the annual strawberry festival of the Iroquois held in early summer (Parker 1912). A decoction of strawberry is effective for diarrhea and strawberries are especially rich in ascorbic acid and citric acid (Beckstrom-Sternberg and Duke 1994, 2000).

Witchhazel
Evidence for witchhazel was found only at Bull's Point. A decoction made from bark, leaves, and berries is used to relieve colds and coughs (Herrick 1995). Witchhazel is rich in tannins (Beckstrom-Sternberg and Duke 1994, 2000). This plant currently is common around Cootes Paradise.

Greens and Grains

The seeds of some of the plants in this category may not preserve well in the archaeological record as some starchy seeds tend to have a proclivity for popping or bursting during the process of carbonization rendering their presence invisible in the archaeological record (Saunders 1993). Furthermore, plants used for their leafy greens are difficult to identify archaeologically as the part of the plant used is consumed without leaving a trace.

Edible greens probably comprised a large part of the pre-contact diet; however, their presence is difficult to detect as the leafy part of a plant will decompose readily whether fresh or cooked. Parker (1912:93) notes that greens were eaten young and tender when not more than six to ten inches high. The Iroquoian considered all greens good for the liver, the blood, and as a remedy for rheumatism.

Chenopod

Chenopod is one of the most common plants recovered in this study and somewhat less commonly in that of Ounjian (1998) (see Plate 12). Many studies have focused on the domestication of chenopod (cf. Asch and Asch 1977; Heiser 1985; Gremillion 1993; Smith 1995) and this topic is discussed in Chapter Four (Plant Evidence: Identification and Quantification). The plant is a member of the starchy-seed complex (chenopod, knotweed, maygrass, and little barley) that dominates Middle and Late Woodland assemblages in the Northeast (Asch and Asch 1985; Ford 1985; Smith 1995).

Both the greens and the seeds of chenopod can be used as a food source. Medicinally, the whole plant can be used as a poultice (Herrick 1995:142). Vitamin A (retinol) content and vitamin C (ascorbic acid) content of chenopod is very high. Other compounds identified in chenopod leaf include calcium, leucine, oxalic acid, potassium, and threonine (Arnason *et al.* 1981; Beckstrom-Sternberg and Duke 1994, 2000).

Grasses

Several species of grasses are identified in this study and in Ounjian's (1998). Grasses are found at Grand Banks, Meyer, and Bull's Point and those specimens that I was unable to identify to the species level are identified as grasses (Poaceae) in general. Many members of the Poaceae family are very similar in morphological make-up and, this, combined with distortion from charring and preservation, makes grasses notoriously difficult to identify to species.

As in Ounjian's study (1998), switch grass (or panic grass, see Plate 8), rye grass (see Plate 9), little barley (tentative identification, see Plate 10), and manna grass are identified. Ounjian identified 13 species and notes a quantity of unknown and unidentifiable grasses. Most of the switch grass seeds and the unknown or unidentifiable grasses from Ounjian's study are from the Glen Meyer Calvert site. A decoction can be made with the roots of grasses for general health and for the heart and kidneys (Herrick 1995:239). Corn kernels were soaked in a mixture of grass roots and water before planting to encourage their growth (Herrick 1995:243).

One wild rice grain (*Zizania* sp.) is identified in a sample from Grand Banks. The distinctive sulcus of this species is visible (see Plates 6 and 7). Ounjian reports two grains from the Glen Meyer Kelly site. Wild rice is the only wild grain crop in North America and there is extensive

ethnohistoric evidence for the use of wild rice (cf. Jenks 1900, Vennum 1988), particularly amongst Midwestern groups, including the Sauk, Fox, Mascoutin, Potawatomi, and Menominee. Parker (1912:109) notes that although wild rice was an important food for those living in the Midwest, wild rice was not commonly used by the Iroquois.

Thirty-seven sites in the Northeast and adjacent areas report archaeological evidence for wild rice (Crawford and Smith 2001). The earliest archaeological record for wild rice dates to the Late Archaic in west-central Kentucky (Crawford 1982) and the Dunn Farm site in Michigan (Ford and Brose 1975). The Laurel occupation at the Big Rice site in Minnesota dates to about 1700 B.P. (Valppu 1989). Recent studies in Minnesota report phytoliths from wild rice chaff in charred food residues on potsherds dating over 2000 years ago (Kluth and Thompson 1995). Some 165 wild rice grains are identified from two sites that date from 1250 to 1000 B.P. in the upper Wisconsin River drainage system (Moffatt and Arzigian 2000). High densities of grass pollen between 800 and 2,000 years ago provide evidence that wild rice was growing and present in the Cootes Paradise wetlands during the time that the area was inhabited by Princess Point people (Lee *et al.* n.d.). Although this group would have had direct access to the wild rice, no grains were recovered in assemblages from Cootes Paradise.

A parasitic fungus or ergot (*Claviceps purpurea*) that commonly grows on members of the Poaceae family is particularly common on wild rice grains (Aiken *et al.* 1988). Boyd (1986) argues that ergot may be overlooked at archaeological sites due to its broad morphological variability and relative scarcity; the shape is not distinctive or readily recognizable. One of the few reports of carbonized ergot recovered from archaeological samples is from a site in Scotland dating to 2000 B.P. (Barclay 1984).

Consumption of ergot can have grave consequences, ranging from hallucinations to death (Wasson *et al.* 1978). Occurrences of ergotism and death from consuming infected bread grains are well documented during the Middle Ages in Europe. However, ergot also was used to stop bleeding during childbirth (Wasson *et al.* 1978:212). The Iroquoian made the most extensive use of fungi of any native group in eastern Canada (Arnason *et al.* 1981). Many fungi contain compounds that are effective in killing bacteria (e.g., *Penicillium, Cordyceps*; see Plotkin 2000) and parasites, such as stomach worms (Johns 1996:273).

Erect Knotweed

Erect knotweed is found at Grand Banks, Lone Pine, and Meyer (see Plate 17). Ounjian (1995) reports a number of erect knotweed seeds (or achenes) at four Glen Meyer sites. Evidence for the plant occurs at most Late Woodland sites in Ontario (Crawford and Smith 2001).

Erect knotweed, a starchy-seed plant, has been documented as an economically important prehistoric species from the upper Mississippi and Illinois valleys. In west-central Illinois, knotweed is dominant in Middle and Late Woodland assemblages and is also common in Middle and Late Woodland components in the American Bottom (Asch and Asch 1985:183). Few seeds of the plant are found in pre-Middle Woodland assemblages.

Changes in morphology and size do not appear between prehistoric and modern samples and the natural range for the plant is throughout the Northeast. Erect knotweed seeds are trigonal in shape (one side is shorter than the other two) and there are striations along the long axis (Montgomery 1977). The achenes of erect knotweed are dimorphic and the two types occur on the same plant. One type is slightly shorter and wider with a thicker reticulate pericarp and the other is longer and narrower with a smooth thin pericarp. The percentage of smooth seeds increases late in the fruiting season. Both types occur in prehistoric collections (Asch and Asch 1985:184). Seventeen erect knotweed achenes were identified in this study, all of the first mentioned type (that is, shorter and wider with a thicker reticulate pericarp).

Erect knotweed naturally occurs in disturbed habitats. An effective harvest is only possible when the species is abundant but dense stands are uncommon as a single plant yields a small amount of seed by weight (Asch and Asch 1985:185). Therefore, as Asch and Asch (1985:186) note, the occurrence of erect knotweed is difficult to reconcile as a common, even dominant species, in archaeological assemblages unless some form of plant management took place. Selective pressures may have promoted dense stands of erect knotweed; however, no clear evidence exists, either by seed morphology or size, that this plant was domesticated. Together with being a good source of plant oils and starch, erect knotweed had many medicinal uses, including its use as an aphrodisiac (Herrick 1995). However, there is no chemical evidence for the plant being a stimulant or depressant. The root of the plant contains emodin (an antioxidant) and tannins (Beckstrom-Sternberg and Duke 1994, 2000).

Purslane
This seed, while found only at Grand Banks and Bull's Point, is found in great numbers at these two sites (see Plate 18). Purslane is also very common in Glen Meyer assemblages (Ounjian 1998). Yarnell (1976) indicates that purslane was grown in cultivated plots of the Huron. Ford (1985) suggests that purslane seeds may have been disseminated by accident while gathered as a potherb. Iroquoian ethnographic evidence points to purslane being used for burns and bruises (Herrick 1995). The succulent leaves of purslane are very rich in all the essential fatty acids, making the plant a healthy summer green (Beckstrom-Sternberg and Duke 1994, 2000).

Other Taxa

Arrowhead
Seeds, numerous stem fragments, and several tubers of arrowhead occur in samples from Grand Banks and Forster (see Plates 20 to 23). The stems from this plant are variable in size but consistent in shape and distinguished by their internodes. The tubers have a rounded shape. Ounjian (1998) recovered several tubers and corms and suspects that some derive from arrowhead. The starchy tubers of arrowhead are edible and can be boiled with water to make a decoction for general malaise. Parker (1912:104) notes that roots and tubers were rarely eaten by the Iroquois and only when other more preferred foods were unavailable. However, arrowhead tubers were one exception to this practice and were eaten regularly. The Iroquoian soaked maize kernels with arrowhead before planting to encourage growth (Herrick 1995:239).

Cat-tail
Cat-tail seeds are very small and are the only seeds to be recovered from below the 0.212 mm sieve. Evidence for this plant was recovered from Grand Banks, Meyer, and Bull's Point. Plate 16 displays the diversity of preservation with which the analyst can be confronted and making some identifications difficult. In Ounjian's (1998) study, cat-tail is found in great numbers and is present at every site, sometimes numbering in the thousands. Cat-tail can be a versatile plant; its various parts used for food, medicine, and utilitarian purposes. The young shoots of cat-tail are eaten as they emerge in the spring and the flower is eaten in early summer (Herrick 1995:243). The rhizomes can be eaten raw or cooked (Elliot 1995). The root of cat-tail can be used as a poultice for cuts and burns (Herrick 1995:243). The Iroquoian commonly used the dried and pulverized roots of cat-tail to make a sweet white flour to make bread or pudding. Juice also was extracted from the roots (Parker 1912:108).

Cinquefoil
Cinquefoil is recovered only from Feature 210, Grand Banks. The seed coat is distinctive (see Plate 15). Ounjian (1998) reports minimal evidence of this plant. Tea can be made with cinquefoil leaves (Peterson 1977:180) and the fleshy roots of this plant are edible (Peterson 1977:70). Its root was used by the Iroquoian to relieve diarrhea (Herrick 1995:164).

Cleaver (or Bedstraw)
Cleaver is found at all sites in this study except for Meyer. Ounjian (1998) reports cleaver to be somewhat common. Herrick (1995) notes that cleaver can be used to treat venereal disease by washing the infected area with the plant. This plant contains tannins which would serve well as an astringent to dry out infected skin. Cleaver also contains the compounds coumarin and nicotinic acid, both of which are sedatives or depressants (Beckstrom-Sternberg and Duke 1994, 2000).

Milkvetch

Grand Banks and Forster revealed evidence for milkvetch. Plate 11 illustrates the morphological diversity of these seeds. They are distinguishable by their size, curled appearance, and embryo scar to the top of the seed. None is reported by Ounjian (1998). This weedy plant blooms late June through to September and although not too common in southern Ontario today, was relatively common in the last century and is still common in the Midwest prairies (Barnaby 1964). Milkvetch carries various potentially toxic substances, including swainsonine, miserotoxin, and dangerously high levels of selenium metabolites (Davis 1984:972-975). The ingestion of milkvetch can cause hyperactivity, spontaneous locomotor activity, and an inability to coordinate one's movements (Beckstrom-Sternberg and Duke 1994, 2000). The plant contains the compound arabinogalactan, a stimulant that can be mildly addictive (Beckstrom-Sternberg and Duke 1994, 2000).

Mint

A small amount of mint was recovered from Grand Banks. Ounjian also reports the presence of mint (Ounjian 1998). A decoction or tea can be made with mint that will ease a sore stomach (Herrick 1998:207).

Sassafras

One carbonized sassafras seed was recovered from Bull's Point. The roots of sassafras can be made into a tonic to ease stomach disturbances and fever (Herrick 1995:114). Sassafras flowers, berries, and leaves were used as a diuretic, condiment, and smoked in pipes (Moerman 1982). Sassafras has been used as a remedy for poison ivy (Elliott 1995) and, interestingly, poison ivy is presently common in the area of Bull's Point. Numerous large sassafras trees still grace the woodlands surrounding Cootes Paradise.

Sassafras is rich in tannins and the root of sassafras has a spicy, cinnamon scent that derives from the compound cinnamolaurine (Beckstrom-Sternberg and Duke 1994, 2000). The main compound found in sassafras, safrole, has anaesthetic and relaxant qualities which likely account for it being used as smoking material. This compound is a known carcinogen. Sassafras also contains reticuline, a compound that can cause uncontrolled locomotor activity (Beckstrom-Sternberg and Duke 1994, 2000).

St. John's Wort

Evidence for St. John's wort is found at Grand Banks, Meyer, and Bull's Point. Ounjian (1998) found low quantities of this seed. St. John's wort, a plant currently popularly used to treat anxiety, is reported to have been used for menstrual problems and to treat sterility (Herrick 1995). This plant is rich in the compounds cadinene and cadmium which are mild relaxants. St. John's wort also contains mannitol, an anti-inflammatory, and rutin, an antioxidant (Beckstrom-Sternberg and Duke 1994, 2000).

Sumac

Grand Banks and Bull's Point both produced evidence for sumac. Ounjian (1998) found this seed one of the most common recovered in the Glen Meyer assemblages. Its most common use by the Iroquoian was as a beverage and sumac was also used as a tonic for fever and stomach problems. The red ripe fruit was used as a poultice (Herrick 1995:188).

Wood Sorrel

Wood sorrel was recovered from Grand Banks and Bull's Point (see Plate 14). Herrick (1995:190)) notes the use of this plant by the Iroquois to ease complaints of general malaise. The plant is crushed in water to make a tea. Oxalic acid, found in wood sorrel, is a strong chelating agent which, if consumed regularly, can promote chronic problems, such as vomiting, diarrhea, muscle cramps, reduced ability for blood to coagulate, and low levels of calcium in the body. Blanching can reduce the levels of water-soluble oxalates somewhat but regular ingestion over time can cause health problems (D'Mello 1997:346).

Nuts

The most common nut recovered from Princess Point sites is acorn (*Quercus* sp.). Butternut is found second most commonly and then hickory. Although evidence for nuts is found at all sites, the evidence is in small quantities and the remains are very fragmented. As such, the identification of the remains to species is difficult and they are categorized as nuts in general. Walnut and trace quantities of oak and hickory are represented at the Princess Point Holmedale site (Monckton 1999). Spence (1990:146) reports black walnut, hickory, and acorn from the Middle Woodland Couture site. Most Glen Meyer nut remains are acorn; butternut, black walnut, and shagbark hickory are next most common (Ounjian 1998).

Ounjian (1998) notes a general decline in nuts from the Glen Meyer to the prehistoric Neutral, together with a decline in diversity. Most Glen Meyer sites have a least four nut species represented and the prehistoric Neutral sites have one or two. The relative importance of nuts to northeastern populations is not well known at this time and needs further investigation (Crawford and Smith 2001). Basgall (1987:26) notes that variation in nut productivity results from fluctuations in environmental conditions, such as precipitation and temperature.

Nut production is tied to environmental change and ubiquity of nut bearing trees exhibits regional variability (Basgall 1987:26). Stands of nut trees may have not been particularly productive and stopped producing large masts for periods of time. Acorn production is especially variable from year to year and many taxa have good crops perhaps only once every three years (Basgall 1987:23). Nut production is variable and a risk for those depending on nuts as a food source. As such, Princess Point peoples may have preferred more dependable food stuffs. Crawford and Smith (2001) also note that there is less evidence generally for nut use on sites to the north than is found at more southerly sites probably because there are fewer nut-bearing species in the north.

Nut consumption in the Eastern Woodlands of North America appears to have generally increased from the Archaic to the Middle Woodland, then began a steady decline starting in early Late Woodland times and continuing through to contact (Johannessen 1984; Asch and Asch 1985; Smith 1990). Regional variation is a factor. For example, McCorriston (1994:101) explains that the degree to which southern California Indian groups depended on acorn harvest varied greatly over time and according to other resource availability. The variable evidence also could reflect cultural biases or changes in preference (McCorriston 1994:102).

Perhaps other oily plants, such as corn, purslane, sunflower or wild rice, were preferred by the Princess Point and superceded nut exploitation. Monckton's (1990) study of the Late Woodland Hurons found only traces of nuts in the plant assemblages but large collections of fleshy fruits. Evidence for nuts in Ontario may be common (see Crawford 1986; Monckton 1992; Ounjian 1998; and this study) but not always in abundant quantities.

Nuts were used for food (Ford 1979:306) and can be a good source of fats in the diet. The caloric value of acorn is approximately half that of walnut, hickory, and butternut (Ford 1979:306). Some nuts, especially acorn, can be difficult to process and can be bitter because of their objectionable high tannic acid content (Basgall 1987:27). The eastern North American tradition of acorn processing involves gathering, shelling, boiling, and roasting (Basgall 1987:26-27; McCorriston 1994:99). Nuts were not ground in the Northeast tradition; however, tannins are removed faster by grinding nuts prior to boiling and leaching, as was practiced in the California western tradition (Basgall 1987:28; McCorriston 1994:99).

Ford (1979) also notes that the flavour of acorn nuts varies according to the amount of tannic acid and actually varies from one tree to the next. Nuts were an important part of the historic Iroquoian diet and great quantities were consumed year-round (Parker 1912:99). The favoured nuts were hickory, chestnut, and acorn. Fresh nut meats were crushed, boiled in water, and the oil then skimmed. This oil was considered a delicacy used with corn bread and pudding.

Chapter Six

Discussion and Conclusions

Introduction

The Princess Point people represent one of a number of precontact groups that lived in the southern Ontario Lower Great Lakes region, some 1000 to 1500 years ago. This population appears to have occupied a place on a continuum between foragers and food producers, and likely was ancestral to Iroquoian farming societies (Smith and Crawford 1997; Dieterman 2001:290). These early hunter-gatherer-horticulturalists made considerable use of river terraces, floodplains, and wetlands. The lands along the Grand River and the wetlands of Cootes Paradise would have provided two attractive settlement areas (Crawford *et al.* 1998; Walker *et al.* 1998; Dieterman 2001). People gathered wild plant food resources and practiced limited cultivation on river flats. Cultivation of corn gradually gained in intensity. By 1000 B.P., Princess Point was entrenched in a subsistence economy that was based on both food production (Smith and Crawford 1997:27) and wild plant food gathering, together with fishing and hunting

Research Methods

Botanical Remains Analysis

The identification of ancient plant remains enables the reconstruction of prehistoric environments and an understanding of the place of plants in the lifeways of past cultures (Ford 1979). The recovery of plant remains requires extensive logistical preparation, but the increasing use of flotation systems in archaeological projects confirms the important role of plant remains for understanding prehistory. The recovery, identification, and quantification of charred macrobotanical evidence is crucial and essential. Comparisons are made between data sets (sites and features) by quantifying counts and percentages by category and taxa, and by determining density ratios by weight, volume, and number. The frequency of categories and taxa found in flotation samples is also calculated.

This study compares the results of Princess Point data (including Bowyer 1995 and Monckton 1999) to Ounjian's (1998) conclusions regarding the Glen Meyer. Comparisons are also made to the palaeoethnobotany of Middle and Late Woodland populations to the south of Ontario. These comparisons spatially and temporally seat Princess Point within the larger archaeological setting of eastern North America, specifically among those populations within the major drainage system of the Mississippi River and the Lower Great Lakes of southern Ontario.

The range of plant taxa represented in this study of Princess Point indicates that these past peoples used diverse plants for a number of purposes. In varying numbers and densities, there are 36 plant taxa identified within the categories of cultigens, fleshy fruits, greens and grasses, other taxa, and nuts. Results of the analyses are discussed in detail further in this chapter.

Throughout the Northeast, people lived in different areas with a mixed economy, variably dependent on crops and wild resources (Crawford 1999). Continued work on the nature of the variation between hunter-gatherers and agricultural people is important. Data accumulated from research projects should be published and shared for solid comparisons between cultures. The publication of conclusions is insufficient. Absolute numbers, densities, and sample volumes need to be accessible for confident regional comparisons. For consistent presentation of data, Crawford (1999) prefers a cascading tabular system that moves from general to specific categories, with plant names across the top and samples/contexts down the left (see Monckton 1990, 1992; Bowyer 1995; Ounjian 1998; and this manuscript).

Summary of Evidence

The most common category at all Princess Point sites, by absolute count and by percentage, is greens and grains, followed by fleshy fruits, other taxa, and cultigens. Fleshy fruits and greens/grains are the categories with the highest seed density per litre, followed by other taxa and cultigens. By density of seeds per gram of wood charcoal, the most common category is the fleshy fruit category, followed by greens and grains, other taxa, and cultigens.

Feature 210 at Grand Banks stands out for its exceptional seed preservation and high densities. In this feature, the category of greens and grains has the highest density (8.13), followed by fleshy fruits, other taxa, and cultigens. Feature 56 at Meyer produced somewhat greater densities than the Meyer palaeosol or sheet midden. All samples from Forster are from a feature (Feature 1) and are no more dense than other samples that originated from the palaeosol. The average density for all Princess Point sites is about one seed per litre. Cultigen densities range from 0 to 0.56, with an average of 0.15. The density for the fleshy fruits category averages 0.35 (0.1 to 0.83); for greens and grains, 0.35 (1.33 to 0.04); and, for other taxa, 0.12 (0.02 to 0.26). The most common category in Feature 210, by density, is greens and grains; followed by fleshy fruits, other taxa, and cultigens.

Grand Banks produced more plant remains by absolute count than any other site, largely due to the richness of Feature 210. The highest density of plant remains is from

Feature 210; the second highest is from the Grand Banks site in general. Evidence for maize is found at all sites and in the highest percentage of samples from Lone Pine. Next to Grand Banks Feature 210, Meyer has the greatest density of maize per litre. The frequency of maize at these three sites, which are within close proximity, suggests that the cultigen played an important role in this area of the Grand River.

At Bull's Point site, Cootes Paradise, evidence for maize is minimal and the material remains are fragmented. Bull's Point has the lowest density of wood charcoal and produced the most seeds per gram of charcoal. Lone Pine produced the highest density of wood charcoal per litre and the lowest density of seeds per gram of wood charcoal (the converse of Bull's Point). The feature with the highest density of charcoal is Grand Banks Feature 210; Forster Feature 1 has the lowest.

Fleshy fruits are identified at all sites. Bull's Point boasts a high diversity of fleshy fruits (seven species, exceeded only by Grand Banks with eight species), with American nightshade being the most common taxon. Forster has the highest density and highest absolute count of fleshy fruits. All these seeds are bramble, except for one (a blueberry seed).

The highest density of greens and grains is from Grand Banks and this category accounts for the majority of seeds recovered from Feature 210. One wild rice grain is identified from the Grand Banks palaeosol. Grand Banks produced arrowhead and cat-tail, which are both, like wild rice, wetland plants. Arrowhead is also identified from Forster from a large quantity of rhizome fragments, together with a number of tubers. Milkvetch, in the category of other taxa, is found only at Grand Banks and Forster. Sassafras is identified from Bull's Point (sassafras currently does grow at Cootes Paradise) and cat-tail is also present at this site. Biomolecular tests on a sherd from Bull's Point identified sitosterol. The identification of this compound only, and no evidence of animal compounds, indicates that the vessel was used exclusively for cooking plant material.

Comparison of Princess Point and Glen Meyer Plant Remains

This chapter compares the results of this Princess Point study to the analysis conducted on several samples from Lone Pine and Grand Banks by Bowyer (1995), the Holmedale site (Monckton 1999), and Glen Meyer (Ounjian 1998). Princess Point precedes the Glen Meyer, a period when horticulture was well entrenched. The prehistoric Neutral follow the Glen Meyer, and then, the Huron. By comparing Princess Point and Glen Meyer, we are able to examine apparent differences and similarities of two cultural groups that are spatially and temporally linked, together with extending the connection between these southern Ontario populations back in time. Documenting the span or linkage of populations through

time is important. Dramatic changes in subsistence patterns emerge over the some thousand years that these populations represent.

Absolute Numbers

Bowyer's (1995) analysis of Grand Banks and Lone Pine concludes that people exploited a range of local wild resources and incorporated maize into their subsistence regime. At both sites, maize, nut, bramble, sumac, and American nightshade occur. At Grand Banks, a wider spectrum of plant remains includes strawberry, cleavers, chenopod, and grasses. The four Lone Pine samples Bowyer analyzed came from two features. Maize is the most common plant remain (including kernels, cupules, and fragments) by weight. Her analysis identified nut fragments and 12 seeds (six bramble, three American nightshade, three sumac).

Twenty-seven samples were analyzed from Grand Banks, including one pit feature (Feature 1). The feature contained three maize cupules, 19 maize kernel fragments, and 13 seeds (four chenopod, four grasses, one American nightshade, four cleavers). One kernel fragment was dated to 1060 B.P. (Crawford et al. 1997). From other site samples, Bowyer identified fragments of maize kernels and cupules. One fragment was AMS radiocarbon dated to 1250 B.P. (Crawford et al. 1997). She also identified nut fragments and 21 seeds (six chenopod, nine grasses, two bramble, one strawberry, one American nightshade, one cleaver, one sumac).

Monckton (1999) concludes that a variety of fleshy fruits and greens composes most of the plant taxa at the Holmedale site, followed in density by the cultigens, maize and tobacco. Monckton recovered 885 charred seeds and seed fragments from 35 flotation samples. About 21% of the remains were cultigens (maize and tobacco). In this study, cultigens also compose 21% of the remains at Lone Pine (the highest percentage). At Holmedale, fleshy fruits contribute about 16%, consisting of American nightshade, strawberry, bramble, cherry, hawthorn, and grape. Bramble is the most common fleshy fruit. Greens/grains and other taxa include chenopod, cleavers, spikenard, pepper-grass, sumac, cat-tail, and grasses. Nut remains are also identified. Common to Princess Point analyses, Monckton (1998) notes that Holmedale maize remains (kernels and cupules) are very fragmented. Three taxa represented in this study that are common in later Iroquoian sites, but not identified by Bowyer or Monckton, are sunflower, erect knotweed, and purslane.

In Ounjian's (1998) comparison of Glen Meyer to prehistoric Neutral, she found no significant difference between the suite of plants used by these two cultural groups. She concludes that both cultures had stable subsistence systems with their palaeoethnobotanical profiles being almost indistinguishable; although nut remains are more common in Glen Meyer. The Glen

Meyer and prehistoric Neutral practiced mixed collecting and horticultural subsistence patterns. The preference for individual taxa varied over time. This study suggests that the economic pattern saw its beginnings with Princess Point.

There is a continuity of some plants from Princess Point through Glen Meyer and the prehistoric Neutral. Thirty-six species are identified in this Princess Point study, including two cultigens, eleven fleshy fruits, and nine taxa from the greens and grains category. There are ten species from the other taxa category and three types of nuts. Sixty-eight plant species are present in Ounjian's (1998) Glen Meyer study. Of the 36 species found in Princess Point, 27 continue to be present in Glen Meyer assemblages: maize, cucurbit (possibly), sunflower, American nightshade, blueberry, bramble, dogwood, elderberry, grape, hawthorn, strawberry, chenopod, erect knotweed, purslane, wild rice, five grass species, cat-tail, cleaver, mint, sumac, and three nut species. Nine species are found only at Princess Point sites: crowberry, hackberry, witchhazel, milkvetch, St. John's wort, wood sorrel, cinquefoil, arrowhead, and sassafras. Of these species, St. John's wort, wood sorrel, and cinquefoil, although not recovered from Glen Meyer, are recovered from the later prehistoric Neutral.

The most common plant in Princess Point assemblages by absolute number is the grasses, followed by purslane. The most common plant remain in the Glen Meyer samples by absolute number is cat-tail, followed by maize. Nearly 5500 maize kernels are identified in Glen Meyer samples. Tobacco is the next most common remain. Table 16 compares the 14 most common Princess Point and Glen Meyer plant remains by rank. Other plant species are present in smaller numbers, often represented by one seed.

Ounjian (1998) concludes that the most common category in Glen Meyer is other taxa, closely followed by fleshy fruits. Cultigens is the third most common, followed by greens and grains. Ounjian (1998) notes that the other taxa category is skewed by very large numbers of cat-tail and, if this species was not included, fleshy fruits would be the most common category.

Density

Ranking taxa by number per litre results in a different order from that of absolute count; not all species are identified at all five sites and the sample size from each site varies (see Table 19). The density of plant remains for Princess Point is lower than for the Glen Meyer samples. As densities are low at all Princess Point sites, but show higher levels at Feature 210 (Grand Banks), densities for individual taxa are calculated only for this feature. The feature produced a large number of plant remains and has greater potential to provide a meaningful comparison with Glen Meyer samples.

The density range for Princess Point sites is from 0.37 (Lone Pine) to 2.17 (Grand Banks), with an average of less than one. Feature 210 at Grand Banks has the highest density: 3.1. Except for Feature 210, all densities are lower for Princess Point than for Glen Meyer samples. Cultigen densities average from 0.09 to 5.32 per litre for the Glen Meyer, with an average of 1.76, increasing through the prehistoric Neutral from 0.05 to 57.77, with an average of 7.03. The cultigen density for Feature 210 is 0.23. Princess Point densities are discussed in greater detail in Chapter Four.

The density for the Glen Meyer fleshy fruits category averages 2.13 and, for the other taxa category, 3.39. The category of greens/grains is poorly represented in the Glen Meyer assemblages (average density 0.15) and is more prevalent in prehistoric Neutral sites (average density 0.28). The most common category by density is other taxa, followed by fleshy fruits, cultigens, and greens and grains (Ounjian 1998). Cultigens is the most common category reported for the prehistoric Neutral, followed by fleshy fruits, other taxa, and greens and grains. Average cultigen densities for Huron samples range from two to 13 seeds per litre (Monckton 1992).

The Princess Point site with the highest density of wood charcoal (grams) to soil volume (litres) is Lone Pine. Ounjian (1998:726) calculates that the average density of wood charcoal for Glen Meyer is nearly 2 g per litre, over twice the density calculated from Lone Pine. The assemblage with the highest charcoal density is from Feature 210, Grand Banks. The highest density from a Glen Meyer assemblage is about one and a half times the density for Feature 210. Bull's Point has the lowest density of wood charcoal. As in this Princess Point study, wood charcoal dominates Glen Meyer samples.

The highest density of seeds per gram of wood charcoal is from Feature 210: over three seeds per gram of wood charcoal. The next highest densities are from the Grand Banks site palaeosol and Bull's Point (over one seed per gram). By comparison, the average Glen Meyer density is eight seeds per gram (Ounjian 1998:728), that is, over twice that from the highest density Princess Point samples. Lone Pine exhibits the lowest density of seeds per gram of charcoal.

Cultigens

Although maize is found at all Princess Point sites in this study, cultigens is the least common category by density. Cultigens is the third most dominant category in Glen Meyer samples, increasing considerably in importance in prehistoric Neutral samples to become the most common category. Maize is the most common Princess Point and Glen Meyer cultigen. Although kernels, cupules, and fragments are identified in Princess Point samples, the vast majority of remains are fragments (nearly three times that of kernels and cupules combined). Twice as many cupules as kernels are identified. From the Glen Meyer samples, maize kernels (5498) as well as cupules (2354) are identified in large numbers; fragments are infrequent. On average, nearly two cultigen remains per litre were recovered from the Glen Meyer samples, compared to about one-tenth of a remain from Princess Point. The density for Feature 210, however, is similar to that of Glen Meyer samples (about one and a half remain per litre). Feature 210 is dated to about 970 B.P., late Princess Point.

Sunflower, cucurbit, bean, and tobacco are other cultigens present in Glen Meyer assemblages. Ounjian (1998:261) notes that bean increases in number and density during Glen Meyer times and first appears at the Calvert site, dating to about 850 B.P. Cucurbit seeds are the least frequent cultigen and the earliest confirmed evidence for cucurbit is from the Glen Meyer Elliott site, dating about 1000 B.P. Tobacco seeds are the second most abundant cultigen.

Although tobacco density shows a decrease from Glen Meyer to prehistoric Neutral, Ounjian (1998:261) notes that this level may be skewed because of the extremely large number of tobacco seeds recovered from one pit at the Elliott site. If the tobacco from this pit is removed from the averages, tobacco then increases slightly from Glen Meyer to prehistoric Neutral. The Elliott site provides the earliest evidence for tobacco in Ontario (1000 B.P.). Tobacco is not recovered from Princess Point assemblages in this study; however, smoking pipes were unearthed at the Lone Pine and Holmedale sites. The presence of pipes suggests that people engaged in the social behaviour of smoking at an early date. Also, Monckton (1999) identified eight tobacco seeds from the Princess Point Holmedale site.

Fleshy Fruits

The most common category for both Princess Point and Glen Meyer is fleshy fruits, both by absolute count and density. In Princess Point samples, however, the commonality of the two categories is virtually identical. Fleshy fruits has a slightly higher density. Seeds such as bramble, elderberry, and strawberry appear in the highest densities and largest numbers, especially in Glen Meyer samples. American nightshade and bramble appear frequently in Princess Point samples. These seeds are common at Glen Meyer sites and are found in large numbers (Ounjian 1998). Bramble, American nightshade, elderberry, and strawberry account for most of the fleshy fruit seeds recovered at Glen Meyer sites. In Princess Point samples, American nightshade is very common and bramble is relatively common. However, strawberry is rare and elderberry is not recovered.

The density for fleshy fruits recovered from Feature 210 is nearly three seeds per litre and is about two seeds per litre for Glen Meyer. Ounjian did not detect any trends for this category from the Glen Meyer to prehistoric Neutral; some species decline, some increase, and some

remain unchanged. Fleshy fruits appear to have remained a common and stable food source throughout Princess Point, Glen Meyer, and prehistoric Neutral times. Monckton's (1992) study on Huron palaeoethnobotany also comments on the frequency of fleshy fruits, indicating a long-term reliance in southern Ontario.

Greens/Grains

The most striking difference between Princess Point and Glen Meyer is the frequency of the greens and grains category for Princess Point, represented especially by grasses and purslane. The number of chenopod seeds is also high. Greens and grains rank low for Glen Meyer; however, some evidence for chenopod, purslane, and grasses is found. Two wild rice grains are identified in Glen Meyer samples, and one grain, in the Princess Point samples. Erect knotweed is not present in Glen Meyer, but is present in the later prehistoric Neutral and in the earlier Princess Point.

Greens and grains are plentiful from the Grand Banks assemblage, and account for the vast majority of seeds recovered from Feature 210. Grass taxa are especially common. Greens and grains is the second most frequent category by seed density (0.35) in this Princess Point study (by a slight margin over fleshy fruits). This is the least common category in Ounjian's (1998) Glen Meyer study. Greens and grains are present at all Glen Meyer sites but often in minimal numbers. Ounjian calculates a greens and grains seed density of just over one-tenth of a seed per litre. In this study, Feature 210 produced about eight seeds per litre, much richer than the Glen Meyer samples.

The highest density of a pit feature in the Glen Meyer samples is an exterior pit at the Elliott site (an average density for all taxa of 13 seeds per litre). Ounjian notes an increase in the use of greens and grains from the Glen Meyer to the prehistoric Neutral, with an overall increase in the diversity of taxa in prehistoric Neutral. As at Princess Point sites, the most abundant seeds are purslane, knotweed, and chenopod.

Other Taxa

From the category of other taxa, arrowhead is found at Forster and, like at Grand Banks, a large quantity of rhizome fragments provides evidence for this plant. Milkvetch is found also only at Grand Banks and Forster. The other taxa category is the most frequent plant type recovered in Glen Meyer samples, present at all sites (Ounjian 1998). By prehistoric Neutral times, this category is the third most common.

In the Glen Meyer, most seeds in this category are infrequent and low in density, with the notable exception of cat-tail and sumac. As with greens and grains, there is an increase in the variety of taxa from the Glen Meyer to the prehistoric Neutral. Cat-tail has the highest density in

Glen Meyer samples (probably positively skewed by one assemblage), representing about 85% of the other taxa category (Ounjian 1998). Cat-tail is less frequently identified in Princess Point. Seeds representative of the other taxa category (milkvetch, cleavers, cat-tail, St. John's wort, wood sorrel, and sumac) are present in Princess Point samples but are absent in Glen Meyer, with the exception of cat-tail and sumac.

Nuts

In the Princess Point assemblages, nut remains, although present at all sites, are in small quantities and are very fragmented. Like the Glen Meyer samples, the most common nut is acorn; butternut (walnut) and hickory are also found. Nuts are present at all Glen Meyer sites, with four or more species represented (Ounjian 1998). Nuts decline from the Glen Meyer to the prehistoric Neutral (Ounjian 1998:262). Walnut and trace quantities of oak and hickory are represented at the Princess Point Holmedale site (Monckton 1999). Ounjian (1998) reports a considerably higher frequency of nut remains from the Glen Meyer than is at Princess Point sites (64 times more mass). The average density of nuts present during the Glen Meyer is much higher (0.01 g per litre) than during Princess Point (0.006 g per litre). The Princess Point site with the highest density is Lone Pine (0.02 g per litre). The highest total weight of nut remains is from Grand Banks, Feature 210 at less than one gram: just 0.4 per cent of the total sample, and 21% of the combined total for maize and nut. The total weight of nuts from Glen Meyer is over 628 g and accounts for over 55% of the combined total for maize and nut. In Princess Point, the amount of nut is considerably less than the amount of corn; however, this trend is reversed in the Glen Meyer. By prehistoric Neutral times, nut remains are again minimal (Ounjian 1998).

Generally, the Glen Meyer remains present more variability than those of the prehistoric Neutral; but, overall, Ounjian's study represents stability and continuity of a subsistence system spanning from the early Late Woodland through to the late Late Woodland. Ounjian (1998) proposes that there is no indication of agriculturally induced changes at the beginning of Glen Meyer in the late Woodland, nor later, and that the changes associated with the origins of agriculture took place prior to Glen Meyer. She argues that a pattern of stable plant use was already well entrenched in the early Glen Meyer culture and that the introduction and adjustment to agriculture occurred earlier, that is, with Princess Point.

Contextual Analysis

Contextual analysis plays an important role in understanding plant distributions at a site, and provides a broader picture of plant distribution from site to site. It can provide considerable information for the interpretation of prehistoric subsistence patterns. The comparison of contexts helps to determine if any variable is preferentially deposited. Sites with similar contexts can be compared to determine the level of similarity between sites. Intersite and intrasite comparisons explore variation between sites and contexts. Crawford (1999) notes that in Ontario Iroquoian sites from 750 B.P. and later, maize densities exhibit considerable variation. For example, the average maize kernel density at the Wallace site is about 30 per litre (Crawford 1986). At Glen Meyer and prehistoric Neutral sites, densities range from 1.3 to 33 per litre (Ounjian 1998). The range for Princess Point sites is from zero (a calculated value of no kernels per litre at Bull's Point, although maize fragments were recovered) to 0.1 per litre at Meyer (Forster, 0.02; Grand Banks, 0.05; Lone Pine, 0.08). Feature 210 at Grand Banks has the highest density, 0.23 per litre. The sample with the highest maize kernel density is from Feature 210, 1.21 kernels per litre.

To better understand what these varying densities mean, the comparison of cultures that post-date Princess Point, as well as earlier Middle Woodland sites, is important. Intensive sampling and analysis should be continued not only on later sites (see Monckton 1990, 1992; Ounjian 1998), but on the earlier Middle Woodland sites for development of a solid comparative model.

There are five pit features in this Princess Point study; three are from Grand Banks, one from Forster, and one from Meyer. Feature 210 from Grand Banks, the feature with the best preservation, has higher density than the remaining sheet midden. This difference in density between site and feature is not as clearly exhibited elsewhere. Feature 210 presents higher absolute counts of cultigens but by weight (although the difference is not as large), the ratio is higher for the palaeosol. This suggests that the maize recovered from Feature 210 is less fragmented than the remains recovered from the palaeosol. This is likely a reflection of preservation quality and also may indicate that the inhabitants were purposefully storing or disposing maize in the pit.

Feature 210 is dated to later Princess Point (about 970 B.P.). Densities for corn are highest from Princess Point features, as opposed to sheet middens. Seed density is considerably higher for Feature 210 than for the palaeosol. Wood charcoal also is more concentrated in this feature than the remaining palaeosol. The other features do not display such obvious differences. The sites located along the Grand River produced significantly higher densities than Bull's Point at Cootes Paradise.

Ounjian's (1998) Glen Meyer and prehistoric Neutral study, and Monckton's (1990, 1992) Huronia study more easily incorporated context as an analytical variable, as the remains from these sites are better preserved, and contexts, such as hearths, middens, houses, are more commonly identified. Ounjian (1998) concludes that wood charcoal is concentrated in the Glen Meyer houses.

Other than for Feature 210, Princess Point sites did not reveal a similar difference in charcoal densities between features and sites.

In the Glen Meyer, small seeds, nuts, and horsetail stems are most common in exterior pits. Cat-tail and sumac seeds tend to be mostly found in the houses. Non-cultigens are more concentrated in exterior pits, but cultigens tend to be evenly distributed throughout Glen Meyer sites. Monckton (1992) found that there were significant differences between hearth, midden, and house samples in his Huronia study. Hearths had a much lower density of seeds than middens and pits. External house middens were more consistent in composition than hearths and pits, which exhibited higher diversity. Ongoing statistical observations being conducted by Monckton (personal communication) suggest that the density of fleshy fruits in external pits is significantly higher than for any other context. Monckton (personal communication) suspects that this difference illustrates differential preparation and disposal methods for plant foods.

Discussion of Plant Use

Crawford and Smith (1996) define the diverse subsistence pattern of the Great Lakes Late Woodland people as a Northern Mixed Economy. This model, consisting of an economy based on agriculture, hunting, fishing, and gathering wild plants, includes a plant component that consists of cultigens, potential cultigens, fleshy fruits, grains and greens, nuts, and weedy plants. Crawford *et al.* (1997) note that the Northern Mixed Economy, firmly entrenched by Iroquoian times, was being practiced in the Lower Great Lakes by 1000 B.P. With corn as the foundation of local horticulture, intensification of food production systems occurred in Ontario with Princess Point and continued to Glen Meyer (Crawford and Smith 2001).

Further to the south, sunflower, marsh elder, chenopod, maygrass, erect knotweed, and little barley compose the Eastern Agricultural Complex (first proposed by Linton (1924)) that is typical of the Middle and Late Woodland (pre-Mississippian) of Ohio and Illinois. Three of these plants (chenopod, erect knotweed, and sunflower) help define the Princess Point assemblage. Two plants (chenopod and erect knotweed) are often recovered in high densities at northeastern sites and occur at most Late Woodland sites in Ontario (Crawford and Smith 2001). Little barley may be present (currently a tentative identification) in the assemblage from this study. The presence of little barley is reported from the Late Woodland Harrietsville site (Ounjian 1998) and from the early Late Woodland Memorial Park site in Pennsylvania (Hart and Asch Sidell 1996). Princess Point evidence for some of the plants that define the Eastern Agricultural Complex appears to indicate some similarity to their neighbours to the south. Fleshy fruits and greens/grains are the most common categories. The most common

seeds for Princess Point (by absolute numbers and densities) are grasses, purslane, American nightshade, and chenopod.

Maize is a central component of Iroquoian culture and was important during the Princess Point period, but not to the extent as during Glen Meyer or Iroquoian times. With the consumption of maize, the Princess Point diet (as well as the Glen Meyer and later groups' diets) remained varied and incorporated a number of wild plant foods. Carbohydrates, starches, and oils are an important component of a well-rounded, healthy diet. This study produced evidence for plants containing these compounds, such as maize, sunflower, chenopod, wild rice, and arrowhead. Wild rice and arrowhead are not as common. Numerous arrowhead rhizomes and several tubers recovered from this study suggest that arrowhead provided a good source of carbohydrates for Princess Point people.

A wide variety of plants serve to fill the dietary, medicinal, spiritual, and social needs of humans. Many of the plants identified in this study could be used for various purposes, often over-lapping. Evidence suggests that the Princess Point people had a diet rich in starchy and oily-seeded plant foods (including corn), supplemented with a variety of fleshy fruits and greens.

Princess Point and Glen Meyer Plant Use

While plant use by the Princess Point and the Glen Meyer exhibits similarities, there are striking differences between the importance of botanical categories and in the importance of specific plants. While the beginning of agriculture and increasing levels of agricultural intensification do not denote the end of wild plant use, the preference given to some wild plant species over others appears to change with intensification (for example, compare Princess Point, Glen Meyer, prehistoric Neutral, and Huron). The differences in plant use reflect a temporal difference, as well as regional habitat differences, between Princess Point and the more westerly Glen Meyer.

The presence of a quantity of carbonized maize remains suggests that the Princess Point people practiced horticulture. A series of AMS radiocarbon dates on maize from the Grand Banks site includes the earliest Ontario dates from 1570 to 970 B.P. (Crawford *et al.* 1997; Crawford and Smith 2000). Corn appears to have been added to an earlier stable subsistence pattern, rather than having been a replacement, and gardening was likely small-scale, supplemented with wild plant food gathering.

A reliance on corn increased over time, and by 1000 B.P. Princess Point people had increasingly incorporated corn into their subsistence regime (Crawford *et al.* 1997; also see Ounjian 1998). By the Glen Meyer period, four other cultigens were present: beans, cucurbit, sunflower, and tobacco. Chenopod, frequently found in this Princess

Point study and less commonly in Ounjian's (1998) Glen Meyer study, is recovered as a domesticate from more southerly sites in the Northeastern Woodlands (see Gremillion 1993; Smith 1995). Chenopod seeds recovered from both Princess Point and Glen Meyer samples appear to exhibit the morphology of wild plants (*Chenopodium berlandieri*). Future research should explore the morphology of these remains in detail to confirm their wild or domesticated status.

Princess Point and Glen Meyer samples present differences in the quantity and frequency of the greens and grains category. The use of indigenous, starchy and oily-seeded plant foods, such as chenopod, during Princess Point may have created the appropriate conditions for subsistence practices that, in time, would lead to agriculture. A diet that focused on indigenous, starchy and oily-seeded plant foods could include wild rice, various tubers, purslane, maize, and sunflower.

The proximity of Princess Point sites to rivers and wetlands links these people to the use of wetland resources, including plants such as arrowhead, cat-tail, and wild rice. Support for the importance of starchy plants is reflected in the archaeobotanical evidence of this study. A large number of arrowhead rhizome and tuber fragments are identified; the tubers likely were a relatively reliable, if not important, food source. Although just one wild rice grain was recovered, the potential importance of this food source is suggested by association through the identification of other wetland plant foods.

Oily-seeded annuals, including chenopod and erect knotweed, are commonly found in late Middle and early Late Woodland sites to the south. Later assemblages are characterized by a general lack of reliance on indigenous starchy seeds (Fritz 1993; Smith 1995). Starchy seeds in the greens and grains category in this study indicate that these foodstuffs were more important to the Princess Point than to the Glen Meyer, as evidenced by a decrease in frequency over time. The trend away from small indigenous oily-seeded annuals appears to have begun with Glen Meyer, concomitant with a greater reliance on maize.

Fleshy fruits exhibit high levels of use for both Princess Point and Glen Meyer. The most common plants of this type during Princess Point are American nightshade and bramble, and with the Glen Meyer, bramble, strawberry, and elderberry. Princess Point samples suggest considerable reliance on wild plant foods, as evidenced by the frequency of greens and grains, fleshy fruits, and other taxa.

Nuts were not used by the Princess Point to the extent that the resource was used by the Glen Meyer. Glen Meyer depended on nut resources in conjunction with maize cultivation and foraging, significantly more than either Princess Point or prehistoric Neutral. This may

reflect local and temporal availability; climatic variations can have a marked effect on the distribution of nut resources. A dependence on nuts by the Glen Meyer is one example of regional variation found throughout northeastern North America.

This research suggests that a continuum of subsistence behaviours existed in southern Ontario, increasing in intensity from Princess Point to Glen Meyer and to the prehistoric Neutral. Princess Point peoples were plant gatherers who cultivated maize on a supplemental basis. They modified their subsistence pattern to fit their own needs and resources. This study points to the emergence of a distinctive Princess Point economic pattern defined by indigenous starchy, oily-seeded annuals, maize, and wetland resources.

Human - Plant Interrelationship

This research explores the interrelationship between Princess Point people and their environment, together with the adaptive strategies pursued towards the development of a distinctive Princess Point subsistence pattern. The interrelationship between people and plants tends to be dynamic and variable. The genetic changes that plants undergo as a result of human involvement and manipulation, and the resultant cultural and organizational changes that can occur in human societies, add a dynamic aspect to the study of ecological and anthropological questions (Smith 1992). The environment affects cultural development by providing cultural groups with a particular set of resources (Popper and Hastorf 1988), and people choose how to use the resources. A culture defines appropriate resources, and the behavioural consequence of plant use modifies the structure and composition of local plant communities (Ford 1979:290).

Plants from archaeological sites are a by-product of human cognitive patterns of behaviour, as evidenced by inclusions from the local plant environment (Ford:320-323). Plants were not selected at random. The context for the use of each plant is culturally prescribed (see Yarnell 1964) and the associated plant remains reflect that activity for the archaeologist. In many instances, nothing may be preserved of these activities except for carbonized plant remains.

Like other cultures, Princess Point peoples would have used plants for food, medicine, fuel, dyes, building material, clothing, toys, weapons, and household purposes (Yarnell 1964; Ford 1979). These people likely perceived the many uses of plants as inextricably intertwined and looked to the general power of plants, rather than categorizing them into individual uses (see Herrick 1995; Moerman 1998). The economic pattern of the Lower Great Lakes region entailed a mix of subsistence activities, including horticulture, gathering, hunting, and fishing, that was practiced by extracting a variety of resources from various biotic zones and ecological niches (see Yarnell 1964; Ellis and Ferris

1990; Monckton 1992; Shen 1997; Smith and Crawford 1997; Ounjian 1998; Dieterman 2001.

The plant component of this pattern was composed of cultigens, fleshy fruits, grains, greens, nuts, and weedy annuals and perennials. Variability and regional development are important concepts that underlie the archaeology of the Lower Great Lakes. An understanding of how past peoples incorporated plants into their lives is an important component to understanding prehistory and, in this study, palaeoethnobotany illuminates the relationship between the Princess Point and their natural world, specifically, that of plants.

Plant biology imposes constraints on a culture (Ford 1979:289). The choice of a plant, however, is not dictated by its biological properties to the exclusion of human cognition. The selection of plants depends upon cultural specification and classification (Ford 1979:289-290). For example, the choices of certain plants for medicinal use are partially explainable because of their biochemical constituents, but they also are chosen for cultural reasons. The chemical properties of plants are detectable by scientific analysis, and this knowledge can help explain (but not determine) the use of some plants. Plant use ultimately is defined by cultural principles (Ford 1979:289; Johns 1996; Moerman 1998) and uses often seemingly can defy reason.

For example, Moerman (1998:14) explains that plants can be used for opposite purposes by different peoples (and sometimes even the same peoples). The Iroquoian use a decoction of the roots of cup plant (*Silphium perfoliatum*) as an emetic (to cause vomiting); whereas the Meskwaki use the root of the same plant to alleviate vomiting and nausea that may accompany pregnancy (Moerman 1998:15). Similar cases in other cultures were found by Moerman (1998) in which a plant is used as both a stimulant and a sedative. A plant can even be considered poisonous by one group and, for another, be used as an antidote for poisoning (Moerman 1998:15).

Anthropogenesis

Levels of Impact

Anthropogenesis is defined as the process by which humans impact their environment (Crawford 1997:87). Resulting ecosystems are characterized by spatial and temporal patchiness with disturbance as the main factor. Ecological disruption can be of advantage to people, as the result can mean an increased biomass production. Evidence for anthropogenic impact may be detected in palaeosols, pollen profiles, wood charcoal, and carbonized seeds. As the impact is specific to an environment, each region where agriculture began needs to be examined individually. For example, Crawford (1997) explores anthropogenic conditions correlating with the development of food production in prehistoric Japan. Crawford (1997:102) notes that Early through Late

Jomon exhibits a consistent pattern of annual and perennial weed use, while subsequent periods have weed assemblages consistent with wet rice production and dryland plant husbandry, as well as seeds of domesticated species.

Some of the more routine aspects of prehistoric life had the potential for dramatically altering the environment. For example, the quantity of wood used for building, heating, and cooking would affect the landscape, together with land cleared for gardening activities (Yarnell 1964, 1969; Ford 1979). The impact of human activities on plants often may be unintended; however, people alter the environment, often drastically (Yarnell 1964, 1969). Plants may be gathered without humans deliberately affecting the plant population's survival, but unintended consequences can occur which benefit or alter the plant population. These changes do not necessarily lead to domestication, however, as plants may be collected after being tended in some manner without detectable genetic changes occurring.

Yarnell (1969:215) contends that the disturbance to the environment will be more intensive with increasing complexity of technological development and more extensive archaeological remains. Disturbance will be less intensive with less complex technological development and less extensive archaeological remains. The Glen Meyer assemblage reflects a greater complexity of technological development and higher density of archaeological remains than the Princess Point. The continuum from hunter-gatherer to agriculturalist is marked by an increasingly intense impact on the environment. The Princess Point population appears to occupy a phase along this continuum, between foragers and food producers (Smith and Crawford 1997; Dieterman 2001).

The genetic modification of plants is the last step along a continuum of human-plant interactions that starts with the gathering of wild plants (Ford 1979:316). In the past, humans intervened in the growth cycle of local plant populations, enhancing the competitive advantage and chances for reproductive success of individual plants (Harlan 1995). With transplanting or storing and dispersing seeds to assure their availability for germination, these manipulated or cultivated plants may have developed morphological changes, such as a thinner seed coat (for example, chenopod; see Smith 1992, and Chapter Four), which is indicative of intensive human interaction. These human-manipulated plants may still be viable and reproduce when humans are not involved.

Mechanisms of germination dormancy (such as a thicker seed coat) function to prevent the premature germination of mature seeds that have been naturally dispersed and are present in the soil. A thicker seed coat blocks germination of a portion of the seeds naturally dispersed until the next growing season, ensuring the presence of seeds in the soil the subsequent spring (Smith 1992:114).

In the case of chenopod, the presence of a thick, hard outer seed coat restricts the enlargement and germination of the embryo, as well as blocking water and other external elements that are essential for embryo emergence and development. A thick outer seed coat is of selective advantage in wild plants but is maladaptive in domesticated crops. Humans select for crops that come up when planted and have reduced dormancy, thus assuming the controlled responsibility for maintaining the proper temperature and moisture for plant growth (Smith 1992:114).

Continuum of Interaction

Shipek (1989) explains that agriculture initially began by people favouring wild plants that produced food. The example of the historic Kumeyaay Indians of southern California, provided by Shipek (1989), reinforces the concept that plant husbandry can, but does not necessarily lead to the domestication of plants. A number of changes in the human-plant interrelationship can occur without the selection for particular genetic traits. The Kumeyaay planted oak trees and tended various other plant foods, including grains. This area of California was not naturally productive and the climate varied tremendously from coast to mountains to desert and riverine. Shipek (1998) contends that the inhabitants developed a wide range of foods in response to the dynamic weather conditions. Rather than reducing plant diversity by concentrating on a few productive taxa, they increased diversity by interplanting various species in ecological niches and, thus, acquired a level of insurance against possible failure of some plant foods. No plants, however, were selected to the point of domestication.

Shipek (1989) explains that a stratified hierarchy of specialists (such as shamans) in southern California was necessary to develop, maintain, and manage the activities and knowledge needed to ensure the survival of these plants. Shipek (1989) argues that perhaps under less erratic climatic conditions, the plant-husbandry system practiced by the Kumeyaay may have led to the domestication of some species. On the continuum of increasing human-plant interaction, the Princess Point also likely had specialists with particular knowledge about individual plants or environments.

Societies do not simply practice agriculture with domesticated plants or forage for wild plants but, rather, a continuum of complex interactions within particular ecological niches occurs. Populations interact with their environments at different levels of intensity. Periods of broadly classified cultures (such as early Late Woodland), cultures within periods (such as Princess Point), individual groups of a specific culture, and individuals themselves, interact with their particular environments and available resources through behaviours that are restricted by cultural and personal definitions of what is appropriate and what is not.

Because of the innate complexity and idiosyncratic nature of cultural and human interactions with environments, broad assumptions about plant use should not be made. A number of environmental variables (temperature, precipitation, daylight hours, season, plant disease, soil, natural predation), together with a wide range of individual cultural characteristics (social structure, trading patterns, kinship patterns, ritual, symbolism, technology, genetics), result in a complex task for the interpretation of palaeoethnobotanical patterns of cultures and time periods.

Yarnell notes (1969:215) that palaeoethnobotany deals with feedback systems that are more than simple cause and effect models. There is no simple dichotomy between cultigens and wild plants. The category for the remains of plants, which may or may not have been intentionally cultivated, covers a wide continuum (Yarnell 1969). For this reason, the intermediate nature of the Princess Point period is particularly important to understanding human-plant interrelationships in general. Princess Point stands on the threshold of agriculture.

Agricultural Origins

Regional Variability

Domesticated plants are dependent upon humans for their existence. These plants are a cultural artifact resulting from human selection for genetically controlled features that would be disadvantageous under natural conditions (Ford 1979:316; Harlan 1995). Corn is one such plant. With the introduction of cultivated crops, people generally maintain their pattern of gathering and hunting, while slowly incorporating cultigens for added economic stability (see Harris and Hillman 1989; Smith 1992; Cowan and Watson 1992a; Gebauer and Price 1992; Scarry 1993; Harris 1996). Crops gradually become increasingly important to sustain the group. With horticulture, there is a general shift towards permanent, settled villages (see Ellis and Ferris 1990; Rogers and Smith 1995; McNutt 1996).

The development of food production systems ultimately helps to fuel the process of cultural change. While difficult to accurately define or pinpoint the shift towards a more sedentary lifestyle, evidence of maize in this study suggests that Princess Point represents the start of a move away from a mobile foraging strategy to a horticultural economic pattern that was more sedentary (Smith and Crawford 1997; Crawford and Smith 2001; Dieterman 2001).

Subsistence patterns in the Eastern Woodlands of North America formed a continuum that varied in intensity and expression across time and space. Proximity to other populations, their subsistence behaviours, as well as population movement, location, and population size would affect the economic pattern of Princess Point. While this area of southern Ontario exhibits ecological variability (Allen *et al.* 1990), the late Middle Woodland and early Late Woodland generally saw regional cultural adaptations, together with some level of uniformity in settlement and subsistence patterns (see Asch and Asch 1985; Ford 1985; Keegan 1987; Ellis and Ferris 1990; Smith 1990, 1992; Monckton 1990, 1992; Scarry 1993; Smith and Crawford 1997; Shen 1997; Ounjian 1998; Hart 1999a; Dieterman 2001).

To the south of the Princess Point area, plant remains reflect regional variation, but there is an overlapping suite of plants that form the Eastern Agricultural Complex (Linton 1924). Late Middle Woodland and early Late Woodland populations, located directly or indirectly within the drainage basin of the Mississippi River, generally are marked by a high reliance on wild plant resources, as well as a suite of indigenous crop plants, with a focus on starchy and oily-seeded plants (Asch and Asch 1985; Ford 1985; Keegan 1987; Fritz 1990; Smith 1990, 1992, 1995a; Scarry 1993; Hart 1999a). There is evidence for this small-scale seed-crop cultivation steadily intensifying to the Late Woodland. Corn fragments, dating to about 2000 years ago, also are recovered, indicating that corn was grown, but, as the remains are fragmented and not in large quantity, the crop probably was not a staple (Asch and Asch 1985).

Throughout the Northeast, fleshy fruits and nuts are major plant foods as well, and some sunflower seeds and tobacco seeds are recovered. The plants comprising the Eastern Agricultural Complex (sunflower, marsh elder, chenopod, maygrass, erect knotweed, and little barley) become increasingly important through the Middle Woodland, with regional variations among cultural groups. Chenopod, erect knotweed, and sunflower are found in Princess Point assemblages. Other seeds commonly found further south, and also found at Princess Point sites, include a number of grasses, hackberry, bramble, sumac, grape, elderberry, cleaver, purslane, American nightshade, and mint.

In Ontario, evidence from this study suggests a localized variation of this typical Middle and Late Woodland pattern found further south. The most thoroughly developed model for the domestication of plants in eastern North America involves the creation and maintenance of open, disturbed, and enriched human habitation areas on river terraces (Fritz 1993:55; Smith 1995a,b). Princess Point sites characteristically also are located adjacent to water on river terraces, on floodplains, and along wetlands (Crawford *et al.* 1998; Dieterman 2001). An open, disturbed environment could provide abundant, readily available sources of food and other resources.

Like their neighbours to the south, Princess Point subsistence exhibits a persistent reliance on gathering wild plant resources, especially fleshy fruits, starchy and oily-seeded plants, greens and grains, augmented with the cultigen maize. To the south, the extensive and continued

exploitation of some of these annual weedy plants, such as chenopod, ultimately led to their domestication (Asch and Asch 1985; Smith 1995a, 1998). The Princess Point foraged and perhaps also practiced small-scale gardening of some indigenous plants.

The disruption of the natural landscape by humans, whether intentionally or unintentionally, provided a wealth of weedy resources. These activities set the stage for human manipulation of plants through weeding, tending, gardening, and cultivation. Anthropogenesis was an important factor contributing to plant resources in the Great Lakes region (Yarnell 1964). A past knowledge of plant manipulation and encouragement, establishment of open-habitats, and increasing intervention in the life cycles of plants, would have made the efforts needed to tend and cultivate maize readily accepted (Ford 1979). The introduction of maize may have represented an extension of a pre-existing subsistence (Smith 1995b).

Maize: How and Why?

Between 1100 and 800 B.P., food production intensified throughout much of the Northeast and increasingly significant amounts of corn are identified archaeologically. In the late Late Woodland, corn dramatically increases in importance and rapidly replaces the starchy and oily-seeded plants, and other plant foods (see Asch and Asch 1985; Ford 1985; Keegan 1987; Scarry 1993; Johannessen and Hastorf 1994; Smith 1992, 1995; Rogers and Smith 1995; McNutt 1996; Hart 1999a). After this time period, cultivated crops become important staples.

The earliest dates for macrobotanical evidence of maize in northeastern North America date about 2000 years ago from the Holding site (Riley *et al.* 1994); however, maize played a minor role in subsistence activities during the first 600 years after its initial introduction. Flotation of 5340 litres of soil at the Holding site yielded eleven kernels, four cupules, three cob fragments, and one embryo. In another intensively sampled site, the first evidence for corn in Ontario is from the Princess Point Grand Banks site (part of this research), which dates from about 1570 to 970 B.P. (Crawford *et al.* 1997).

When maize becomes common at archaeological sites in a region, there is often evidence for increased reliance on storage, suggesting the use of maize over extended periods of time (Hart 1999b). Except for the recovery of cobs, maize generally is recovered in relatively small quantities compared to the number of fragments a cob can produce. Hart (1999b:161) submits that prior to intensive use, maize may have entered the archaeological record only rarely, and that which did, represents more than casual use. Maize often seems to appear suddenly in an area. However, evidence of a sudden adoption of maize agriculture cannot be assumed by the occurrence of maize without intensive efforts to find maize in earlier contexts.

The timing of maize's introduction into southern Ontario can only be determined with intensive sampling of Middle Woodland sites, prior to Princess Point. Sample size has an important effect on the number of taxa represented, and the discovery of rare or unusual taxa requires large samples be analyzed (Hart 1999b). The highest density of corn in this study is from Grand Banks Feature 210, which dates a few hundred years later than the initial evidence for corn (Smith and Crawford 1997). The high density of corn in this feature suggests that the cultigen was becoming increasingly important in the Princess Point diet.

As well as being reflected by archaeobotanical evidence, the increasing use of C_4 plants (such as corn) in the diet is seen in isotope studies of human skeletal remains from Ontario, which exhibit a gradual increase in heavy carbon from 1300 to 700 B.P. (Katzenberg et al.1995). Corn horticulture substantially increases in intensity from the Glen Meyer to the prehistoric Neutral and other cultigens are added to the diet. By 1200 B.P., maize is widespread and abundant in the archaeological record of the Northeast. Within 300 years, agricultural economies dominated by maize are well-established in eastern North America (Asch and Asch 1985; Ford 1985; Keegan 1987; Smith 1990, 1992, 1995; Scarry 1993; Hart 1999a). In the Lower Great Lakes, maize becomes an increasingly important crop slightly later, after about 1000 or 1100 B.P. (Smith and Crawford 1997).

There are a number of explanations for the introduction of maize. Regionally specific frameworks to explain the origins of agriculture are necessary, as suites of plants involved in economic patterns include indigenous taxa that, together with cultigens, represent a culture's subsistence regime. In the Northeastern Woodlands, horticultural origins are secondary (see Smith 1990, 1992; Scarry 1993; Cowan and Watson 1992a). Horticulture in the Lower Great Lakes is the result of secondary origins either from cultural diffusion or migration, or both (Smith and Crawford 1997).

The question of diffusion or migration concerns *how* agriculture arrived, and the issues of population resources and social demands involve causality or *why* foragers became farmers (Price 1996:35). Hart (1999b:142) explains that *how* questions are functional and explore proximate causes. Ultimate causes are evolutionary and are the subject of *why* questions. Maize was introduced into southern Ontario either by the actual migration of peoples from the Midwest or eastern North America, or by diffusion of the economic pattern into the Middle Woodland subsistence pattern (Snow 1995, 1996; Crawford and Smith 1996). Price (1996) contends that, in general, agriculture spread through the diffusion of ideas and products, rather than through the migration of people. Simply put, foragers became farmers (Price 1996:359).

Snow (1995) proposed that Iroquoian-speaking peoples migrated into the area about 1000 years ago, bringing with them maize horticulture and displacing indigenous groups of Algonkian hunter-gatherers. Crawford and Smith (1996) contend that Princess Point was not an Algonkian-speaking group displaced by horticulturalists from the south, but should be considered an early Late Woodland culture, arguing that the Princess Point practiced corn horticulture considerably earlier than 1000 B.P., as evidenced by much earlier AMS dates (1570 B.P.) (Crawford *et al.* 1997). Maize could have been introduced to a variety of groups out of which arose the Iroquoian.

An explanation for the gap of several hundred years between the time when maize was first introduced and the time when it became a focal point in Northeastern subsistence can be provided by genetics. Cowan and Watson (1992b) explain that, initially, maize was a tropical cultigen, adapted to much different growing conditions than those in northeastern North America, but through genetic manipulation people selected for plants with desired characteristics. By about 1000 B.P., the variety grown in the north was well adapted to the area's cooler mean annual temperature and shorter day-length. This variety of maize grew well and was as productive, if not more, than the wild starchy and oily-seeded plants and fleshy fruits that the Princess Point and others had enjoyed.

One of the main hypotheses concerning the transition to agriculture suggests that population growth resulted in too many people and too little food (Binford and Binford 1968; Cohen 1977). That is, agriculture was adopted either as a result of growing populations or of declining resources, with an imbalance between population and resources.

Some suggest that the transition to agriculture was caused by factors involving social structure and the emergence of hierarchies (Bender 1978; Hayden 1990, 1992). Individuals may have directed others to adopt agriculture to produce a food surplus for increasing exchange and trade. Price (1996) agrees that, in southern Scandinavia, the primary correlates of the transition to agriculture are increasing status differentiation and trade. Price (1996) contends that agriculture first appeared in areas with abundant resources, rather than in marginal or poor environments. New strategies are initiated where risk is affordable.

Hart (1999b) argues that a single introduction of maize is unlikely to account for the perpetuation of maize as a crop in the Eastern Woodlands. His theory makes a good argument for trade being an important factor with Princess Point. At the time of its introduction(s) into the area, maize had been a domesticate for millennia, dependent on humans. Like all plants, maize is sensitive to its immediate environment and individual plant populations would adapt to their local environments, some adapting better than others (Hart 1999b:149). The number of plants that produced grain determined the population from which next year's crop would be selected and, likely, not all plants reached vegetative and sexual maturity and were viable.

Maize may have been integrated into an existing system that evolved with gardening of native plants, or inhabitants may have tried to recreate the management techniques described by a population that donated or traded maize into the area (Hart 1999b:150). Corn would be subject to selective pressures from its new environment, together with human cultural pressures. Human behaviour would, in large part, determine the size of the corn crop. The inhabitants would have to have been willing and knowledgeable to provide the necessary care for this new crop to become established. Indifference towards the crop would have decreased, or even eliminated, its chances of survival. Hart (1999b:150) contends that factors, such as ceremonial and religious reasons, may have encouraged adopting populations to effectively manage the new maize crop. In some instances, the cost of maize production may have been low enough for the crop to be easily accepted and tended.

Maize is particularly susceptible to decreases in yield as a result of inbreeding over short periods of time. In the absence of gene flow, a new small maize population would become extinct if inbred (Hart 1999b:152). For early maize agriculture to be successful, multiple introductions of different maize populations (for example, through trade) were necessary to increase genetic diversity (Hart 1999b:152). The diffusion of maize from different areas would result in greater genetic variation; and maize fitness would increase as humans sowed more kernels, increasing the number of plants and, consequently, genetic diversity.

Symbolism and Plants

The introduction of maize would have been seen as a likely extension of related, pre-existing attitudes toward manipulation, management, and control of the environment (Smith 1995b:193-214). Domesticated plants would have provided impressive proof of an expanding control over the environment. Presumably, planting is a precondition for domestication, not only as an activity, but as a behavioural mind-set. A cluster of interrelated variables would have occurred just prior to the appearance of maize. Archaeology does not deal with psychology or intentions but, rather, human behaviour, that is, what people actually did. Nonetheless, peoples' behaviours can follow goals, such as maximizing caloric acquisition. Specific strategies and the values that guided those strategies can be inferred (Smith 1995b:193-214).

Plants are crucial to the spiritual world of people and often are a metaphor for life itself (Ford 1979; Herrick 1995; Ingold 1996). Communication between humans and noncorporal beings is maintained with the use of medicinal plants (see Overholt and Callicott 1982; Gow

1995). Communication with the spiritual world is facilitated with tobacco and other psychoactive plants which may even mentally transport the human spirit to the spiritual world (Schultes and Hofmann 1980; Gow 1995). Although these relationships are difficult to interpret without ethnographic analogies, Ford (1979) notes that it may be possible, more or less, to reconstruct the symbolic world of ancient societies with archaeobotanical remains where no other kind of evidence is available. Although evidence for the symbolic component of a society may not preserve in every site, the possibility of this pervasive component of a culture should be acknowledged (Ford 1979). As Ford (1979:289) notes, "Unless such evidence is sought and its importance for cultural reconstruction recognized, valuable information about past lifeways can easily be dismissed as beyond the archaeologist's grasp for lack of evidence".

Conclusions

The Princess Point, Glen Meyer, prehistoric Neutral, and Huron cultures across southern Ontario increasingly used cultivated crops, including maize, and continued to use wild plant foods (Monckton 1990, 1992, 1999; Bowyer 1995; Smith and Crawford 1997; Ounjian 1998). These groups exhibit spatial and temporal variability in their settlement patterns, material cultures, and economic patterns. However, there is some level of continuity in their subsistence behaviours. Nonetheless, differences among the botanical categories are evident, as well as shifts in the importance of certain taxa. The differences reflect local variation of a Northeastern Woodland subsistence pattern as affected by availability, need, and cultural preference. Regional variations include differences in indigenous crop preferences, varying maize cultivation intensity, and a diversity of use of wild plant resources.

Although the inhabitants added corn to their subsistence, the cultigen did not replace the existing economic pattern, but, rather, added to a broad-based reliance on plant foods that included both domesticated and undomesticated plants. The Princess Point began to incorporate maize into their subsistence regime as early as 1570 B.P., but probably not much earlier, considering its earliest evidence in areas to the south is about 2000 B.P. (Crawford *et al.* 1997). Maize is found at all sites in this study, indicating that the cultigen was an important component of Princess Point subsistence, and became increasingly important over time through the Glen Meyer and early prehistoric Neutral (Ounjian 1998).

The reoccupation and reuse of specific locations on floodplain locations would have provided disturbed anthropogenic habitats where weedy annuals, such as chenopod, purslane, and American nightshade would thrive. These plants would be attracted to disturbed soil that would have been overturned as a result of the construction of pits, houses, and hearths, together with a range of everyday processing and manufacturing activities. Gardening of indigenous species may have been intentionally practiced, coinciding with the occupation of floodplains along the Grand River. Grand Banks, Forster, and Cayuga Bridge sites are located on the floodplain; Bull's Point, along a wetland; and Lone Pine and Meyer are located on a terrace along the Grand River.

The plants identified in this study served to fill the dietary, medicinal, spiritual, and social needs of the Princess Point people. Some plants, such as maize, chenopod, wild rice, and arrowhead are easily stored and are high in starch and oils. Many plants could be used for various purposes, often over-lapping. For example, bramble could be used as a food (berries) or as a healthful tonic (leaves). Together with the presence of Princess Point smoking pipes, some plants suggest the ingestion of mind-altering plant material, such as American nightshade and milkvetch. Although tobacco is not present at the sites in this study, Monckton (1999) reports tobacco at the Holmedale site. The range of taxa for which there is evidence suggests that Princess Point peoples were well aware of the richness of their environment and exploited it accordingly.

The most common categories present in Princess Point sites are fleshy fruits and greens/grains, followed by other taxa and cultigens. For the Glen Meyer, the most common plant type is other taxa, closely followed by fleshy fruits, then cultigens and greens and grains. (As previously noted, the other taxa category for the Glen Meyer is skewed by the very large number of cat-tail at the Calvert site. If this large number were reduced to the average found at other Glen Meyer sites, the most common plant category would be fleshy fruits.) By prehistoric Neutral times, the most common category is cultigens, followed by fleshy fruits, other taxa, and greens and grains. The greens and grains category dramatically decreases in frequency over time and with the increased use of maize (Ounjian 1998).

In comparing the archaeobotany of Princess Point to that of Glen Meyer, a number of similarities, yet several differences are evident, as well as shifts in the importance of some plant taxa. Horticulture emerges during Princess Point with the first evidence of corn (Crawford *et al* 1997). Corn is the only domesticate present in Princess Point but that does not imply that other plants were not being tended and manipulated. By the later Glen Meyer, evidence for other cultigens (such as bean, sunflower, and tobacco) are common with corn remaining the most frequent cultigen.

The density of cultigens (mostly maize) increases significantly (nearly 20%) from Princess Point to Glen Meyer. Much of the material evidence for corn in Princess Point assemblages is fragmentary. Maize remains recovered at Middle Woodland and early Late Woodland sites to the south also commonly are fragmented. By the Glen Meyer, corn kernels tend to be better preserved, suggesting an increase in use (see Asch and Asch 1985). Nonetheless, in Princess Point assemblages, there are some well-preserved kernels and a greater number of intact cupules.

The size of sunflower achenes from the Ontario Late Woodland does not fit the model of increasing size through time (Crawford 1999). Achenes from the Late Woodland are similar in size to Early and Middle Woodland achenes in the Midwest. Glen Meyer sunflower seeds are larger than those measured in this Princess Point study. The achene size increased in size over time in Ontario but, as Crawford (1999:231) suggests, the overall smaller size may relate to the shorter growing season in the north, other growing conditions, or a unique variety of sunflower growing in the area. Achene sizes are variable on individual plants, depending on their location on the seed head. The three sunflower achenes in this study are small and not yet identified as common sunflower, woodland sunflower, or Jerusalem artichoke. A sample size of three is too small for meaningful statistical conclusions. Ethnographic accounts report that the Iroquoian used sunflower for its oil rather than its grain potential (Parker 1912), and the Princess Point may have favoured a different variety of sunflower than their southerly neighbours.

The earliest evidence for another cultigen, tobacco, dates to about 1000 B.P. from the Elliott site (Ounjian 1998). Although no tobacco was identified in this study, Monckton (1999) reports eight tobacco seeds from the Princess Point Holmedale site. Smoking pipes were recovered from Lone Pine. Tobacco seeds are reported from the Stratford Flats site dating to about 950 B.P. (MacDonald 1986; Fox 1990). Evidence for tobacco is found in the northeastern United States, at the Smiling Dan site, several hundred years earlier, about 1800 B.P. (Asch and Asch 1985).

As Monckton (1990, 1992) and Ounjian (1998) point out, with an increasing reliance on cultigens in southern Ontario over time, there was not necessarily a concomitant decrease in the use of wild plant foods. On the contrary, it can be argued that with an increase in disturbed soil due to increasing sedentism and agricultural activities, some wild weedy species would thrive. There could be an actual increased reliance on weedy plants (Smith 1992, 1993). With an increase in population and more people requiring more resources, plant species occupying the margins of crop fields and other disturbed areas would provide an attractive food resource.

Monckton's (1990, 1992) Huron research and Ounjian's (1998) Middle Iroquoian research show that, although intensively involved in maize agriculture, these past populations also relied on a significant amount of wild plant foods. Monckton (1990, 1992) concludes that the most commonly used wild plants during Huron times are those that fall under the category of fleshy fruits, and that these were used extensively. Ounjian (1998) also concludes that fleshy fruits were an important component of the early Iroquoian diet. Cultigens likely were more important during some seasons than others, or under certain circumstances. Rather than simply replacing wild plants, cultigens augmented the prehistoric diet. The intensity at which crop plants were used varied regionally from population to population, underlain with a basic pattern of continuity. The Princess Point also incorporated maize horticulture into their economic pattern and continued to be dependent on wild plant foods.

One of the more obvious differences between Princess Point and Glen Meyer is in the greens and grains category. The importance of the category decreases from Princess Point to the Glen Meyer. The trend away from starchy and oily-seeded annuals begins with the Glen Meyer, but oily-seeded annuals, such as chenopod, knotweed, and purslane, are commonly found at late Middle and early Late Woodland sites to the south. Like their neighbours to the south, the use of starchy and oily-seeded plants by the Princess Point may have created the appropriate conditions for subsistence practices that would lead to horticulture. This would eventually lead to the intensive horticulture practiced during the Glen Meyer.

Together with maize, the starchy grains of wild rice may have been included in a diet that focused on starchy and oily-seeded plants. Evidence for the exploitation of wild rice is found at the Grand Banks site along the Grand River, and palynological evidence at Cootes Paradise shows that wild rice was growing in this wetland during Princess Point times. In general, the proximity of Princess Point sites to rivers and wetlands, together with macrobotanical evidence, links this culture to wetland resources. The large number of arrowhead rhizome and tuber fragments also lends support for the importance of starchy plants. Tubers could provide a fairly reliable, if not important, food source. Although often not found at archaeological sites, numerous tubers and tuber fragments were recovered in this study.

The Princess Point modified their subsistence pattern to fit their needs and local resources. Their individuality is reflected by the frequency of starchy and oily-seeded annuals, maize, wetland resources, and fleshy fruits, together with the scarcity of nut remains. These people were plant gatherers who cultivated maize on a supplemental basis. Horticulture increased in intensity from Princess Point to Glen Meyer and, subsequently, to the prehistoric Neutral and to contact. The Princess Point relied on a variety of plant resources along the Grand River and in Cootes Paradise, incorporating maize into a subsistence pattern, while wild plant gathering remained an important focus. There was an interconnectedness between Princess Point and other populations, underlain with a level of variability and regional development.

Princess Point plant use generally exhibits many similarities to Middle Woodland, Late Woodland, and Iroquoian populations in southern Ontario, and to Middle and Late Woodland populations in the Northeast.

Future Research

Intensive sampling and analysis should be continued on later sites (for example, see Monckton 1990, 1992; Ounjian 1998). Ongoing, research is filling in gaps for the Late Woodland. These efforts must be continued to better understand the significant changes that occurred during this dynamic period: a time when people moved away from a foraging lifestyle to one that eventually concentrated on horticulture. The earlier Middle Woodland must be better understood for the development of a solid comparative model through time. The timing of maize's introduction into southern Ontario can be determined only with intensive sampling of Middle Woodland sites, prior to Princess Point. Evidence for maize during the Middle Woodland in southern Ontario is not present (Spence *et al.* 1990; Fox 1990; Crawford and Smith 2001). A fine-grained research method that entails the analysis of large quantities of soil samples (such as conducted for the Princess Point research project) must be initiated.

If southern Ontario populations engaged in the tending and cultivating of indigenous plants to the point that the plants would be morphologically and genetically modified needs to be explored. A visual inspection of chenopod seeds recovered from southern Ontario sites suggests that some seeds might fall within the domesticated category. To establish the presence of cultivated *Chenopodium* during Princess Point, through the Glen Meyer, prehistoric Neutral, and Huron, analysis by SEM is necessary. Seed coat changes can be discreet and minute. Establishing the presence of cultivated chenopod would imply human involvement with the plant. This would provide support for the proposition of a general exploitation of oily and starchy-seeded plants over a long period. Smith (1992:125) notes the identification of early horticulture or gardening from different regions will result in a better understanding of the timing and geographical location of domestication.

Palaeoethnobotany needs to better understand what Crawford (1999) calls the "middle ground" between hunter-gatherers and agricultural people. People were living throughout the Northeast with a mixed economy, variably dependent on crops and wild resources. Princess Point, Glen Meyer, prehistoric Neutral, and Huron exhibit this pattern of maize horticulture, together with wild plant use. Each cultural group exhibits some level of temporal and spatial variation, within their individual sites, and from one period to another. Continued work on the nature of this variation within southern Ontario and, generally, the Northeast, will shed light on past populations, and will be important for modeling behaviour elsewhere. Continued analysis of flotation samples will provide more data and information, and the opportunity for greater interpretation. This research addresses a key area of palaeoethnobotanical research: the intermediate or transitional phase between forager and horticulturalist. By exploring the continuum of mild interaction with the environment to extensive interaction, all phases of the human-plant interrelationship, together with the dynamic interrelationship of one population to another, will be better understood. For this reason, the intermediate nature of Princess Point is particularly important to understanding the human-plant interrelationship.

References

Adams, K.R., and R.E. Gasser
 1980   Plant Microfossils from Archaeological Sites: Research Considerations, and Sampling Techniques and Approaches. *The Kiva* 45(4):293-300.
Aiken, S.G., P.F. Lee, D. Punter, and J.M. Stewart
 1988   *Wild Rice in Canada.* NC Press Limited, Toronto.
Alexander, M.M., and J.A. Paredes
 1998   Possible Efficacy of a Creek Folk Medicine through Skin Absorption: An Object Lesson in Ethnopharmacology. *Current Anthropology* 39(4):545-549.
Allen, G. M., P.F.J. Eagles, and S.D. Price, eds.
 1990   *Conserving Carolinian Canada.* University of Waterloo Press, Waterloo.
Anderson, E.
 1952   *Plants, Man, and Life.* Little Brown and Co., Boston.
 1956   Man as a Maker of New Plants and New Plant Communities. In *Man's Role in Changing the Face of the Earth*, edited by W.L. Thomas, pp. 763-777. University of Chicago Press, Chicago.
Anderson, R.A.
 1976   Wild Rice: Nutritional Review. *Cereal Chemistry* 53:949-955.
Arnason, T., R.J. Hebda, and T. Johns
 1981   Use of Plants for Food and Medicine by Native Peoples of Eastern Canada. *Canadian Journal of Botany* 59:2189-2325.
Asamarai, A.M., P.B. Addis, R.J. Epley, and T.P. Krick
 1996   Wild Rice Hull Antioxidants. *Journal of Agricultural Food Chemistry* 44:126-130.
Asch, D.L. and N.E. Asch
 1977   Chenopod as cultigen: a reevaluation of some prehistoric collections from eastern North America. *Midcontinental Journal of Archaeology* 2(1):3-45.
 1985   Prehistoric Plant Cultivation in West-Central Illinois. In *Prehistoric Food Production in North America*, edited by R. Ford, pp. 149-203. Anthropological Papers 75, University of Michigan Museum of Anthropology, Ann Arbor.
Barclay, G.J., and A.D. Fairweather
 1984   Rye and Ergot in the Scottish Later Bronze Age. *Antiquity* 58:126-127.
Barnaby, R.C.
 1964   *Atlas of North American Astragalus* sp. New York Botanical Garden, New York.
Basgall, M.E.
 1987   Resource Intensification among Hunter-Gatherers: acorn economies in prehistoric California. *Research in Economic Anthropology* 9:21-52.

Begossi, A.
 1996   Use of Ecological Methods in Ethnobotany: Diversity Indices. *Economic Botany* 50(3):280-289.
Bekerman, A.
 1995   *Relative Chronology of Princess Point Sites.* Unpublished M.Sc. research paper on file at the Department of Anthropology, University of Toronto, Toronto.
Bender, B.
 1978   From gatherer-hunter to farmer: a social perspective. *World Archaeology* 19:204-222.
Berg, D.J.
 1988   *The Analysis of Faunal Material from Flotation Samples from Fifteen London (Ontario) Region Sites.* Unpublished manuscript on file at the Department of Anthropology, Erindale Campus, University of Toronto, Toronto.
Bettinger, R. L.
 1991   *Hunter-gatherers: archaeological and evolutionary theory.* Plenum Press, New York.
Binford, S.R. and L.R. Binford
 1968   *New perspectives in archaeology.* Aldine, Chicago.
Bird, R.M.
 1994   Manual for the Measurements of Maize Cobs. In *Corn and Culture in the Prehistoric New World,* edited by S. Johannessen and C. Hastorf, pp 5-22. Westview Press, Boulder.
Black, M.J.
 1980   *Algonquin Ethnobotany.* National Museum of Man Mercury Series, Canadian Ethnology Series, Paper No. 65, Ottawa.
Bonzani, R.M.
 1997   Plant Diversity in the Archaeological Record: A Means toward Defining Hunter-Gatherer Mobility Strategies. *Journal of Archaeological Science* 24:1129-1139.
Bowyer, V.E.
 1995   *Paleoethnobotanical Analysis of Two Princess Point Sites: Grand Banks (AfGx-3) and Lone Pine (AfGx-113) in the Grand River Area, Ontario.* Unpublished M.Sc. research paper on file at the Department of Anthropology, University of Toronto, Toronto.
Boyd, W.E.
 1986   Rye and Ergot in the Ancient History of Scotland. *Antiquity* 60:45-49.
Brown, A. G.
 1997   *Alluvial Geoarchaeology: Floodplain Archaeology and Environmental Change.* Cambridge University Press, Cambridge.
Budak, M.K.
 1985   Laurel Ceramics: A Pointed Question. *The Minnesota Archaeologist* 44(2):31-40.

Butzer, K.W.
1993   Human Ecosystem Framework for Archaeology. In *The Ecosystem Approach in Anthropology, From Concept to Practice*, edited by E.F. Moran, pp. 91-130. The University of Michigan Press, Ann Arbor.

Bye, R.A.
1985   Botanical Perspectives of Ethnobotany of the Greater Southwest. *Economic Botany* 39(4):375-386.

Cabaceiras, D.
1994   *Faunal Report of the Lone Pine Site AfGx-113.* Unpublished manuscript on file at the Department of Anthropology, University of Toronto, Toronto.

Caldwell, J.R.
1958   *Trend and Tradition in the Prehistory of the Eastern United States.* American Anthropological Association Memoir No. 88.

Caruso, F.L., and D.C. Ramsdell
1995   *Compendium of Blueberry and Cranberry Diseases.* APS Press, St. Paul.

Chapman, C.J., and D. F. Putnam
1984   *The Physiography of Southern Ontario.* Ontario Geological Survey, Toronto.

Chapman, J. and P.J. Watson
1993   The Archaic Period and the Flotation Revolution, in *Foraging and Farming in the Eastern Woodlands*, edited by C.M. Scarry, pp. 27-38. University Press of Florida, Gainesville.

Cohen, M.N.
1977   *The food crisis in prehistory.* Yale University Press, New Haven.

Cowan, C.W.
1978   The Prehistoric Use and Distribution of Maygrass in Eastern North America: Cultural and Phytogeographical Implications. In *The Nature and Status of Ethnobotany*, edited by R. Ford, pp. 163-288. Anthropological Papers 67, University of Michigan Museum of Anthropology, Ann Arbor.

Cowan, C.W., and P.J. Watson, eds.
1992a   *The Origins of Agriculture: An International Perspective.* Smithsonian Institution Press, Washington D.C.

1992b   Some Concluding Remarks. In *The Origins of Agriculture: An International Perspective*, edited by C.W. Cowan and P.J. Watson, pp. 207-212. Smithsonian Institution Press, Washington D.C.

Cowgill, G.L.
1989   Formal approaches in archaeology. In *Archaeological Thought in America*, edited by C.C. Lamberg-Karlovsky, pp. 74-88. Cambridge University Press, Cambridge.

Crawford, G.W.
1982   Late Archaic Plant Remains from West-Central Kentucky. *Midcontinental Journal of Archaeology* 7(2):205-224.

1983   *Paleoethnobotany of the Kameda Peninsula Jomon.* University of Michigan Anthropological Papers No. 73. Museum of Anthropology, Ann Arbor.

1985   *Subsistence Ecology of the Seed Site.* Unpublished manuscript on file at the Department of Anthropology, University of Toronto, Toronto.

1986   *The Wallace Site.* Unpublished manuscript on file at the Department of Anthropology, University of Toronto, Toronto.

1992   The Transitions to Agriculture in Japan. In *Transitions to Agriculture in Prehistory*, edited by A.B. Gebauer and T.D. Prince, pp. 117-132. Monographs in World Archaeology No. 4, Prehistory Press, Madison.

1997   Anthropogenesis in Prehistoric Northeastern Japan. In *People, Plants, and Landscapes: Studies in Paleoethnobotany*, edited by K.J. Gremillion, pp. 86-103. The University of Alabama Press, Tuscaloosa.

1999   Palaeoethnobotany in the Northeast. In *Current Northeast Palaeoethnobotany*, edited by John Hart, pp. 225-234. New York State Museum Bulletin 494, Albany.

Crawford, G.W., and D.G. Smith
1996   Migration in Prehistory: Princess Point and the Northern Iroquoian Case. *American Antiquity* 61(4):782-790.

2001   *Palaeoethnobotany in the Northeast.* Draft manuscript on file at the University of Toronto, Toronto.

n.d.   *Updating the Princess Point Project.* Draft manuscript on file at the University of Toronto, Toronto.

Crawford, G.W., D.G. Smith, and V.E. Bowyer
1997   Dating the Entry of Corn (Zea Mays) into the Lower Great Lakes Region. *American Antiquity* 62(1):112-119.

Crawford, G.W., D.G. Smith, J.R. Desloges, and A.M. Davis
1998   Floodplains and Agricultural Origins: A Case Study in South-Central Ontario, Canada. *Journal of Field Archaeology* 25(2):123-137.

Davis, D.
1984   Isolation and characterization of swainsonine from locoweed. *Plant Physiology* 76:972-975.

D'Mello, J.P.F.
1997   Toxic compounds from fruit and vegetables. In *Phytochemistry of Fruit and Vegetables*, edited by F.A. Tomas-Barberan and R.J. Robins, pp. 331-352. Oxford Science Publications, Oxford.

Densmore, F.
1928   *Use of Plants by the Chippewa Indians.* Bureau of American Ethnology, Annual Report (1926-1928).

Dice, L. R.
1943   *The Biotic Provinces of North America.* University of Michigan Press, Ann Arbor.

Dickason, O.P.
1991   For Every Plant There is a Use: The Botanical

World of Mexica and Iroquoians. In *Aboriginal Resource Use in Canada: Historical and Legal Aspects,* edited by K. Abel and J. Friesen, pp. 11-34. University of Manitoba Press, Winnipeg.

Dieterman, F.
2001 *Princess Point: The Landscape of Place.* Ph.D. dissertation on file at the Department of Anthropology, University of Toronto, Toronto.

Dore, W.G.
1969 *Wild Rice.* Research Branch of Canada, Department of Agriculture, Ottawa.

Elliott, D.
1995 *Wild Roots.* Healing Arts Press, Rochester.

Etkin, N.L.
1990 Ethnopharmacology: Biological and Behavioural Perspectives in the Study of Indigenous Medicines. In *Medical Anthropology, Contemporary Theory and Method,* edited by T.M. Johnson and C.F. Sargent, pp. 149-158. Praeger, New York.

Fecteau, R.D.
1983 *A preliminary report on plant remains from three early Iroquoian sites in southwestern Ontario.* Report on file at the Heritage Branch, Ontario Ministry of Citizenship and Culture, London.
1985 *The Introduction and Diffusion of Cultivated Plants in Southern Ontario.* Unpublished M.A. thesis on file at the Department of Geography, York University, Toronto.

Finlayson, W.D.
1977 *The Saugeen Culture: A Middle Woodland Manifestation in Southwestern Ontario.* National Museum of Man, Archaeological Survey of Canada, Mercury Series No. 61.

Flannery, K.V.
1972 The cultural evolution of civilizations. *Annual Review of Ecology and Systematics* 3:399-426.

Flannery, K.V., ed.
1986 *Guila Naquitz: Archaic Foraging and Early Agriculture in Oaxaca, Mexico.* Academic Press, New York.

Food and Agriculture Organization of the United Nations (FAO)
1992 *Maize in Human Nutrition.* FAO Food and Nutrition Series, No. 25. Food and Agriculture Organization of the United Nations, Rome.

Ford, R.I.
1974 Northeastern Archaeology: Past and Future Directions. *Annual Review of Anthropology* 4:385-414.
1979 Paleoethnobotany in American Archaeology. In *Advances in Archaeological Method and Theory, Vol. 2,* pp. 285-336. Academic Press, New York.
1985 *Prehistoric Food Production in North America.* Anthropological Papers 75. University of Michigan Museum of Anthropology, Ann Arbor.

Ford, R. and D. Brose
1975 Prehistoric Wild Rice from the Dunn Farm Site, Leelanau County, Michigan. *The Wisconsin Archeologist* 56:9-15.

Fox, W.S.
1982 The Princess Point Concept. *Arch Notes* 2:17-26.
1984 The Princess Point Complex: An Addendum. *Kewa* 84(5.5):2-10.
1990 The Middle Woodland to Late Woodland Transition. In *The Archaeology of Southern Ontario to A.D. 1650,* edited by C.J. Ellis and N. Ferris, pp. 171-188. Publication Number 5. Occasional Publication of the London Chapter, Ontario Archaeological Society, London.

Fox, A., C. Heron, and M.Q. Sutton
1995 Characterization of Natural Products on Native American Archaeological and Ethnographic Materials from the Great Basin Region, U.S.A.: a preliminary study. *Archaeometry* 37(2):363-375.

Fritz, G.J.
1990 Multiple Pathways to Farming in Precontact Eastern North America. *Journal of World Prehistory* 4(4):387-476.
1993 Early and Middle Woodland Period Paleoethnobotany. In *Foraging and Farming in the Eastern Woodlands,* edited by C.M. Scarry, pp. 39-56. University Press of Florida, Gainesville.

Gebauer, A.B. and T. D. Price, eds.
1992 *Transitions to Agriculture in Prehistory.* Prehistory Press, Madison.

Gow, P.
1995 Land, People, and Paper in Western Amazonia. In *The Anthropology of Landscape: Perspectives on Place and Space,* edited by E. Hirsch and M. O'Hanlon, pp. 62-93, Clarendon Press, Oxford.

Gremillion, K.J.
1993 Crop and Weed in Prehistoric Eastern North America: The Chenopodium Example. *American Antiquity* 58(3):496-509.

Gremillion, K.J., ed.
1997 *People, Plants, and Landscapes: Studies in Paleoethnobotany.* The University of Alabama Press, Tuscaloosa.

Hammett, J.E.
1997 Interregional Patterns of Land Use and Plant Management in Native North America. In *People, Plants, and Landscapes: Studies in Paleoethnobotany,* edited by K.J. Gremillion, pp. 195-216. The University of Alabama Press, Tuscaloosa.

Harbourne, J.B.
1997 Phytochemistry of fruit and vegetables: an ecological overview. In *Phytochemistry of Fruit and Vegetables,* edited by F.A. Tomas-Barberan and R.J. Robins, pp. 353-368. Oxford Science Publications, Oxford.

Harlan, J.R.
1995 *The Living Fields: our agricultural heritage.* Cambridge University Press, Cambridge.

Harlan, J.R., J.M.J. deWet, and E.G. Price
1973 Comparative Evolution of Cereals. *Evolution* 27:311-325.

Harris, D.R.
1996 *The Origins and Spread of Agriculture and Pastoralism in Eurasia.* UCL Press, London.

Harris, D.R., and G.C. Hillman, eds.
1989 *Foraging and Farming: The Evolution of Plant Exploitation.* Unwin Hyman, London.

Harris, M.
1979 *Cultural Materialism: The Struggle for a Science of Culture.* Random House, New York.

Hart, J.P.
1999a *Current Northeast Palaeoethnobotany.* New York State Museum Bulletin 494, Albany.
1999b Maize Agriculture Evolution in the Eastern Woodlands of North America: A Darwinian Perspective. *Journal of Archaeological Method and Theory* 6(2):137-180.
2001 Maize, Matrilocality, Migration, and Northern Iroquoian Evolution. *Journal of Archaeological Method and Theory* 8(2):151-182.

Hart, J.P. and N. Asch Sidell
1996 Prehistoric Agricultural Systems in the West Branch of the Susquehanna River Basin, A.D. 800 to A.D. 1350. *Northeast Anthropology* 52:1-32.

Hastorf, C.
1988 The Use of Paleoethnobotanical Data in Prehistoric Studies of Crop Production, Processing, and Consumption. In *Current Paleoethnobotany: Analytical Methods and Cultural Interpretations of Archaeological Plant Remains*, edited by C.A. Hastorf and V.S. Popper, pp. 119-144. The University of Chicago Press, Chicago.
1999 Recent Research in Paleoethnobotany. *Journal of Archaeological Research* 7(1):55-106.

Hastorf, C.A. and S. Johannessen
1994 Becoming Corn-Eaters in Prehistoric North America. In *Corn and Culture in the Prehistoric New World*, edited by S. Johannessen and C.A. Hastorf, pp. 427-442. Westview Press, Oxford.

Hastorf, C.A., and V.S. Popper (eds.)
1988 *Current Paleoethnobotany: Analytical Methods and Cultural Interpretations of Archaeological Plant Remains.* The University of Chicago Press, Chicago.

Hather, J. G.
1993 *An Archaeological Guide to Root and Tuber Identification.* Oxbow Books, Oxford.

Hayden, B.
1981 *Archaeology: Science of Once and Future Thing.* W.H. Freeman and Co., New York.
1992 Models of domestication. In *Transitions to Agriculture in Prehistory*, edited by A.B.

Gebauer and T. D. Price, pp. 11-20. Prehistory Press, Madison.

Health Canada
1999 *Nutrient Value of Some Common Foods.* Health Canada, Ottawa.

Heidenreich, C.E.
1971 *Huronia: A History and Geography of the Huron Indians, 1600-1650.* McClelland and Stewart, Toronto.

Heiser, C.B.
1985 *Of Plants and People.* University of Oklahoma Press, Norman.

Herrick, J.W.
1995 *Iroquois Medical Botany.* Syracuse University Press, Syracuse.

Hirsch, E.
1995 Landscape: Between Place and Space. In *The Anthropology of Landscape: Perspectives on Place and Space*, edited by E. Hirsch and M. O'Hanlon. Clarendon Press, Oxford.

Hodder, I.
1982 *Symbols in Action: Ethnoarchaeological Studies of Material Culture.* Cambridge University Press, Cambridge.
1990 *The Domestication of Europe.* Basil Blackwell, Oxford.
1992 *Theory and Practice in Archaeology.* Routledge, London.

Hoover, R., Y. Sailaja, and F.W. Sosulski
1996 Characterization of starches from wild and long grain brown rice. *Food Research International* 7(2):99-107.

Huxtable, R.
1992 The Pharmacology of Extinction. *Journal of Ethnopharmacology* 37:1-11.

Ingold, Tim
1987 *The appropriation of nature: Essays on human ecology and social relations.* Iowa City, University of Iowa Press.
1996 Hunting and Gathering as Ways of Perceiving the Environment, in *Redefining Nature: ecology, culture, and domestication*, edited by R. Ellen and K. Fukui. Berg Publishers, Oxford.

Jackson, L.J.
1983 Early Maize in South Central Ontario. *Arch Notes* 83(3):9-11.

Jarman, H. N., A.J. Legge, and J.A. Charles
1972 Retrieval of Plant Remains from Archaeological Sites by Froth Flotation. In *Papers in Economic Prehistory*, edited by E. Higgs, pp. 39-48. Cambridge University Press, Cambridge.

Jarman, M. R., G.N. Bailey, and H.N. Jarman, eds.
1982 *Early European Agriculture: Its Foundations and Development.* Cambridge University Press, Cambridge.

Jenks, A.R.
1900 *The Wild Rice Gatherers of the Upper Lakes.* Government Printing Office, Washington.

93

Johannessen, S.

    1984   Paleoethnobotany. In *American Bottom Archaeology*, edited by C. Bareis and J. Porter, pp. 197-214. University of Illinois Press, Urbana.

    1988   Plant Remains and Culture Change: Are Paleoethnobotanical Data Better than We Think? In *Current Paleoethnobotany*, edited by C. Hastorf and V. Popper, pp. 145-166. University of Chicago Press, Chicago.

    1993   Farmers of the Late Woodland. In *Foraging and Farming in the Eastern Woodlands*, edited by C.M. Scarry, pp. 57-77. University Press of Florida, Gainesville.

Johannessen, S. and C.A. Hastorf, eds.

    1994   *Corn and Culture in the Prehistoric New World.* Westview Press, Boulder.

Johns, T.

    1996   *The Origins of Human Diet and Medicine.* The University of Arizona Press, Tucson.

Kadane, J.B.

    1988   Possible Statistical Contributions to Paleoethnobotany. In *Current Paleoethnobotany*, edited by C.A. Hastorf and V.S. Popper, pp. 206-214. The University of Chicago Press, Chicago.

Katzenberg, A., H.P. Schwartz, M. Knyf, and F.J. Melbye

    1995   Stable Istotope Evidence for Maize Horticulture and Paleodiet in Southern Ontario, Canada. *American Antiquity* 60:335-350.

Keegan, W.F., ed.

    1987   *Emergent Horticultural Economies of the Eastern Woodlands.* Occasional Paper 7. Southern Illinois University, Carbondale.

Keeley, L.M.

    1992   The Introduction of Agriculture to the Western European Plain. In *Transitions to Agriculture in Prehistory*, edited by A.B. Gebauer, and T.D. Price, pp. 81-95. Prehistory Press, Madison.

King, F.B.

    1994   Variability in Cob and Kernel Characteristics of North American Maize Cultivars. In *Corn and Culture in the Prehistoric New World*, edited by S. Johannessen and Christine Hastorf, pp. 35-54. Westview Press, Boulder

Kuris, K.

    1998   *A Contextual Analysis of Plant Remains at Bull's Point.* Unpublished paper on file. Department of Anthropology, University of Toronto at Mississauga, Mississauga.

Lamberg-Karlovsky, C.C., ed.

    1989   *Archaeological Thought in America.* Cambridge University Press, Cambridge.

Lee, G.A.

    1998   *Identification of Pollen Grains of Wild Rice in Cootes Paradise, Ontario: Palynological and Archaeological Reviews.* Unpublished paper on file. Department of Geography, University of Toronto, Toronto.

Lee, G.A., A.M. Davis, D.G. Smith, and J.H. McAndrews

    2004   Identifying fossil wild rice (Zizania) pollen from Cootes Paradise, Ontario: a new approach using scanning electron microscopy. *Journal of Archaeological Science* 31:411-421.

Lee, T.E.

    1951   *A Preliminary Report on an Archaeological Survey of Southwestern Ontario in 1949.* National Museum of Canada, Bulletin 123:42-48.

    1952   *A Preliminary Report on an Archaeological Survey of Southwestern Ontario for 1950.* National Museum of Canada, Bulletin 126:64-75.

Lennox, P.A., and B. Morrison

    1990   *The Ramsey Site: A Princess Point Camp, Brant County, Ontario.* Report on file. Ontario Ministry of Transportation, Toronto.

Lennstrom, H.A., and C.A. Hastorf

    1995   Interpretation in Context: Sampling and Analysis in Paleoethnobotany. *American Antiquity* 60(4):701-721.

Leone, M.P.

    1982   Some opinions about recovering mind. *American Antiquity* 47:742-760.

Leonard, R.D., and G.T. Jones, eds.

    1989   *Quantifying Diversity in Archaeology.* Cambridge University Press, Cambridge.

Linton, R.

    1924   North American Maize Culture. *American Anthropologist* 26:345-59.

    1936   *The Study of Man.* Appelton-Century-Crofts, New York.

MacNeish, R.

    1952   *Iroquois Pottery Types.* National Museum of Canada, Bulletin 124.

MacDonald, J.D.

    1986   *The Varden Site: A Multi-Component Fishing Station on Long Point, Lake Erie.* Report on file, Ontario Ministry of Culture and Communications, Toronto.

Mangelsdorf, P.C.

    1974   *Corn: Its Origin, Evolution, and Improvement.* The Belknap Press of Harvard University, Cambridge.

Mason, R.

    1981   *Great Lakes Archaeology.* Academic Press, New York.

McAndrews, J.H.

    1969   Paleobotany of a Wild Rice Lake in Minnesota. *Canadian Journal of Botany* (47):1671-1679.

McAndrews, J.H., and M. Boyko-Diakonow

    1989   Pollen Analysis of the Varved Lake Sediment at Crawford Lake, Ontario: Evidence of Indian and European Farming. In *Quaternary Geology of Canada and Greenland*, edited by R.J. Fulton, J.A. Heginbottom, and R.J. Funder, pp. 528-530. Geological Survey of Canada, Ottawa, Ontario.

McCorrison, J.

    1994   Acorn eating and agricultural origins:

California ethnographies as analogies for the ancient Near East. *Antiquity* 68:97-107.

McCorriston, J., and F. Hole
1964 The Ecology of Seasonal Stress and the Origins of Agriculture in the Near East. *American Anthropologist* 93:39-62.

McGlade, J.
1995 Archaeology and the ecodynamics of human-modified landscapes. *Antiquity* 69:113-132.

McNutt, C.H.
1996 *Prehistory of the Central Mississippi Valley.* University of Alabama Press, Tuscaloosa.

Miksicek, C.H.
1987 Formation Processes of the Archaeobotanical Record. In *Advances in Archaeological Method and Theory, Volume 10,* edited by M.B. Schiffer. Academic Press Inc., San Diego.

Miller, N.
1988 Ratios in Paleoethnobotanical Analysis. In *Current Paleoethnobotany*, edited by C. Hastorf and V. Popper, pp. 72-85. University of Chicago Press, Chicago.

Moerman, D.E.
1982 *Geraniums for the Iroquois.* Reference Publications, Algonac.
1998 *Native American Ethnobotany.* Timber Press, Portland.

Moffatt, C.R. and C.M. Arzigian
2000 New Data on the Late Woodland Use of Wild Rice in Northern Wisconsin. *Midcontinental Journal of Archaeology* 25(1):49-81.

Monckton, S.G.
1990 *Huron Paleoethnobotany.* Ph.D. dissertation on file at the Department of Anthropology, University of Toronto, Toronto.
1992 *Huron Paleoethnobotany.* Ontario Archaeological Reports 1. Ontario Heritage Foundation, Toronto.
1999 Plant Remains. In *Turning the First Millennium: the Archaeology of the Holmedale Site (AgHb-191), a Princess Point Settlement on the Grand River,* edited by R.H. Pihl, pp. 81-84. Archaeological Services Inc., Toronto.

Morse, D.F., and P. Morse
1990 Emergent Mississippian in the Central Mississippi Valley. In *The Mississippian Emergence*, edited by B.D. Smith, pp. 153-174. Smithsonian Institution Press, Washington, D.C.

Muller, J.D.
1987 Lower Ohio Valley Emergent Horticulture and Mississippian. In *Emergent Horticultural Economies of the Eastern Woodlands*, edited by W. Keegan, pp. 243-273. Occasional Paper 7, Southern Illinois University Center for Archaeological Investigations, Carbondale.

Murphy, C., and Ferris, N.
1990 The Late Woodland Western Basin Tradition in Southwestern Ontario. In *The Archaeology of Southern Ontario to A.D. 1650,* edited by C.J.

Ellis and N. Ferris, pp. 189-278. Publication Number 5, Occasional Publications of the London Chapter, Ontario Archaeological Society, London.

Noble, W.C.
1975 Corn and the Development of Village Life in South Ontario. *Ontario Archaeology* 25:37-46.

Noble, W.C. and I.T. Kenyon
1972 Porteous (AgHb-1): A Probable Early Glen Meyer Village In Brant County, Ontario. *Ontario Archaeology* 19:11-18.

O'Brien, M.J. and R.C. Dunnell
1998 *Changing Perspectives on the Archaeology of the Central Mississippi River Valley.* University of Alabama Press, Tuscaloosa.

Ormerod, T.
1994 *The Lone Pine Flaked Lithic Aggregate: Behavioural Implications for a Transitional Woodland Site.* Unpublished M.Sc. research paper on file at the Department of Anthropology, University of Toronto, Toronto.

Ounjian, G.L.
1998 *Glen Meyer and Prehistoric Neutral Paleoethnobotany.* Unpublished Ph.D. dissertation on file at the Department of Anthropology, University of Toronto, Toronto.

Overholt, T. W. and J. B. Callicott
1982 *Clothed-in-Fur and Other Tales: An Introduction to Ojibwa World View.* University Press of America, Lanham.

Parker, A.C.
1912 *Parker on the Iroquois* (edited by W.C. Fenton, 1968). Syracuse University Press, Syracuse.

Payne, S.
1972 Partial Recovery and Sample Bias: The Results of Some Sieving Experiments. In *Papers in Economic Prehistory*, edited by E.S. Higgs. Cambridge University Press, London.

Pearsall, D.M.
1989 *Paleoethnobotany: A Handbook of Procedures.* Academic Press, San Diego.
1996 Reconstructing Subsistence in the Lowland Tropics. In *Case Studies in Environmental Archaeology*, edited by E.J. Reitz, L.A. Newsom, and S.J. Scudder, pp. 233-254. Plenum Press, New York.

Pengelly, J.W., K.J. Tinkler, W.G. Parkins, and F.M. McCarthy
1997 12600 years of lake level changes, changing sills, ephemeral lakes, and Niagara Gorge erosion in the Niagara Peninsula and Eastern Lake Erie basin. *Journal of Paleoliminology* 17:377-402.

Perez, R.M., J.A. Perez, L.M. Garcia, and H. Sossa
1998 Neuropharmacological activity of *Solanum nigrum* fruit. *Journal of Ethnopharmacology* 62:43-48.

Peros, M.
1997 *Pollen Analysis and the Environmental History of Cootes Paradise, Ontario, Canada.*

Unpublished undergraduate research paper on file at the Departments of Anthropology and Geography, University of Toronto, Toronto.

Peterson, L.A.
1977   *Edible Wild Plants.* Houghton Mifflin Company, Boston.

Pihl, R.H. and D.A. Robertson
1999   Introduction. In *Turning the First Millennium: the Archaeology of the Holmedale Site (AgHb-191), a Princess Point Settlement on the Grand River,* edited by R.H. Pihl, pp. 1-3. Archaeological Services Inc., Toronto.

Plotkin, M.J.
2000   *Medicine Quest: In Search of Nature's Healing Secrets.* Viking, New York.

Popper, V.
1988   Selecting Quantitative Measures in Paleoethnobotany. In *Current Paleoethnobotany*, edited by C. Hastorf and V. Popper, pp. 53-71. University of Chicago Press, Chicago.

Popper, V., and C.A. Hastorf
1988   Introduction. In *Current Paleoethnobotany*, edited by C. Hastorf and V. Popper, pp. 1-16. University of Chicago Press, Chicago.

Price, T.D. and A.B. Gebauer, eds.
1995   *Last Hunters - First Farmers.* School of American Research Press, Sante Fe.

Price, T.D.
1996   The first farmers of southern Scandinavia. In *The origins and spread of agriculture and pastoralism in Eurasia*, edited by D.R. Harris, pp. 346-362. UCL Press Limited, London.

Quin, J.
1996   *Chert Sourcing in the Lower Grand River Valley: A Study in Methods and Applications.* Unpublished M.Sc. research paper on file at the Department of Anthropology, University of Toronto, Toronto.

Rindos, D.
1984   *The Origins of Agriculture: An Evolutionary Perspective.* Academic Press, Orlando.

Ritchie, W.A.
1944   *The Pre-Iroquoian Occupations of New York State.* Rochester Museum of Arts and Sciences, Research Records 5, Rochester.
1965   *The Archaeology of New York State.* Natural History Press, Garden City, New York.

Ritchie, W.A., and Funk, R.E.
1973   *Aboriginal Settlement Patterns in the Northeast.* Service Memoir 20. New York State Museum of Science, New York.

Robbins, M.K., A.D. Bavage, and P. Morris
1997   Options for the genetic manipulation of astringent and antinutritional metabolites in fruit and vegetables. In *Phytochemistry of Fruit and Vegetables*, edited by F.A. Tomas-Barberan and R.J. Robins, pp. 251-262. Oxford Science Publications, Oxford.

Rogers, E.S.
1953   *Aboriginal and Post-Contact Traits of the Montagnais-Naskapi Culture.* University of New Mexico Press, Albuquerque.

Rogers, J.D. and B.D. Smith, ed.
1995   *Mississippi Communities and Households.* University of Alabama Press, Tuscaloosa.

Rowe, J.S.
1977   *Forest Regions of Canada.* Department of the Environment, Canadian Forestry Service, Ottawa.

Rudgley, R.
1993   *Essential Substances: A Cultural History of Intoxicants in Society.* Kodansha International, New York.

Salmon, M.H.
1982   *Philosophy and Archaeology.* Academic Press, New York.

Saunders, D.
1993   *Experiments on the Effects of Charring and Flotation Recovery Rates.* Unpublished M.Sc. research paper on file at the Department of Anthropology, University of Toronto, Toronto.
1994   *Biochemical Analyses of Pottery Sherds from Nestor Falls Site, Big Rice Lake Site, and Grand Banks Site.* Unpublished M.Sc. research paper on file at the Department of Anthropology, University of Toronto, Toronto.

Schaaf, J.M.
1981   A Method for Reliable and Quantifiable Subsampling of Archaeological Features for Flotation. *Mid-Continental Journal of Archaeology* 6(2):219-248.

Scarry, C.M., ed.
1993   *Foraging and Farming in the Eastern Woodlands.* University Press of Florida, Gainesville.

Schultes, R.E., and A. Hofmann
1980   *The Botany and Chemistry of Hallucinogens.* Charles C. Thomas Publisher, Springfield.

Shen, C.
1997   *Towards a Comprehensive Understanding of the Lithic Production System of the Princess Point Complex, Southwestern Ontario.* Unpublished Ph.D. dissertation. Department of Anthropology, University of Toronto, Toronto.

Shennan, S.
1990   *Quantifying Archaeology.* Academic Press, San Diego.

Shipek, F.C.
1989   An example of intensive plant husbandry: the Kumeyaay of southern California. In *Foraging and Farming: The evolution of plant exploitation*, edited by D.R. Harris and G.C. Hillman, pp. 159-170. Unwin Hyman, London.

Skibo, J.M.
1992   *Pottery Function: A Use-Alteration Perspective.* Plenum Press, New York.

Smith, B.D.
1984   Chenopodium as Prehistoric Domesticate in

Eastern North America: Evidence from Russell Cave, Alabama. *Science* 266:165-167.

1987   Domesticated Chenopodium in Prehistoric Eastern North America: New Accelerator Dates from Eastern Kentucky. *American Antiquity* 52:355-357.

1990   *The Mississippian Emergence.* Smithsonian Institution Press, Washington, D.C.

1992   *Rivers of Change: Essays on Early Agriculture in Eastern North America.* Smithsonian Institution Press, Washington, D.C.

1995a   *Seed Plant Domestication in Eastern North America.* School of American Research Press, Santa Fe.

1995b   Seed Plant Domestication in Eastern North America. In *Last Hunters - First Farmers,* edited by T.D. Price and A.B. Gebauer, pp. 193-214. School of American Research Press, Sante Fe.

Smith, C.E., Jr.

1985   Recovery and Processing of Botanical Remains. In *The Analysis of Prehistoric Diets,* edited by R.I. Gilbert and J.H. Mielke. Academic Press, Orlando.

Smith, D.G.

1990   Iroquoian Societies in Southern Ontario: Introduction and Historic Overview. In *The Archaeology of Southern Ontario To A.D. 1650,* edited by C.J. Ellis and N. Ferris, pp. 279-290. Publication Number 5. Occasional Publication of the London Chapter, Ontario Archaeological Society, London.

1997   Radiocarbon Dating the Middle To Late Woodland Transition and Earliest Maize in Southern Ontario. *Northeast Anthropology* 54:37-74.

1997   Recent Investigation of Late Woodland Occupations at Cootes Pardise, Ontario. *Ontario Archaeology* 63:4-16.

in press Northeast Middle Woodland and Initial Late Woodland. In *Encycopedia of Prehistory*, edited by L. Ember and P. Peregrine, pp. 358-376. Kluwer Academic/Plenum Publishers, New York.

Smith, D.G., and G.W. Crawford

1995   The Princess Point Complex and the Origins of Iroquoian Societies in Ontario. In *Origins of the People of the Longhouse*, edited by A. Beckerman and G.A. Warrick, pp. 43-54. Proceedings of the 21st Annual Symposium of the Ontario Archaeological Society. Ontario Archaeological Society, Toronto.

1997   Recent Developments in the Archaeology of the Princess Point Complex in Southern Ontario. *Canadian Journal of Archaeology* 21:9-32.

Smith, D.G., T. Ormerod, and A. Bekerman

1996   *Small Princess Point Sites in Cootes Paradise.* Paper presented at the 23rd Annual Symposium of the Ontario Archaeological Society, Toronto.

Smith, E.A., and B. Winterhalder, eds.

1992   *Evolutionary Ecology and Human Behaviour.* Aldine de Gruyter, New York.

Smith, M.A.L., K.A. Marley, D. Seigler, K.W. Singletary, and B. Meline

2000   Bioactive Properties of Wild Blueberry Fruits. *Journal of Food Science* 65(2):352-356

Snow, D.R.

1995   Migration in Prehistory: The Northern Iroquoian Case. *American Antiquity* 60:59-79.

1996   More on Migration in Prehistory: Accommodating New Evidence in the Northern Iroquoian Case. *American Antiquity* 61:791-796.

Sosulski, F.

1993   Wild Rice. In *Encyclopaedia of Food Science, Food Technology, and Nutrition,* Volume 7, edited by R. Macrae and R.K. Robinson, pp. 4917-4921. Academic Press, New York.

Spector, J. D.

1970   Seed Analysis in Archaeology. *Wisconsin Archaeologist* 51:163-190.

Spence, M.W., and R.H. Pihl

1984   The Early and Middle Woodland Occupations of Southern Ontario: Past, Present and Future Research. *Arch Notes* 84(2):32-48.

Spence, M.W., R.H. Pihl, and C.R. Murphy

1990   Cultural Complexes of the Early and Middle Woodland Periods. In *The Archaeology of Southern Ontario to A.D. 1650*, edited by C.J. Ellis and N. Ferris, pp. 125-169. Publication Number 5. Occasional Publication of the London Chapter, Ontario Archaeological Society, London.

Steward, J.H.

1955   *Theory of Culture Change.* University of Illinois Press, Urbana.

Stewart, R.M.

1994   *Prehistoric Farmers of the Susquehanna Valley: Clemson Island Culture and the St. Anthony Site.* Occasional Publications in Northeastern Anthropology, 13.

Stothers, D.M.

1973   Early Evidence of Agriculture in the Great Lakes. *Canadian Archaeological Association Bulletin* 5:62-76.

1977   *The Princess Point Complex.* Mercury Series 58. National Museum of Man. Archaeological Survey of Canada, Ottawa.

Stothers, D.M., and R.A. Yarnell

1977   An Agricultural Revolution in the Lower Great Lakes. In *Geobotany*, edited by R.D. Romans, pp. 209-232. Plenum Publishing, New York.

1979   The Western Basin Tradition: Algonquin or Iroquois? *Pennsylvania Archaeologist* 49(3):13-30.

Stothers, D.M. and M. Pratt

1981   New Perspectives on the Late Woodland Cultures of the Western Lake Erie Region. *Mid-Continental Journal of Archaeology* 6:91-121.

Sykes, C.M.
1981 Northern Iroquois Maize Remains. *Ontario Archaeology* 35:23-34.

Timmins, P.A.
1985 *The Analysis and Interpretation of Radiocarbon Dates in Iroquoian Prehistory.* Research Report No. 19, Museum of Indian Archaeology, London.
1992 *The Alder Creek Site (AiHd-75): Interior Paleo-Indian and Princess Point Settlement Patterns in the Region of Waterloo, Ontario.* Unpublished report. Ontario Ministry of Transportation, Toronto.

Toll, M.S.
1988 Flotation Sampling: Problems and Some Solutions, with Examples from the American Southwest. In *Current Paleoethnobotany*, edited by C.A. Hastorf and V.S. Popper, pp. 36-52. The University of Chicago Press, Chicago.

Trigger, B.G.
1981 Prehistoric Social and Political Organization: An Iroquoian Study. In *Foundations of Northeast Archaeology*, edited by D. Snow, pp. 1-44. Academic Press, New York.
1985 *Natives and Newcomers: Canada's 'Heroic Age' Reconsidered.* McGill-Queen's University Press, Montreal.

Trigger, B.G.
1989 History and contemporary American archaeology: a critical analysis. In *Archaeological Thought in America*, edited by C.C. Lamberg-Karlovsky, pp. 19-34. Cambridge University Press, Cambridge.

Valppu, S.H.
1989 *Palaeoethnobotany of Big Rice Site, St. Louis County, Minnesota: Early Wild Rice (Zizania aquatica L.) in Archaeological Context.* Unpublished M.A. thesis on file at the University of Minnesota.

Van der Merwe, N. and H. Tschauner
1998 C$_4$ Plants and the Development of Human Societies. In *The Biology of C$_4$ Plants*, edited by R. Sage, pp. 509-549. Academic Press, New York.

Vennum, T., Jr.
1988 *Wild Rice and the Ojibway People.* Minnesota Historical Society Press, St. Paul.

Von Gernet, A.D.
1993 Hallucinogens and the Origins of the Iroquoian Pipe/Tobacco/Smoking Complex. In *Proceedings of the 1989 Smoking Pipe Conference*, edited by C.F. Hayes, pp. 171-185. Research Records No. 22. Rochester Museum and Science Center, Rochester.

Walker, I.J., J.R. Desloges, G.W. Crawford, and D.G. Smith
1997 Floodplain Formation Processes and Archaeological Implications at the Grand Banks Site, Lower Grand River, Southern Ontario. *Geoarchaeology* 12(8):865-887.

Wasson, R.G., C.A.P. Ruck, and A. Hofmann
1978 *The Road to Eleusis.* Harcourt, Brace, Jovanovich, New York.

Watson, P.J.
1976 In Pursuit of Prehistoric Subsistence: A Comparative Account of Some Contemporary Flotation Techniques. *Midcontinental Journal of Archaeology* 1:77-100.

Watts, C.
1997 *A Quantitative Analysis and Chronological Seriation of Riviere au Vase Phase Ceramics from Southwestern Ontario.* Unpublished M.Sc. research paper on file at the Department of Anthropology, University of Toronto, Toronto.

Waugh, F.W.
1916 *Iroquois Foods and Food Preparation.* Canada Department of Mines, Memoir No. 86.

Welch, P.D.
1990 Mississippian Emergence in West-Central Alabama. In *The Mississippian Emergence*, edited by B. Smith, pp. 197-226. Smithsonian Institution Press, Washington D.C.

de Wet, J.M.J., and J.R. Harlan
1975 Weeds and Domesticates: Evolution in the Man-Made Habitat. *Economic Botany* 29:99-107.

White, M.E.
1963 Settlement Pattern Change and the Development of Horticulture in the New York - Ontario Area. *Pennsylvania Archaeologist* 33:1-12.

Willey, G.R., and P. Phillips
1958 *Method and Theory in American Archaeology.* University of Chicago Press, Chicago.

Williamson, R.F.
1990 The Early Iroquoian Period of Southern Ontario. In *The Archaeology of Southern Ontario To A.D. 1650*, edited by C.J. Ellis and N. Ferris, pp. 291-320. Publication Number 5. Occasional Publication of the London Chapter, Ontario Archaeological Society, London.

Wills, W.H.
1995 Archaic Foraging and the Beginning of Food Production in the American Southwest. In *Last Hunters-First Farmers*, edited by T.D. Price and A.B. Gebauer, pp. 215-242. School of American Research Press, Santa Fe.

Wing, E.S., and S.R. Wing
1995 Prehistoric Ceramic Age Adaptation to Varying Diversity of Animal Resources along the West Indian Archipelago. *Journal of Ethnobiology* 15(1):119-148.

Winterhalder, B., and E.A. Smith, eds.
1981 *Hunter-Gatherer Foraging Strategies: ethnographic and archaeological analysis.* University of Chicago Press, Chicago.

Wilson, H.
1980 Artificial hybridization among species of *Chenopodium. Systematic Botany* 5:263-273.

Wright, J.V.
   1966   *The Ontario Iroquois Tradition.* Bulletin 210, National Museum of Canada, Ottawa.
   1972   *Ontario Prehistory.* National Museum of Man, Ottawa.
   1984   The Cultural Continuity of Iroquoian-Speaking Peoples. In *Extending the Rafters*, edited by M. Foster, J. Campisi, and M. Mithun, pp. 283-299. State University of New York, Albany.

Wylie, A.
   1982   Epistemological issues raised by a structuralist archaeology. In *Symbolic and Structural Archaeology*, edited by I. Hodder, pp. 39-46. Cambridge University Press, Cambridge.
   1994   Matters of fact and matters of interest. In *Archaeological Approaches to Cultural Identity*, edited by S. Shennan, pp. 94-109. Routledge, New York.

Wyman, L.C., and W.C. Boyd
   1937   Blood Group Determinations of Prehistoric American Indians. *American Anthropologist* 39:583-592.

Wymer, D.A.
   1993   Cultural Change and Subsistence: The Middle Woodland and Late Woodland Transition in the Mid-Ohio Valley. In *Foraging and Farming in the Eastern Woodlands*, edited by C.M. Scarry, pp. 138-156. University of Florida Press, Gainesville.

Yarnell, R. A.
   1964   *Aboriginal Relationships Between Culture and Plant Life in the Upper Great Lakes Region.* Anthropological Papers 23. University of Michigan Museum of Anthropology, Ann Arbor.
   1969   Palaeo-Ethnobotany in America. In *Science in Archaeology: a survey of progress and research*, edited by D. Brothwell and E. Higgs, pp. 215-228. Thames and Hudson, Bristol.
   1976   Early Plant Husbandry in Eastern North America. In *Culture Change and Continuity*, edited by C. Cleland, pp. 265-273. Academic Press, Orlando.
   1974   Plant Food and Cultivation of the Salts Cavers. In *Archaeology of the Mammoth Cave Area*, edited by P.J. Watson, pp. 113-122. Academic Press, New York.
   1978   Domestication of Sunflower and Sumpweed in Eastern North America. In *Nature and Status of Ethnobotany*, edited by R.I. Ford, pp. 289-299. Museum of Anthropology, University of Michigan, Anthropological Papers 67, Ann Arbor.
   1993   The Importance of Native Crops during the Late Archaic and Woodland Periods. In *Foraging and Farming in the Eastern Woodlands*, edited by C.M. Scarry, pp. 13-26. University of Florida Press, Gainesville.

Zvelebil, M.
   1986   *Hunters in Transition.* Cambridge University Press, Cambridge.

Plate 1: Maize kernel (dorsal view)

Plate 2: Maize kernel (dorsal view)

Plate 3: Maize kernel (distal end)

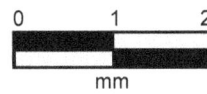

Plate 4: Maize cupules

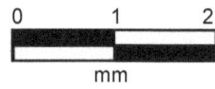

Plate 5: Sunflower

Plate 6: Wild Rice

Plate 7: Wild Rice

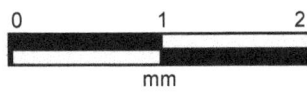

0   1   2
mm

Plate 8: Switch Grass

Plate 9: Rye Grass

Plate 10: Little Barley (probable)

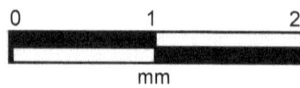

Plate 11: Milkvetch

Plate 12: Chenopod

Plate 13: Wild Grape

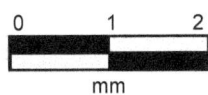

```
0        1        2
mm
```

Plate 14: Wood Sorrel

Plate 15: Cinquefoil

Plate 16: Cat-tail seeds

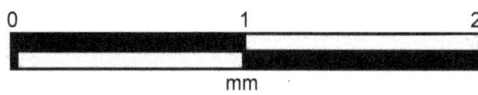

Plate 17: Erect Knotweed

Plate 18: Purslane

Plate 19: Bramble

Plate 20: Arrowhead (seed)

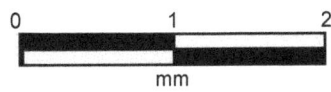

0 1 2
mm

Plate 21: Arrowhead (rhizomes)

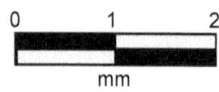

0   1   2

mm

Plate 22: Arrowhead (tuber)

Plate 23: Arrowhead (tuber)

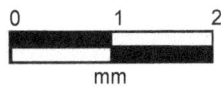

Plate 24: Arrowhead tuber (probable)

Plate 25: American Nightshade

Plate 26: American Nightshade (germinating)

Plate 27: American Nightshade seeds (mass)

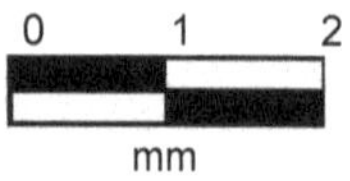

www.ingramcontent.com/pod-product-compliance
Lightning Source LLC
Chambersburg PA
CBHW061005030426
42334CB00033B/3369